FREE Study Skills DVD Offer

Dear Customer,

Thank you for your purchase from Mometrix! We consider it an honor and privilege that you have purchased our product and want to ensure your satisfaction.

As a way of showing our appreciation and to help us better serve you, we have developed a Study Skills DVD that we would like to give you for <u>FREE</u>. **This DVD covers our "best practices" for studying for your exam, from using our study materials to preparing for the day of the test.**

All that we ask is that you email us your feedback that would describe your experience so far with our product. Good, bad or indifferent, we want to know what you think!

To get your **FREE Study Skills DVD**, email <u>freedvd@mometrix.com</u> with "FREE STUDY SKILLS DVD" in the subject line and the following information in the body of the email:

    a.   The name of the product you purchased.

    b.   Your product rating on a scale of 1-5, with 5 being the highest rating.

    c.   Your feedback. It can be long, short, or anything in-between, just your impressions and experience so far with our product. Good feedback might include how our study material met your needs and will highlight features of the product that you found helpful.

    d.   Your full name and shipping address where you would like us to send your free DVD.

If you have any questions or concerns, please don't hesitate to contact me directly.

Thanks again!

Sincerely,

Jay Willis
Vice President
jay.willis@mometrix.com
1-800-673-8175

Praxis II

Middle School
English Language Arts (5047)

SECRETS

Study Guide
Your Key to Exam Success

Praxis II Test Review for the
Praxis II: Subject Assessments

Published by
Mometrix Test Preparation
Praxis II Exam Secrets Test Prep Team

Written and edited by the Praxis II Exam Secrets Test Prep Staff

Printed in the United States of America

This paper meets the requirements of ANSI/NISO Z39.48-1992 (Permanence of Paper).

Mometrix offers volume discount pricing to institutions. For more information or a price quote, please contact our sales department at sales@mometrix.com or 888-248-1219.

Praxis II® is a registered trademark of Educational Testing Services ® (ETS®), which was not involved in the production of, and does not endorse, this product.

ISBN 13: 978-1-63094-595-4
ISBN 10: 1-63094-595-1

Dear Future Exam Success Story:

Congratulations on your purchase of our study guide. Our goal in writing our study guide was to cover the content on the test, as well as provide insight into typical test taking mistakes and how to overcome them.

Standardized tests are a key component of being successful, which only increases the importance of doing well in the high-pressure high-stakes environment of test day. How well you do on this test will have a significant impact on your future, and we have the research and practical advice to help you execute on test day.

The product you're reading now is designed to exploit weaknesses in the test itself, and help you avoid the most common errors test takers frequently make.

How to use this study guide

We don't want to waste your time. Our study guide is fast-paced and fluff-free. We suggest going through it a number of times, as repetition is an important part of learning new information and concepts.

First, read through the study guide completely to get a feel for the content and organization. Read the general success strategies first, and then proceed to the content sections. Each tip has been carefully selected for its effectiveness.

Second, read through the study guide again, and take notes in the margins and highlight those sections where you may have a particular weakness.

Finally, bring the manual with you on test day and study it before the exam begins.

Your success is our success

We would be delighted to hear about your success. Send us an email and tell us your story. Thanks for your business and we wish you continued success.

Sincerely,

Mometrix Test Preparation Team

Need more help? Check out our flashcards at: http://MometrixFlashcards.com/PraxisII

TABLE OF CONTENTS

Top 20 Test Taking Tips

1. Carefully follow all the test registration procedures
2. Know the test directions, duration, topics, question types, how many questions
3. Setup a flexible study schedule at least 3-4 weeks before test day
4. Study during the time of day you are most alert, relaxed, and stress free
5. Maximize your learning style; visual learner use visual study aids, auditory learner use auditory study aids
6. Focus on your weakest knowledge base
7. Find a study partner to review with and help clarify questions
8. Practice, practice, practice
9. Get a good night's sleep; don't try to cram the night before the test
10. Eat a well balanced meal
11. Know the exact physical location of the testing site; drive the route to the site prior to test day
12. Bring a set of ear plugs; the testing center could be noisy
13. Wear comfortable, loose fitting, layered clothing to the testing center; prepare for it to be either cold or hot during the test
14. Bring at least 2 current forms of ID to the testing center
15. Arrive to the test early; be prepared to wait and be patient
16. Eliminate the obviously wrong answer choices, then guess the first remaining choice
17. Pace yourself; don't rush, but keep working and move on if you get stuck
18. Maintain a positive attitude even if the test is going poorly
19. Keep your first answer unless you are positive it is wrong
20. Check your work, don't make a careless mistake

Reading

William Shakespeare

William Shakespeare lived in England from 1564-1616. He was a poet and playwright of the Renaissance period in Western culture. He is generally considered the foremost dramatist in world literature, and the greatest author to write in the English language. He wrote many poems, particularly sonnets, of which 154 survive today, and approximately 38 plays. Though his sonnets were larger in number and are very famous, he is best known for his plays, including comedies, tragedies, tragicomedies and historical plays. His play titles include: *All's Well That Ends Well, As You Like It, The Comedy of Errors, Love's Labour's Lost, Measure for Measure, The Merchant of Venice, The Merry Wives of Windsor, A Midsummer Night's Dream, Much Ado About Nothing, The Taming of the Shrew, The Tempest, Twelfth Night, The Two Gentlemen of Verona, The Winter's Tale, King John, Richard II, Henry IV, Henry V, Richard III, Romeo and Juliet, Coriolanus, Titus Andronicus, Julius Caesar, Macbeth, Hamlet, Troilus and Cressida, King Lear, Othello, Antony and Cleopatra,* and *Cymbeline.*

William Faulkner

[handwritten: Early 20th C. A Rose for Emily, Absalom, Absalom!, The Sound & the Fury, As I lay dying — from the south]

William Faulkner lived in the state of Mississippi in the United States of America from 1897-1962. He is known as one of the greatest authors of Southern literature in America, and of American literature in general. Faulkner wrote one play, poems, essays, screenplays, and especially novels and short stories. He based his writing on his experience living in Mississippi during the early 20th century. Many of his short stories and novels are set in a fictional Southern county modeled on the two counties where he lived. Faulkner was awarded the 1949 Nobel Prize for Literature and two Pulitzer Prizes for Fiction, both for novels: one for *A Fable* in 1954, and another for *The Reivers*, his final novel, in 1962. Titles of some of his best-known works include the novels *The Sound and the Fury; As I Lay Dying; Light in August; Absalom, Absalom!;* and the short story *A Rose for Emily.*

Geoffrey Chaucer *[handwritten: "Father of English Literature"]*

The Canterbury Tales

[handwritten in margin: Canterbury Tales, Parliament of Fowles]

Medieval poet Geoffrey Chaucer (c. 1343-1400), called the "Father of English Literature," chiefly wrote long narrative poems, including *The Book of the Duchess, Anelida and Arcite, The House of Fame, The Parlement of Foules, The Legend of Good Women,* and *Troilus and Criseyde.* His most famous work is *The Canterbury Tales.* Its historical and cultural context is life during the Middle Ages, representing a cross-section of society—tradespeople, professionals, nobility, clergy, and housewives, among others, and religious pilgrimages, a common practice of the time. Its literary context is a frame-tale, that is, a story within a story. Chaucer described a varied group of pilgrims all on their way to Canterbury, taking turns telling stories to amuse the others. Tales encompass a broad range of subjects: bawdy comedy, chivalry, romance, and religion. These include *The Knight's Tale, The Miller's Tale, The Reeve's Tale, The Cook's Tale, The Man of Law's Tale, The Wife of Bath's Tale, The Friar's Tale, The Summoner's Tale, The Clerk's Tale, The Merchant's Tale, The Squire's Tale, The Franklin's Tale, The Physician's Tale, The Pardoner's Tale, The Nun's Priest's Tale,* and others.

The Parlement of Foules

In the brief preface to his poem "The Parlement of Foules," Geoffrey Chaucer refers to ancient Classical Roman author Cicero's "The Dream of Scipio." This was a philosophical dialogue Cicero wrote as a kind of epilogue to his famous longer book, *De re publica* (*"The Republic"*). It narrates that Roman senator and general Scipio the Younger dreams that his grandfather, the renowned general Scipio Africanus, visits him and escorts him to heaven. While viewing the spheres, he tells his grandson how the afterlife is the true life, earthly virtue earns the reward of Heaven, and earthly delights are less important. This reflects Stoic philosophy: Romans adapted Platonic ideals from the Greeks. Whereas "The Dream of Scipio" is a dream-vision on the nature of the universe as macrocosm, Chaucer's poem is a dream-vision on a smaller part of the universe as microcosm. He describes reading "The Dream of Scipio," then also dreaming of a visit from Scipio Africanus, who praises him and promises to reward him for reading Cicero's work.

Influence of Cicero's "Dream of Scipio": During Geoffrey Chaucer's lifetime (1300s), Cicero's philosophical dialogue "The Dream of Scipio," found at the end of his major work *De re publica* (*The Republic*) was a very popular, admired, and influential work. Medieval Christians appreciated Greek and Latin Stoic philosophies for their assigning more importance to spiritual virtues than materialism. They adapted these easily to Christianity for their similarity to Christian values, as they did with many other pagan traditions. Chaucer wrote several dream-vision poems influenced by the Classics, including "The House of Fame," influenced by Virgil's *Aeneid,* and "The Book of the Duchess," influenced by Ovid's *Metamorphoses.* He introduces *The Parlement of Foules* by recounting "The Dream of Scipio," and his own similar dream from the influence of reading this work, as homage to Cicero. He then segues to writing that though personally unsuccessful in love, he writes about love. He contrasts the brevity of life with the lengthiness of learning the poetic art. He concludes his preface asking help from Venus, Roman Goddess of Love.

Drama

early English drama stemmed from religious ritual

Early development

Interestingly, early English drama originally developed from religious ritual. Early Christians established traditions of presenting pageants or mystery plays, each traveling on wagons and carts through the streets of its city, depicting events of the Judeo-Christian Old and New Testaments. Medieval tradition assigned responsibility for performing specific plays to the different guilds. In Middle English, "mystery" meant both religious ritual/truth, and craft/trade. Historically, mystery plays were to be reproduced exactly the same every time as religious rituals. However, by human nature, some performers introduced individual interpretations of roles and/or even improvised. Thus drama was born. Narrative detail and nuanced acting were evident in mystery cycles by the Middle Ages. As individualized performance evolved, plays on other subjects also developed. Middle English mystery plays extant include the York Cycle, Coventry Cycle, Chester Mystery Plays, N-Town Plays, and Towneley/Wakefield Plays. Mystery plays have been revived in the 20th and 21st centuries. Dame Judi Dench (born in York) and other actors began their careers in mystery play revivals.

Middle Ages → plays in verse
Renaissance (Shakespeare & colleagues) mixed blank verse prose, + rhymes

Defining characteristics

In the Middle Ages, it was common to compose plays in verse. Early Christian mystery plays were always written in verse. By the time of the Renaissance, Shakespeare and other dramatists wrote plays that mixed prose, rhymed verse, and blank verse. Shakespeare also often used rhyming couplets in his plays. The traditions of costumes and masks were seen in ancient Greek drama, medieval mystery plays, and Renaissance drama. Conventions like asides, wherein actors make comments directly to the audience unheard by other characters, and soliloquies, i.e., dramatic monologues, were also common during Shakespeare's Elizabethan dramatic period. Monologues dated back to ancient Greek drama. Elizabethan dialogue tended to use colloquial prose for lower-class characters' speech and stylized verse for upper-class characters. Another Elizabethan

Asides, soliloquies popular in Shakespeare's plays

Monologues date back to Greek theater

- 3 -

Elizabethan dialogue = colloquial for lower-class characters, play w/in a play stilted for upper-class, convention was the play-within-a-play, like in *Hamlet*. As drama moved toward realism, dialogue became less poetic and more conversational, as in most modern English-language plays. Contemporary drama, both onstage and onscreen, includes a convention of breaking the fourth wall, wherein actors directly face and address audiences.

(margin note left) Breaking 4th wall more mainstream contemporary

Poetry

Poetry w/o rhyme or meter = free verse
meter = described by number of beats or stressed syllables per verse

(margin note left) See notes on scanning poetry

Unlike prose, which traditionally (except in forms like stream of consciousness) consists of complete sentences connected into paragraphs, poetry is written in verses. These may form complete sentences, clauses, or phrases. Poetry may be written in rhyming verses or unrhymed verse. It can be metered, i.e., following a particular rhythmic pattern, such as iambic, dactylic, spondaic, trochaic, or anapestic, or without regular meter. The terms iamb and trochee, among others, identify stressed and unstressed syllables in each verse. Meter is also described by the number of beats or stressed syllables per verse: dimeter (2), trimeter (3), tetrameter (4), pentameter (5), and so forth. With $\cup$ = unstressed, $/$ = stressed, iambic = $\cup/$; trochaic = $/\cup$; spondaic = $//$; dactylic = $/\cup\cup$; anapestic = $\cup\cup/$. Poetry with neither rhyme nor meter is called free verse. Poems may be in free verse, metered but unrhymed, rhymed but without meter, or using both rhyme and meter. In English, the most common meter is iambic pentameter. Unrhymed iambic pentameter is called blank verse. Rhyme schemes identify which lines rhyme, such as ABAB, ABCA, AABA, and so on.

Major forms

Poetic ballads = rhymed + metered + cover subjects such as love, death, murders + religion

(margin note left) Dramatic monologue poem = poet speaks in voice of character or persona
(margin note left) Elegies = mourn dead + have 3 parts 1 - lament 2 - praise for deceased 3 - solace for loss

The ballad is a form historically and currently used in both musical songs and poems. The *ballade* was very popular in 14th- and 15th-century France; ballads were also common in traditional English and American folk songs and poems. Poetry ballads often are rhymed and metered and cover subjects like love, death, murder, or religious topics. In dramatic monologue poems, the poet speaks in the voice of a character/persona. Elegies are mourning poems, traditionally with three parts: a lament, praise of the deceased, and solace for loss. Epic poems are long, recount heroic deeds and adventures, use very stylized language, and combine dramatic and lyrical conventions. Epigrams are memorable, one- or two-line rhymes. Epistolary poems are written and read as letters. Odes evolved from early poems with music and dance to Romantic poems expressing strong feelings and contemplative thoughts. Pastoral poems (and novels) idealize nature and country living. Limericks typically are two lines of iambic trimeter, two lines of iambic dimeter, and one line of iambic trimeter, usually humorous and/or bawdy.

Haiku

Haiku was originally a Japanese poetry form. In the 13th century, haiku was the opening phrase of renga, a 100-stanza oral poem. By the 16th century, haiku diverged into a separate short poem. When Western writers discovered haiku, the form became popular in English and other languages. A haiku has 17 syllables, traditionally distributed across three verses as 5/7/5, with a pause after the first or second line. Haiku are syllabic and unrhymed. Haiku philosophy and technique are that brevity's compression forces writers to express images concisely, depict a moment in time, and evoke illumination and enlightenment. An example is 17th-century haiku master Matsuo Basho's classic: "Oh, old pond! / A frog jumps in— / the sound of water." Modern American poet Ezra Pound revealed the influence of haiku in his two-line poem "In a Station of the Metro"—line 1 has 5+7 syllables, line 2 has 7, but it still preserves haiku's philosophy and imagistic technique: "The apparition of these faces in the crowd; / Petals on a wet, black bough."

Sonnets

The sonnet traditionally has 14 lines of iambic pentameter, tightly organized around a theme. The Petrarchan sonnet, named for 14th-century Italian poet Petrarch, has an eight-line stanza, the octave, and a six-line stanza, the sestet. There is a change or turn, known as the volta, between the eighth and ninth verses setting up the sestet's answer or summary. The rhyme scheme is ABBA/ABBA/CDECDE or CDCDCD. The Petrarchan sonnet was introduced to 16th-century England by Sir Thomas Wyatt. The English or Shakespearean sonnet has three quatrains and one couplet, with the rhyme scheme ABAB/CDCD/EFEF/GG. This format better suits English, which has fewer rhymes than Italian. The final couplet often contrasts sharply with the preceding quatrains, as in Shakespeare's sonnets—for example, Sonnet 130, "My mistress' eyes are nothing like the sun." Variations on these two forms include 16th-century Edmund Spenser's Spenserian sonnet; 17th-century John Milton's Miltonic sonnet; and sonnet sequences, as used by 17th-century poet John Donne in *La Corona*, 19th-century poet Elizabeth Barrett Browning in *Sonnets from the Portuguese*, 19th-20th-century poet Rainer Maria Rilke, and 20th-century poets Robert Lowell and John Berryman.

Literary terminology

In works of prose such as novels, a group of connected sentences covering one main topic is termed a paragraph. In works of poetry, a group of verses similarly connected is called a stanza. In drama, when early works used verse, these were also divided into stanzas or couplets. Drama evolved to use predominantly prose. Overall, whether prose or verse, the conversation in a play is called dialogue. Large sections of dialogue spoken by one actor are called soliloquies or monologues. Dialogue that informs audiences but is unheard by other characters is called an aside. Novels and plays share certain common elements, such as characters—the people in the story; plot—the action of the story; a climax—when action and/or dramatic tension reaches its highest point; and denouement—the resolution following the climax. Sections dividing novels are called chapters, while sections of plays are called acts. Subsections of plays' acts are called scenes. Novels' chapters are usually not subdivided, although some novels have larger sections divided into groups of chapters.

Novels

Major forms

Historical novels set fiction in particular historical periods—including prehistoric and mythological—and contain historical, prehistoric, or mythological themes. Examples include Walter Scott's *Rob Roy* and *Ivanhoe*; Leo Tolstoy's *War and Peace*; Robert Graves' *I, Claudius*; Mary Renault's *The King Must Die* and *The Bull from the Sea* (an historical novel using Greek mythology); Virginia Woolf's *Orlando* and *Between the Acts*; and John Dos Passos's *U.S.A* trilogy. Picaresque novels recount episodic adventures of a rogue protagonist or *pícaro*, like Miguel de Cervantes' *Don Quixote* or Henry Fielding's *Tom Jones*. Gothic novels originated as a reaction against 18th-century Enlightenment rationalism, featuring horror, mystery, superstition, madness, supernatural elements, and revenge. Early examples include Horace Walpole's *Castle of Otranto*, Matthew Gregory Lewis' *Monk*, Mary Shelley's *Frankenstein*, and Bram Stoker's *Dracula*. In America, Edgar Allan Poe wrote many Gothic works. Contemporary novelist Anne Rice has penned many Gothic novels under the pseudonym A. N. Roquelaure. Psychological novels, originating in 17th-century France, explore characters' motivations. Examples include Abbé Prévost's *Manon Lescaut*; George Eliot's novels; Fyodor Dostoyevsky's *Crime and Punishment*; Tolstoy's *Anna Karenina*; Gustave Flaubert's *Madame Bovary*; and the novels of Henry James, James Joyce, and Vladimir Nabokov.

Novel of manners

Novels of manners are fictional stories that observe, explore, and analyze the social behaviors of a specific time and place. While deep psychological themes are more universal across different historical periods and countries, the manners of a particular society are shorter-lived and more varied; the novel of manners captures these societal details. Novels of manners can also be regarded as symbolically representing, in artistic form, certain established and secure social orders. Characteristics of novels of manners include descriptions of a society with defined behavioral codes; the use of standardized, impersonal formulas in their language; and inhibition of emotional expression, as contrasted with the strong emotions expressed in romantic or sentimental novels. The novels of Jane Austen are examples of some of the finest novels of manners ever produced. In the 20th century, Evelyn Waugh's *Handful of Dust* is a novel of social manners, and his *Sword of Honour* trilogy is a novel of military manners. Another 20th-century example is *The Unbearable Bassington* by Saki (the pen name of writer H. H. Munro), focusing on Edwardian society.

Western-world sentimental novels

Sentimental love novels originated in the movement of Romanticism. Eighteenth-century examples of novels that depict emotional rather than only physical love include Samuel Richardson's *Pamela* (1740) in English, and Jean-Jacques Rousseau's *Nouvelle Héloïse* (1761) in French. Also in the 18th century, Laurence Sterne's novel *Tristram Shandy* (1760-1767) is an example of a novel with elements of sentimentality. The Victorian era's rejection of emotionalism caused the term "sentimental" to have undesirable connotations. In the 19th century, William Makepeace Thackeray and Charles Dickens, while not considered sentimental novelists by any means, both included sentimental elements in some of their novels: for example, in Dickens' *A Christmas Carol.* A 19th-century author of genuinely sentimental novels was Mrs. Henry Wood (e.g., *East Lynne,* 1861). In the 20th century, Erich Segal's sentimental novel *Love Story* (1970) was a popular bestseller, staying on the New York Times Best Seller List for 41 weeks, and was adapted into a movie (also released in 1970) which was also well received by both movie audiences and film critics, receiving numerous award nominations.

Epistolary novel

Epistolary novels are told in the form of letters written by their characters rather than in narrative form. Samuel Richardson, the best-known author of epistolary novels like *Pamela* (1740) and *Clarissa* (1748), widely influenced early Romantic epistolary novels throughout Europe that freely expressed emotions. Richardson, a printer, published technical manuals on letter-writing for young gentlewomen; his epistolary novels were natural fictional extensions of those nonfictional instructional books. Nineteenth-century English author Wilkie Collins' *The Moonstone* (1868) was a mystery written in epistolary form. By the 20th century, the format of well-composed written letters came to be regarded as artificial and outmoded. English novelist Christopher Isherwood tried to revive the form in *Meeting by the River* (1967), but this was criticized for using chatty and informal letters to tell a story with a serious religious theme. A 20th-century evolution of letters was tape-recording transcripts in French playwright Samuel Beckett's drama *Krapp's Last Tape.* Though evoking modern alienation, Beckett still created a sense of fictional characters' direct communication without author intervention as Richardson had.

Pastoral novels

Pastoral novels and fiction (as well as poetry) lyrically idealize country life as idyllic and utopian, akin to the Garden of Eden. *Daphnis and Chloe*, written by Greek novelist Longus around the second or third century, was pastoral and influenced Elizabethan pastoral romances like Philip Sidney's *Arcadia* and Thomas Lodge's *Rosalynde* (both 1590). William Shakespeare based his play *As You Like It* on *Rosalynde.* Jacques-Henri Bernardin de St. Pierre's French work *Paul et Virginie* (1787) demonstrated the early Romantic view of the innocence and goodness of nature. Later non-pastoral novels like *The Rainbow* (1915) and *Lady Chatterley's Lover* (1928), both by D. H. Lawrence, contain pastoral elements. Growing realism transformed pastoral writing into less ideal and more dystopian, distasteful and ironic depictions of country life in George Eliot's and Thomas Hardy's novels. Saul Bellow's novel *Herzog* (1964) may demonstrate how urban ills highlight an alternative pastoral ideal. Some scholars feel the pastoral satire *Cold Comfort Farm* (1932) by Stella Gibbons (also adapted into a movie) has made British novelists less able to take the pastoral tradition's lyricism seriously.

Bildungsroman

Bildungsroman is German, literally meaning "education novel." This term is also used in English to describe "apprenticeship" novels focusing on coming-of-age stories, including youth's struggles and searches for things such as identity, spiritual understanding, or the meaning in life. Johann Wolfgang von Goethe's *Wilhelm Meisters Lehrjahre* (1796) is credited as the origin. Charles Dickens' two novels *David Copperfield* (1850) and *Great Expectations* (1861) also fit this form. H. G. Wells wrote *bildungsromans* about questing for apprenticeships to address modern life's complications in *Joan and Peter* (1918), and from a Utopian perspective in *The Dream* (1924). School *bildungsromans* include Thomas Hughes' *Tom Brown's School Days* (1857) and Alain-Fournier's *Le Grand Meaulnes* (1913). Many Hermann Hesse novels, including *Demian, Steppenwolf, Siddhartha, Magister Ludi,* and *Under the Wheel* are *bildungsromans* about struggling/searching youth. Samuel Butler's *The Way of All Flesh* (written in 1885 and published in 1903) and James Joyce's *A Portrait of the Artist as a Young Man* (1916) are two outstanding modern examples. Variations include J. D. Salinger's *The Catcher in the Rye* (1951), set both within and beyond school, and William Golding's *Lord of the Flies* (1955), a novel not set in a school but one that is a coming-of-age story nonetheless.

Roman à clef

Roman à clef, French for "novel with a key," means the story needs a real-life frame of reference, or key, for full comprehension. In Geoffrey Chaucer's *Canterbury Tales,* the Nun's Priest's Tale contains details that confuse readers unaware of history about the Earl of Bolingbroke's involvement in an assassination plot. Other literary works fitting this form include John Dryden's political satirical poem *Absalom and Achitophel* (1681), Jonathan Swift's satire *A Tale of a Tub* (1704), and George Orwell's political allegory *Animal Farm* (1945), all of which cannot be understood completely without knowing their camouflaged historical contents. *Roman à clefs* disguise truths too dangerous for authors to state directly. Readers must know about D. H. Lawrence's enemies to comprehend *Aaron's Rod* (1922). To appreciate Aldous Huxley's *Point Counter Point* (1928), readers must realize that the characters Mark Rampion and Denis Burlap respectively represent author Huxley and real-life critic John Middleton Murry. Marcel Proust's *Remembrance of Things Past (À la recherché du temps perdu,* 1871-1922) is informed by his social context. James Joyce's *Finnegans Wake* is an enormous *roman à clef* via multitudinous personal references.

Realism

Realism is a literary form whose goal is to represent reality as faithfully as possible. Its genesis in Western literature was a reaction against the sentimentality and extreme emotionalism of the works written in the literary movement of Romanticism, which championed feelings and their expression. Realists focused in great detail on immediacy of time and place, on specific actions of their characters, and the justifiable consequences of those actions. Some techniques of realism include writing in the vernacular, i.e., the characters' ordinary conversational language; writing in specific dialects used by some characters; and emphasizing the analysis and development of characters more than the analysis and development of plots. Realistic literature often addresses various ethical issues. Historically, realistic works have often concentrated on the middle classes of the authors' societies. Realists eschew treatments that are too dramatic or sensationalistic as exaggerations of the reality that they strive to portray as closely as they are able.

Satire

Satire uses sarcasm, irony, and/or humor as social criticism to lampoon human folly. Unlike realism, which intends to depict reality as it exists without exaggeration, satire often involves creating situations or ideas deliberately exaggerating reality to be ridiculous to illuminate flawed behaviors. Ancient Roman satirists included Horace and Juvenal. Alexander Pope's poem "The Rape of the Lock" satirized the values of fashionable members of the 18th-century upper-middle class, which Pope found shallow and trivial. The theft of a lock of hair from a young woman is blown out of proportion: the poem's characters regard it as seriously as they would a rape. Irishman Jonathan Swift satirized British society, politics, and religion in works like *A Tale of a Tub.* In *A Modest Proposal,* Swift used essay form and mock-serious tone, satirically "proposing" cannibalism of babies and children as a solution to poverty and overpopulation. He satirized petty political disputes in *Gulliver's Travels.* Swift was known as a master of the ancient Roman Horatian and Juvenalian satirical styles.

Historical context of change between Middle Ages and Renaissance

The ancient Greek Athenian elite were a highly educated society, developing philosophies and writing about principles for creating poetry and drama. During the Roman Empire, the Romans assimilated and adapted the culture of the Greeks they conquered into their own society. For example, the gods of Roman mythology were essentially the same as in Greek myth, only renamed in Latin. However, after the fall of the Roman Empire, the many European countries formerly united under Roman rule became fragmented. There followed a 1,000-year period of general public ignorance and illiteracy—called the Dark Ages as well as the Middle Ages. Only the Church remained a bastion of literacy: monks and priests laboriously copied manuscripts one at a time by hand. Johannes Gutenberg's 1450 invention of the movable-type printing press changed everything: multiple copies of books could be printed much faster. This enabled a public return to literacy, leading to the Renaissance, or "rebirth"—reviving access and interest for Greek and Roman Classics, and generating a creative explosion in all arts.

[handwritten margin note: examples]

[handwritten margin note: where Dark/middle ages uneducated general public were church where monks copied manuscript]

Christopher Marlowe

Christopher Marlowe was born the same year as William Shakespeare (1564), but died at the age of 29. Some people have proposed Marlowe could have falsified his death and continued writing under Shakespeare's name. Most scholars reject this theory. In the 19th century, an anonymous author also suggested Shakespeare temporarily wrote under the name Christopher Marlowe. In *As You Like It,* Shakespeare pays homage to Marlowe, quoting "Hero and Leander"; in Touchstone's dialogue, mentioning death over a "reckoning," thought to allude to Marlowe's presumed murder over money he owed; and including "in a little room," words from Marlowe's *Jew of Malta.* Shakespeare recycled Marlowe's themes from *Dido* in *Antony and Cleopatra,* from *Jew of Malta* in *The Merchant of Venice,* from *Edward II* in *Richard II,* and from *Dr. Faustus* in *Macbeth.* A speech in *Hamlet* echoes *Dido.* Shakespeare's character Marcadé in *Love's Labour's Lost* acknowledges the god Mercury in Marlowe's play *The Massacre at Paris,* with whom Marlowe identified himself in his poem "Hero and Leander."

Comedy

Today, most people equate the idea of comedy with something funny, and of tragedy with something sad. However, the ancient Greeks defined these differently. Comedy needed not be humorous or amusing: it needed only a happy ending. The Classical definition of comedy, as included in Aristotle's works, is any work that tells the story of a sympathetic main character's rise in fortune. According to Aristotle, protagonists needed not be heroic or exemplary: he described them as not evil or worthless, but as ordinary people—"average to below average" morally. Comic figures who were sympathetic were usually of humble origins, proving their "natural nobility" through their actions as their characters were tested, rather than characters born into nobility—who were often satirized as self-important or pompous. Comedy's mirror-image was tragedy, portraying a hero's fall in fortune. While by Classical definitions, tragedies could be sad, Aristotle went further, requiring their depicting suffering and pain to cause "terror and pity" in audiences; that tragic heroes be basically good, admirable, and/or noble; and that their downfalls be through personal action, choice, or error, not by bad luck or accident.

Shakespearean comedy

Aristotle defined comedy not as a humorous drama, but as one in which the protagonist experiences a rise in fortune, and which has a happy ending. Such Classical definitions of drama were very popular during the Renaissance and the Elizabethan period within it, when William Shakespeare was writing. All of Shakespeare's comedies, as opposed to his tragedies, had happy endings. Not all of them are equally funny, although many are. His play *A Comedy of Errors* fits the comedic genre of the farce. Based and expanding on a Classical Roman comedy, it includes slapstick humor and mistaken identity—not deliberate, but accidental, and is generally light and "fluffy," with disturbing topics only hinted at but soon dissolved in laughter and love. Shakespeare's *Much Ado About Nothing* is a romantic comedy. It incorporates some more serious themes, including social mores; perceived infidelity; marriage's duality as both trap and ideal; and honor and its loss, public shame, and deception, but also much witty dialogue and a happy ending.

Dramatic comedies

Three types of dramas classified as comedy include the farce, the romantic comedy, and the satirical comedy. The farce is a zany, goofy type of comedy that includes pratfalls and other forms of slapstick humor. The characters appearing in a farce tend to be ridiculous or fantastical in nature, markedly more so than characters in other types of comedies. Another aspect of farce is inclusion in the plot of situations so improbable as to be unbelievable—albeit still highly entertaining. Farcical plots frequently feature complications and twists that can go on almost indefinitely. They also often include wildly incredible coincidences that rarely if ever would occur in real life. Mistaken identity, deceptions, and disguises are common devices used in farcical comedies. Shakespeare's play *The Comedy of Errors,* with its cases of accidental mistaken identity and slapstick, is an example of farce. Contemporary examples of farce include the Marx Brothers' movies, the Three Stooges movies and TV episodes, and the *Pink Panther* movie series.

Romantic comedy

Romantic comedies are probably the most popular of the types of comedy, in both live theater performances and movies. They include not only humor and a happy ending, but also love. In the typical plot of a romantic comedy, two people well suited to one another are either brought together for the first time, or reconciled after being separated. They are usually both sympathetic characters, and seem destined to be together yet separated by some intervening complication—

such as an ex-lover(s), interfering parents or friends, or differences in social class. The happy ending is achieved through the lovers' overcoming all these obstacles. William Shakespeare's *Much Ado About Nothing;* Walt Disney's version of *Cinderella* (1950); Broadway musical *Guys and Dolls* (1955); and movies *When Harry Met Sally* (1989), starring Billy Crystal and Meg Ryan, written by Nora Ephron; *Sleepless in Seattle* (1993) and *You've Got Mail* (1998), both directed by Nora Ephron and starring Tom Hanks and Meg Ryan; and *Forget Paris* (1995), co-written, produced, directed by and starring Billy Crystal, are examples of romantic comedies.

Satirical comedy and black comedy

Satires generally mock and lampoon human foolishness and vices. Satirical comedies fit the classical definition of comedy by depicting a main character's rise in fortune, but they also fit the definition of satire by making that main character either a fool, morally corrupt, or cynical in attitude. All or most of the other characters in the satirical comedy display similar foibles. These include cuckolded spouses, dupes, and other gullible types; tricksters, con artists, and criminals; hypocrites; fortune seekers; and other deceptive types who prey on the latter, who are their willing and unwitting victims. Some classical examples of satirical comedies include *The Birds* by ancient Greek comedic playwright Aristophanes, and *Volpone* by 17th-century poet and playwright Ben Jonson, who made the comedy of humors popular. When satirical comedy is extended to extremes, it becomes black comedy, wherein the comedic occurrences are grotesque or terrible. Contemporary movie examples include Quentin Tarantino's *Pulp Fiction* (1994) and the Coen brothers' *Fargo* (1996).

Metaphysical poets

Dr. Samuel Johnson, a famous 18th-century figure, who wrote philosophy, poetry, and authoritative essays on literature, coined the term "Metaphysical Poets" to describe a number of mainly 17th-century lyric poets who shared certain elements of content and style in common. The poets included John Donne (considered the founder of the Metaphysical Poets), George Herbert, Andrew Marvell, Abraham Cowley, John Cleveland, Richard Crashaw, Thomas Traherne, and Henry Vaughan. These poets encouraged readers to see the world from new and unaccustomed perspectives by shocking and surprising them through their use of paradoxes; contradictory imagery; original syntax; combinations of religious, philosophical, and artistic images; subtle argumentation; and extended metaphors called conceits. Unlike their contemporaries, they did not allude to classical mythology or nature imagery in their poetry, but to current geographical and scientific discoveries. Some, like Donne, showed Neo-Platonist influences—like the idea that a lover's beauty reflected Eternity's perfect beauty. They were called metaphysical for their transcendence—Donne in particular—of typical 17th-century rationalism's hierarchical organization through their adventurous exploration of religion, ideas, emotions, and language.

Sir Thomas Browne

Sir Thomas Browne (1605-1682) was a British polymath, a practicing medical physician, scientist, religious philosopher, and author. His writing style was extraordinary and varied widely across his works. Browne was knighted in 1671 by King Charles II in recognition of his accomplishments. Among English-language writers, he has received widespread regard for his high originality. His thinking was paradoxical in that his interests embraced mysticism and other ancient esoteric disciplines, yet also a strong Christian religiosity and the nascent field of inductive scientific reasoning. His original mind produced many fresh ideas and perspectives, expressed with great complexity of both thought and language. Today he is less known and understood than many great authors, due not only to his advanced ideas and wording, but also to his many references to Biblical,

Classical, and esoteric sources. The Oxford English Dictionary credits him with coining over 100 new English vocabulary words, most of which are commonly recognized today. Famous authors have consistently admired and cited him across all four centuries since his death.

Sir Thomas Browne's writing style influenced the literary world from his lifetime in the 17th century through the 21st century today. Eighteenth-century literary authority Dr. Samuel Johnson noted Browne's diverse linguistic sources, as well as his transfer of terminology among different artistic disciplines. He credited Browne with having "augmented our philosophical diction"; defended Browne's "uncommon words and expressions," observing that "he had uncommon sentiments"; and explained that Browne coined new vocabulary because he "was not content to express, in many words, that idea for which any language could supply a single term." The Oxford English Dictionary lists Browne as number 70 of top-cited sources; contains 803 Browne entries; quotes him in 3,636 entries; and credits him with originating over 100 English words, including the following 38: ambidextrous, analogous, approximate, ascetic, anomalous, carnivorous, coexistence, coma, compensate, computer, cryptography, cylindrical, disruption, electricity, exhaustion, ferocious, follicle, generator, gymnastic, herbaceous, insecurity, indigenous, jocularity, literary, locomotion, medical, migrant, mucous, prairie, prostate, polarity, precocious, pubescent, therapeutic, suicide, ulterior, ultimate, and veterinarian. (Hilton, OED, 8/12)

Romanticism

The height of the Romantic movement occurred in the first half of the 19th century. It identified with and gained momentum from the French Revolution (1789) against the political and social standards of the aristocracy and its overthrowing of them. Romanticism was also part of the Counter-Enlightenment, a reaction of backlash against the Enlightenment's insistence on rationalism, scientific treatment of nature, and denial of emotionalism. Though expressed most overtly in the creative arts, Romanticism also affected politics, historiography, natural sciences, and education. Though often associated with radical, progressive, and liberal politics, it also included conservatism, especially in its influences on increased nationalism in many countries. The Romantics championed individual heroes, artists, and pioneers; freedom of expression; the exotic; and the power of the individual imagination. American authors Edgar Allan Poe and Nathaniel Hawthorne, Laurence Sterne in England, and Johann Wolfgang von Góethe in Germany were included among well-known Romantic authors. The six major English Romantic poets were William Blake, William Wordsworth, Samuel Taylor Coleridge, Lord Byron, Percy Bysshe Shelley, and John Keats.

William Blake

William Blake (1757-1827) is considered one of the major English Romantic poets. He was also an artist and printmaker. In addition to his brilliant poetry, he produced paintings, drawings, and notably, engravings and etchings, impressive for their technical expertise, artistic beauty, and spiritual subject matter. Because he held many idiosyncratic opinions, and moreover because he was subject to visions, reporting that he saw angels in the trees and other unusual claims, Blake was often thought crazy by others during his life, though others believed him angelic and/or blessed. His work's creative, expressive character, and its mystical and philosophical elements, led people to consider him both precursor to and member of Romanticism, and a singular, original, unclassifiable artist at the same time. Blake illustrated most of his poetry with his own hand-colored, illuminated printing. He also partially illustrated Dante's *Divine Comedy* a year before dying; the small portion he completed was highly praised. His best-known poetry includes *Songs of Innocence and of Experience*, *The Book of Thel*, *The Marriage of Heaven and Hell*, and *Jerusalem*.

William Wordsworth

William Wordsworth (1770-1850) was instrumental in establishing Romanticism when he and Samuel Taylor Coleridge, another major English Romantic poet, collaboratively published *Lyrical Ballads* (1798). Wordsworth's "Preface to Lyrical Ballads" is considered a manifesto of English Romantic literary theory and criticism. In it, Wordsworth described the elements of a new kind of poetry, which he characterized as using "real language of men" rather than traditional 18th-century poetic style. In this Preface he also defined poetry as "the spontaneous overflow of powerful feelings [which] takes its origin from emotion recollected in tranquility." *Lyrical Ballads* included the famous works "The Rime of the Ancient Mariner" by Coleridge, and "Tintern Abbey" by Wordsworth. His semi-autobiographical poem, known during his life as "the poem to Coleridge," was published posthumously, entitled *The Prelude* and regarded as his major work. Wordsworth was England's Poet Laureate from 1843-1850. Among many others, his poems included "Tintern Abbey," "I Wandered Lonely as a Cloud" (often called "Daffodils"), "Ode: Intimations of Immortality," "Westminster Bridge," and "The World Is Too Much with Us."

Samuel Taylor Coleridge

One of the six major Romantic English Poets, Samuel Taylor Coleridge (1772-1834) was also a philosopher and literary critic, and close friends fellow Romantic poet William Wordsworth, with whom he collaborated in publishing *Lyrical Ballads,* launching the Romantic movement. He wrote very influential literary criticism, including the major two-volume autobiographical, meditative discourse *Biographia Literaria* (1817). Coleridge acquainted English-language intellectuals with the German idealist philosophy. He also coined many now familiar philosophical and literary terms, like "the willing suspension of disbelief," meaning that readers would voluntarily withhold judgment of implausible stories if their authors could impart "human interest and a semblance of truth" to them. He strongly influenced the American Transcendentalists, including Ralph Waldo Emerson. Coleridge's poem *Love,* a ballad (written to Sara Hutchinson), inspired John Keats' poem "La Belle Dame Sans Merci." He is credited with the origin of "Conversational Poetry" and Wordsworth's adoption of it. Some of his best-known works include "The Rime of the Ancient Mariner," "Christabel," "Kubla Khan," "The Nightingale," "Dejection: An Ode," and "To William Wordsworth."

John Keats

John Keats (1795-1821), despite his short life, was a major English Romantic poet. He is known for his six Odes: "Ode on a Grecian Urn," "Ode on Indolence," "Ode on Melancholy," "Ode to a Nightingale," "Ode to Psyche," and "To Autumn." Other notable works include the sonnet "O Solitude," "Endymion," "La Belle Dame Sans Merci," "Hyperion," and the collection *Lamia, Isabella, The Eve of St. Agnes and Other Poems*. The intensity and maturity he achieved in his poetry within a period of only around six years are often remarked since his death, though during life he felt he accomplished nothing lasting. He wrote a year before dying, "I have left no immortal work behind me—nothing to make my friends proud of my memory—but I have lov'd the principle of beauty in all things, and if I had had time I would have made myself remember'd." He was proven wrong. His verse from "Ode on a Grecian Urn" is renowned: "'Beauty is truth, truth beauty'—that is all / Ye know on earth, and all ye need to know."

George Gordon, Lord Byron

George Gordon Byron, commonly known as Lord Byron (1788-1824) was a major English Romantic poet. He is known for long narrative poems "Don Juan," "Childe Harold's Pilgrimage," and the shorter lyric poem "She Walks in Beauty." The aristocratic Byron travelled throughout Europe, living in Italy for seven years. He fought in the Greek War of Independence against the Ottoman Empire, making him a national hero in Greece, before dying a year later from a fever contracted there. He was the most notoriously profligate and flamboyant Romantic poet, with reckless behaviors including multiple bisexual love affairs, adultery, rumored incest, self-exile, and incurring enormous debts. He became friends with fellow Romantic writers Percy Bysshe Shelley, the future Mary Shelley, and John Polidori. Their shared fantasy writing at a Swiss villa the summer of 1816 resulted in Mary Shelley's *Frankenstein*, Byron's *Fragment of a Novel*, and was the inspiration for Polidori's *The Vampyre* establishing the romantic vampire genre. Byron also wrote linguistic volumes on American and Armenian grammars. He loved and kept many animals. His name is synonymous today with the mercurial Romantic.

Percy Bysshe Shelley

Percy Bysshe Shelley (1792-1822), a major English Romantic poet, was not famous during life but became so after death, particularly for his lyric poetry. His best-known works include "Ozymandias," "Ode to the West Wind," "To a Skylark," "Music," "When Soft Voices Die," "The Cloud," "The Masque of Anarchy"; longer poems "Queen Mab"/"The Daemon of the World" and "Adonaïs"; and the verse drama *Prometheus Unbound*. Shelley's second wife, Mary Shelley, was the daughter of his mentor William Godwin and the famous feminist Mary Wollstonecraft (*A Vindication of the Rights of Woman*), and became famous for her Gothic novel *Frankenstein*. Early in his career Shelley was influenced by William Wordsworth's Romantic poetry, and wrote the long poem *Alastor, or the Spirit of Solitude*. Soon thereafter he met Lord Byron, and was inspired to write "Hymn to Intellectual Beauty". He composed "Mont Blanc," inspired by touring the French Alpine commune Chamonix-Mont-Blanc. Shelley also encouraged Byron to compose his epic poem *Don Juan*. Shelley inspired Henry David Thoreau, Mahatma Gandhi, and others to civil disobedience, nonviolent resistance, vegetarianism, and animal rights.

William Butler Yeats

William Butler Yeats (1865-1939) was among the greatest influences in 20th-century English literature. He was instrumental in the Celtic Revival/Irish Literary Revival, founding and initially running the Abbey Theatre, and was the first Irishman awarded the Nobel Prize for Literature (1923). An Irish Nationalist, he was passionately involved in politics. Yeats was believed transitional from Romanticism to Modernism. His earlier verses were lyrical, but later became realistic, symbolic, and apocalyptic. He was fascinated with Irish legend, occult subjects, and historical cycles—"gyres." He incorporated Irish folklore, mythology, and legends in "The Stolen Child," "The Wanderings of Oisin," "The Death of Cuchulain," "Who Goes with Fergus?" and "The Song of Wandering Aengus." Early collections included *The Secret Rose* and *The Wind Among the Reeds*. His later, most significant poetry collections include *The Green Helmet, Responsibilities, The Tower,* and *The Winding Stair*. Yeats's visionary, apocalyptic (1920) poem "The Second Coming" reflects his belief that his times were the anarchic end of the Christian cycle/gyre: "what rough beast, its hour come round at last, / Slouches toward Bethlehem to be born?"

Explanations of Medieval/Renaissance Christian allegory

The student should explain that in literature, authors of allegory use all of the literal plot elements of their writing as symbols to represent more abstract subjects. For example, in *The Divine Comedy*, Dante symbolizes the human soul's efforts to achieve moral beliefs and behaviors and become united with God by narrating his persona's literal adventures as he travels through the kingdoms of Hell, Purgatory, and Heaven (*Inferno, Purgatorio,* and *Paradiso*). What appear literal stories of fantasy experiences are allegorical references to the human spiritual quest. The student should provide textual evidence, for example, quoting the *Inferno*'s opening: "Midway on our life's journey, I found myself / In dark woods, the right road lost". The student could then explain that by the plural first-person possessive in "*our* life's journey", Dante connects his persona's story to all of humanity's universal experience, reinforcing this by referring to "the right road" of which he has lost track. The student should explain the "dark woods" as an allegorical symbol of a human being's sinful, unenlightened Earthly existence and the "right road" symbolizing the life of virtue that unites people with God.

Example student explanation of a poet using a quote from an earlier poet's work

In "The Love Song of J. Alfred Prufrock", Eliot's six-line epigraph is from Canto 27 of Dante's *Inferno*. Eliot quotes Dante's original Italian, spoken by Guido da Montefeltro: "*S'io credesse che mia risposta fosse / A persona che mai tornasse al mondo, / Questa fiamma staria senza piu scosse. /Ma perciocche giammai di questo fondo/Non torno vivo alcun, s'i'odo il vero, / Senza tema d'infamia ti rispondo.*" Eliot omits translation: "If I believed my answer would be to a person who could return to the world, this flame would stay without more motion; but because nobody has ever come back alive from this abyss, if what I hear is true, without fear of infamy I can reply." Guido, fearing worldly ill repute for evil Earthly deeds, believed he could confide these to Dante—also trapped in Hell, hence unable to repeat them. Guido's "flame" represents his disembodied form in Hell: if he believed Dante could return to Earth (which he ultimately did), he/it would move/speak no more. "Prufrock" echoes the hellish setting, depicting hypocrites pretending goodness. Prufrock's concern for his reputation echoes Guido's: *Prufrock*'s dramatic monologue is best safely addressed to nobody who would repeat it.

Interpretation of quotes and references in first section of T. S. Eliot's *The Waste Land*

In *The Waste Land*'s first section, "The Burial of the Dead", Eliot refers to Chaucer's *Canterbury* Tales opening about April—but twisting it from Chaucer's happy depiction of its "sweet showers" to "...the cruelest month, breeding / Lilacs out of the dead land, mixing / memory and desire..." He quotes Wagner's opera *Tristan and Isolde* retelling the Arthurian story of adulterous lovers and the loss experienced through their actions. Eliot used his extensive knowledge of literature to reinforce his depiction of the fragmented, decayed "waste land" of post-World War I twentieth-century society. Two major influences Eliot took were *From Ritual to Romance* by Jessie Weston and *The Golden Bough* by Sir James Frazier—both British contemporaries of Eliot (born in America but resettled in England). Both authors described ancient fertility rites reflected Arthurian legend and modern religion and thought—prominently, the Fisher King legend. His wounds, causing impotence, made his country a "waste land." The land's fertility could be reclaimed by healing the Fisher King. Eliot incorporates the Fisher King theme in *The Waste Land*—yet without healing potential, reinforcing the modern world's lack of mythological or religious narrative to unify it.

Example student explanation of extended metaphor of mechanical object as an animal

In her poem "I like to see it lap the Miles", Emily Dickinson describes a railroad train, a new invention during her time, via extended metaphor comparing it to a horse. She writes of seeing the train "lap the miles—/And lick the Valleys up—/And/...feed itself at Tanks..." She describes seeing it "...prodigious step / Around a Pile of Mountains...And then a Quarry pare / To fit its Ribs..." She describes the train's whistle as "...horrid—hooting stanza" and further characterizes it as a "neigh". She concludes the poem by describing how the train, like a horse, will "...punctual as a Star / Stop—docile and omnipotent / At its own stable door—", representing the train depot/station as a horse's "stable". Juxtaposing the opposites of docility and omnipotence, Dickinson alludes to the way horses are physically powerful, yet often gentle and obedient to much smaller, physically weaker humans. Through the extended metaphor, she moreover likens the train to a horse, for its great power harnessed and controlled by humans.

Student interpretation of imagery

In Act I, Scene V of *Romeo and Juliet,* Shakespeare writes dialogue wherein Romeo describes how beautiful Juliet is using visual imagery: "O, she doth teach the torches to burn bright! / It seems she hangs upon the cheek of night / Like a rich jewel in an Ethiope's ear..." By saying she "teaches" torches to burn brightly, Shakespeare makes the point that Juliet's radiance surpasses that of the flames, contrasting it with the darkness of night. Then, he compares night's darkness to an Ethiopian's skin, and Juliet's contrasting brilliance to a gem's glow in an earring against the dark skin. In "Ode to Autumn", Keats uses auditory imagery to bring the season's "music" alive: "...in a wailful choir the small gnats mourn /...Or sinking as the light wind lives or dies; / And full-grown lambs loud bleat from hilly bourn; / Hedge-crickets sing; and now with treble soft / The redbreast whistles from a garden-croft, / And gathering swallows twitter in the skies." He appeals to readers' hearing, describing intermittent wind; gnats mourning in a "wailful choir"; lambs bleating; crickets singing; a robin's soft treble whistling; and swallows twittering.

Rhetorical devices vs. figures of speech

Although figures of speech and rhetorical devices are very similar and overlap in many aspects of their definitions, one difference is that a figure of speech uses the effect of altering word meanings to express an idea more colorfully or vividly. For example, instead of saying a woman is strong-willed; free-spirited; feisty; attractive, yet unpredictable; and maybe dangerous, some people use the figure of speech, "She's a pistol." When the main purpose of a figure of speech becomes that of convincing or persuading the audience—the writer's readers or the speaker's listeners—of the writer's point or argument, then the figure of speech can be said to become a rhetorical device. One type of rhetorical device is anaphora: the repetition at regular intervals of the same word or phrase, used to create an effect. Walt Whitman used anaphora in his poems *Crossing Brooklyn Ferry:* "Flood-tide below me! I watch you, face to face; / Clouds of the west! sun there half an hour high! I see you also face to face." and *Song of Myself* (Part 51): "Do I contradict myself? / Very well then I contradict myself, / (I am large, I contain multitudes.)"

Both figures of speech and rhetorical devices are used to create calculated effects and communicate specific emphases. One main difference is that figures of speech change the meanings of words. For example, instead of writing, "She is brave", one writes "She is a tiger": this figure of speech employs a metaphor, conveying the same meaning but using a different word than the original. By contrast, an example of a rhetorical device used by some sources (Literary Devices.net 2014, Quizlet.com 2014) uses repetition to create emphasis without changing word meanings: "I am never ever going to rob anyone for you and never, never ever give in to your sinful wish." In Book V of *Paradise Lost,* the great poet John Milton uses rhetoric: "...advise him of his happy state—/ Happiness in his power left free to will, / Left to his own free will, his will though free / Yet mutable..." Describing Adam, Milton emphasized humanity's free will by repeating the words "free" and "will". But he also created ambiguity by writing "though free / Yet mutable", i.e. free will was changeable: Adam could lose freedom by sinning/erring.

Use of rhetoric in poetry

In Holy Sonnet 10 – "Death, be not proud" – the great Metaphysical poet John Donne rhetorically berates Death. In the final sestet, Donne writes: "Thou art slave to fate, chance, kings, and desperate men, / And dost with poison, war, and sickness dwell, / And poppy or charms can make us sleep as well / And better than thy stroke; why swell'st thou then?" This illustrates the message stated in the first quatrain: "Death, be not proud, though some have called thee / Mighty and dreadful, for thou art not so; / For those whom thou think'st dost overthrow / Die not, poor Death, nor yet canst thou kill me." Donne opens denying Death is as powerful or horrible as some say, then adding that some whom Death thinks it kills do not die, and neither can Death kill him. He supports this argument by subsequently diminishing Death's reputed power, characterizing Death as a "slave"; associating it with the poor company of "poison, war, and sickness"; and ultimately asks the rhetorical question, "why swell'st thou then?" meaning Death has no reason to swell with pride—deflating Death's value and strength.

Rhetorical devices

Alliteration and hyperbole

Alliteration is both a literary and rhetorical device, using several words in sequence with the same initial sound. An example as literary device is in Wallace Stevens' (1922) poem "The Emperor of Ice Cream": "And bid him whip in kitchen cups concupiscent curds." Two examples of alliteration as rhetorical devices used by speakers for effect are Julius Caesar's "Veni, vidi, vici" ("I came, I saw, I conquered"), and John F. Kennedy's 1961 Inaugural Address: "Let us go forth to lead the land we love." Both repeated word-initial sounds to make their speeches more memorable. Hyperbole is extreme exaggeration for emphasis or effect. An example is in Andrew Marvell's famous (1650~1652) *carpe diem*-tradition poem "To His Coy Mistress": "My vegetable love should grow / Vaster than empires, and more slow; / An hundred years should go to praise / Thine eyes and on thine forehead gaze; / Two hundred to adore each breast, / But thirty thousand to the rest." Marvell exaggerates his love "Had we but world enough and time" as potentially growing longer than empires, hundreds and thousands of years.

Irony and oxymoron

Irony is the literary and rhetorical device of expressing one meaning by stating it using words that have the opposite meaning. In everyday speech it is also called sarcasm. An example of irony in literature in Shakespeare's tragedy *Julius Caesar* is in Act 3, Scene 2, in Marc Antony's famous eulogy speech at Caesar's funeral: "He was my friend, faithful and just to me. / But Brutus says he was ambitious, / And Brutus is an honorable man." Antony is using irony when he calls Brutus "honorable" to mean he is not. Four lines earlier, he also says "For Brutus is an honorable man; / So are they all, all honorable men..." ironically and indirectly indicting the many dishonorable men involved. Oxymoron juxtaposes apparently contradictory words; some everyday speech examples include "jumbo shrimp", "deafening silence", "conspicuous absence", etc. A literary example is in Shakespeare's *Hamlet,* Act 3, Scene 4: "I must be cruel only to be kind." Shakespeare's phrasing was so popular it has since been adopted into everyday expressions.

Literary irony

In literature, irony demonstrates the opposite of what is said or done. Three types are verbal irony, situational irony, and dramatic irony. Verbal irony uses words opposite to the meaning. Sarcasm may use verbal irony. An everyday example is describing something confusing as "clear as mud." In his 1986 movie *Hannah and Her Sisters,* author/director/actor Woody Allen says to his character's date, "I had a great evening; it was like the Nuremburg Trials." Notice these employ similes. In situational irony, what happens contrasts with what was expected. In dramatic irony, narrative informs audiences of more than its characters know. O. Henry's short story *The Gift of the Magi* uses situational irony: a husband and wife each sacrifice their most prized possession to buy each other a Christmas present. The irony is that she sells her long hair to buy him a watch fob, while he sells his heirloom pocket-watch to buy her the jeweled combs for her hair she had long wanted; in the end, neither of them can use their gifts.

Literal and figurative meaning

When language is used literally, the words mean exactly what they say and nothing more. When language is used figuratively, the words mean something more and/or other than what they say. For example, "The weeping willow tree has long, trailing branches and leaves" is a literal description. But "The weeping willow tree looks as if it is bending over and crying" is a figurative description—specifically, a simile or stated comparison. Another figurative language form is metaphor, or an implied comparison. A good example is the metaphor of a city, state, or city-state as a ship, and its governance as sailing that ship. Ancient Greek lyrical poet Alcaeus is credited with first using this metaphor, and ancient Greek tragedian Aeschylus then used it in *Seven Against Thebes,* and then Plato used it in the *Republic.* Henry Wadsworth Longfellow later famously referred to it in his poem, "O Ship of State" (1850), which has an extended metaphor with numerous nautical references throughout.

Drawing inferences

Inferences about literary text are logical conclusions that readers make based on their observations and previous knowledge. By inferring, readers construct meanings from text relevant to them personally. By combining their own schemas or concepts and their background information pertinent to the text with what they read, readers interpret it according to both what the author has conveyed and their own unique perspectives. Authors do not always explicitly spell out every meaning in what they write; many meanings are implicit. Through inference, readers can comprehend implied meanings in the text, and also derive personal significance from it, making the text meaningful and memorable to them. Inference is a natural process in everyday life. When readers infer, they can draw conclusions about what the author is saying, predict what may reasonably follow, amend these predictions as they continue to read, interpret the import of themes, and analyze the characters' feelings and motivations through their actions, and much more.

Textual evidence to analyze literature

Knowing about the historical background and social context of a literary work, as well as the identity of that work's author, can help to inform the reader about the author's concerns and intended meanings. For example, George Orwell published his novel *1984* in the year 1949, soon after the end of World War II. At that time, following the defeat of the Nazis, the Cold War began between the Western Allied nations and the Eastern Soviet Communists. People were therefore concerned about the conflict between the freedoms afforded by Western democracies versus the oppression represented by Communism. Author Orwell had also previously fought in the Spanish Civil War against a Spanish regime that he and his fellows viewed as oppressive. From this information, readers can infer that Orwell was concerned about oppression by totalitarian governments. This informs *1984*'s story of Winston Smith's rebellion against the oppressive "Big Brother" government of the fictional dictatorial state of Oceania and his capture, torture, and ultimate conversion by that government.

Literary theme

When we read parables, their themes are the lessons they aim to teach. When we read fables, the moral of each story is its theme. When we read fictional works, the authors' perspectives regarding life and human behavior are their themes. Unlike in parables and fables, themes in literary fiction are not meant to preach or teach the readers a lesson. Hence themes in fiction are not as explicit as they are in parables or fables. Instead they are implicit, and the reader only infers them. By analyzing the fictional characters through thinking about their actions and behavior, and understanding the setting of the story and reflecting on how its plot develops, the reader comes to infer the main theme(s) of the work. When writers succeed, they communicate with their readers such that some common ground is established between author and audience. While a reader's individual experience may differ in its details from the author's written story, both may share universal underlying truths which allow author and audience to connect.

Determining theme

In well-crafted literature, theme, structure, and plot are interdependent and inextricable: each element informs and reflects the others. The structure of a work is how it is organized. The theme is the central idea or meaning found in it. The plot is what happens in the story. (Plots can be physical actions or mental processes—e.g., Marcel Proust.) Titles can also inform us of a work's theme. For instance, Edgar Allan Poe's title "The Tell-Tale Heart" informs us of its theme of guilt before we even read about the repeated heartbeat the protagonist begins hearing immediately before and constantly after committing and hiding a murder. Repetitive patterns of events or behaviors also give clues to themes. The same is true of symbols: in F. Scott Fitzgerald's *The Great Gatsby*, for Jay Gatsby the green light at the end of the dock symbolizes Daisy Buchanan and his own dreams for the future. More generally, it symbolizes the American Dream, and narrator Nick Carraway explicitly compares it to early settlers' sight of America rising from the ocean.

Thematic development

In *The Great Gatsby*, F. Scott Fitzgerald portrayed 1920s America as greedy, cynical, and rife with moral decay. Jay Gatsby's lavish weekly parties symbolize the reckless excesses of the Jazz Age. The growth of bootlegging and organized crime in reaction to Prohibition is symbolized by the character of Meyer Wolfsheim and by Gatsby's own ill-gotten wealth. Fitzgerald symbolized social divisions using geography: the "old money" aristocrats like the Buchanans lived on East Egg, while the "new money" bourgeois like Gatsby lived on West Egg. Fitzgerald also used weather, as many authors have, to reinforce narrative and emotional tones in the novel. Just as in *Romeo and Juliet*, William Shakespeare set the confrontation of Tybalt and Mercutio and its deadly consequences on the hottest summer day under a burning sun, in *The Great Gatsby*, Fitzgerald did the same with Tom Wilson's deadly confrontation with Gatsby. Both works are ostensible love stories carrying socially critical themes about the destructiveness of pointless and misguided behaviors—family feuds in the former, pursuit of money in the latter.

In Victor Hugo's novel *Les Misérables*, the overall metamorphosis of protagonist Jean Valjean from a cynical ex-convict into a noble benefactor demonstrates Hugo's theme of the importance of love and compassion for others. Hugo also reflects this in more specific plot events. For example, Valjean's love for Cosette sustains him through many difficult periods and trying events. Hugo illustrates how love and compassion for others beget the same in them: Bishop Myriel's kindness to Valjean eventually inspires him to become honest. Years later, Valjean, as M. Madeleine, has rescued Fauchelevent from under a fallen carriage, Fauchelevent returns the compassionate act by giving Valjean sanctuary in the convent. M. Myriel's kindness also ultimately enables Valjean to rescue Cosette from the Thénardiers. Receiving Valjean's father-like love enables Cosette to fall in love with and marry Marius. And the love between Cosette and Marius enables the couple to forgive Valjean for his past crimes when they are revealed.

In one of his shortest stories, Poe used economy of language to emphasize the murderer-narrator's obsessive focus on bare details like the victim's cataract-milky eye, the sound of a heartbeat, and insistence he is sane. The narrator begins by denying he is crazy, even citing his extreme agitation as proof of sanity. Contradiction is then extended: the narrator loves the old man, yet kills him. His motives are irrational—not greed or revenge, but to relieve the victim of his "evil eye." Because "eye" and "I" are homonyms, readers may infer that eye/I symbolizes the old man's identity, contradicting the killer's delusion that he can separate them. The narrator distances himself from the old man by perceiving his eye as separate, and dismembering his dead body. This backfires in another body part when he imagines the victim's heartbeat, which is really his own. Guilty and paranoid, he gives himself away. Poe predated Freud in exploring the paradox of killing those we love and the concept of projecting our own processes onto others.

William Faulkner contrasts the traditions of the antebellum South with the rapid changes of post-Civil War industrialization in his short story *A Rose for Emily*. The central character, Emily Grierson, denies the reality of modern progress, living inside the isolated world of her house. Contradictorily, she is both a testament to time-honored history and a mysterious, eccentric, unfathomable burden. Faulkner portrays her with deathlike imagery even in life, comparing her to a drowned woman and referring to her skeleton. Emily symbolizes the Old South; as her social status is degraded, so is the antebellum social order. Like Miss Havisham in Charles Dickens' *Great Expectations*, Emily preserves her bridal bedroom, denying change and time's passage. Emily tries to control death through denial, shown in her necrophilia with her father's corpse and her killing Homer Barron to stop him from leaving her, then also denying his death. Faulkner uses the motif of dust throughout to represent not only the decay of Emily, her house, and Old Southern traditions, but also how her secrets are obscured from others.

The great White Whale in *Moby-Dick* plays various roles to different characters. In Captain Ahab's obsessive, monomaniacal quest to kill it, the whale represents all evil, and Ahab believes it his duty and destiny to rid the world of it. Ishmael attempts through multiple scientific disciplines to understand the whale objectively, but fails—it is hidden underwater and mysterious to humans—reinforcing Melville's theme that humans can never know everything; here the whale represents the unknowable and may be interpreted as symbolizing God. Melville reverses white's usual connotation of purity in Ishmael's dread of white, associated with crashing waves, polar animals, albinos—all frightening and unnatural. White is often viewed as an absence of color, yet white light is the sum total of all colors in the spectrum. In the same way, white can signify both absence of meaning, and totality of meaning incomprehensible to humans. As a creature of nature, the whale also symbolizes how 19th-century white men's exploitative expansionistic actions were destroying the natural environment.

Because of the old fisherman Santiago's struggle to capture a giant marlin, some people characterize Ernest Hemingway's story as telling of man against nature. However, it can more properly be interpreted as telling of man's role as part of nature. Both man and fish are portrayed as brave, proud, and honorable. In Hemingway's world, all creatures, including humans, must either kill or be killed. Santiago reflects, "man can be destroyed but not defeated," following this principle in his life. As heroes are often created through their own deaths, Hemingway seems to believe that while being destroyed is inevitable, destruction enables living beings to transcend it by fighting bravely with honor and dignity. Hemingway echoes Romantic poet John Keats' contention that only immediately before death can we understand beauty as it is about to be destroyed. He also echoes ancient Greek and Roman myths and the Old Testament with the tragic flaw of overweening pride/overreaching. Like Icarus, Prometheus, and Adam and Eve, the old man "went out too far."

Universal theme in ancient religious texts

The Old Testament book Genesis, the Quran, and the Epic of Gilgamesh all contain flood stories. Versions differ somewhat: Genesis describes a worldwide flood, attributing it to God's decision that mankind, his creation, had become incontrovertibly wicked in spirit and must be destroyed for the world to start anew. The Quran describes the flood as regional, caused by Allah after sending Nuh (notice the similarity in name to Noah) as a messenger to his people to cease their evil. The Quran stipulates Allah only destroys those who deny or ignore messages from his messengers. Marked similarities also exist: in the Gilgamesh poems Utnapishtim, like Noah, is instructed to build a ship to survive the flood. Both men send out birds afterward as tests, and both include doves and a raven, though with different outcomes. Historians and archeologists believe a Middle Eastern tidal wave was a real basis for these stories. However, their universal themes remain the same: the flood was seen as God's way of wiping out humans whose behavior had become ungodly.

First-person narration

First-person narratives let narrators express inner feelings and thoughts, especially when the narrator is the protagonist as Lemuel Gulliver is in Jonathan Swift's *Gulliver's Travels.* The narrator may be a close friend of the protagonist, like Dr. Watson in Arthur Conan Doyle's *Sherlock Holmes.* Or the narrator can be less involved with the main characters and plot, like Nick Carraway in F. Scott Fitzgerald's *The Great Gatsby.* When a narrator reports others' narratives secondhand or more, s/he is a "frame narrator," like the nameless narrator of Joseph Conrad's *Heart of Darkness* or Mr. Lockwood in Emily Brontë's *Wuthering Heights.* First-person plural is unusual but can be effective, as in Isaac Asimov's *I, Robot;* William Faulkner's *A Rose for Emily;* Maxim Gorky's *Twenty-Six Men and a Girl;* or Jeffrey Eugenides' *The Virgin Suicides.* Author Kurt Vonnegut is the first-person narrator in his semi-autobiographical novel *Timequake.* Also unusual but effective is a first-person omniscient (rather than the more common third-person omniscient) narrator, like Death in Markus Zusak's *The Book Thief* and the dead girl's ghost in Alice Sebold's *The Lovely Bones.*

Second-person narration

While second-person address is very commonplace in popular song lyrics, it is the least used form of narrative voice in literary works. Popular serial books of the 1980s like *Fighting Fantasy* or *Choose Your Own Adventure* employed second-person narratives. In some cases, a narrative combines both second-person and first-person voices, speaking of "you" and "I." This can draw readers into the story, and it can also enable the authors to compare directly "your" and "my" feelings, thoughts, and actions. When the narrator is also a character in the story, as in Edgar Allan

Poe's short story "The Tell-Tale Heart" or Jay McInerney's novel *Bright Lights, Big City,* the narrative is better defined as first-person despite its also addressing "you."

Third-person narration

Narration in the third person is the most often-used type, as it allows authors the most flexibility. It is so common that readers simply assume without needing to be informed that the narrator is not a character in, or involved in the story. Third-person singular is used more frequently than third-person plural, though some authors have also effectively used plural. However, both singular and plural are most often included in stories according to which character(s) is/are being described. The third-person narrator may be either objective or subjective, and either omniscient or limited. Objective third-person narration does not include what the characters described are thinking or feeling, while subjective third-person narration does. The third-person omniscient narrator knows everything about all characters, including their thoughts and emotions, and all related places, times, and events, whereas the third-person limited narrator may know everything about a particular character of focus, but is limited to that character; in other words, the narrator cannot speak about anything that character does not know.

Alternating-person narration

Although authors more commonly write stories from one point of view, there are also instances wherein they alternate the narrative voice within the same book. For example, they may sometimes use an omniscient third-person narrator and a more intimate first-person narrator at other times. In J. K. Rowling's series of *Harry Potter* novels, she often writes in a third-person limited narrative, but sometimes changes to narration by characters other than protagonist Harry Potter. George R. R. Martin's series *A Song of Ice and Fire* (the basis for the popular HBO TV series *Game of Thrones*) changes the point of view to coincide with divisions between chapters. The same technique is used by Erin Hunter (a pseudonym for several authors of the *Warriors, Seekers,* and *Survivors* book series). Authors using first-person narrative sometimes switch to third-person to describe significant action scenes, especially those where the narrator was absent or uninvolved, as Barbara Kingsolver does in her novel *The Poisonwood Bible.*

Classic analysis of plot structure

In *Poetics,* Aristotle defined plot as "the arrangement of the incidents." He meant not the story, but how it is structured for presentation. In tragedies, Aristotle found results driven by chains of cause-and-effect preferable to those driven by the protagonist's personality/character. He identified "unity of action" as necessary for a plot's wholeness; its events must be internally connected, not episodic or relying on *deus ex machina* or other external intervention. A plot must have a beginning, middle, and end. Gustav Freytag adapted Aristotle's ideas into his Triangle/Pyramid (1863). The beginning, today called the exposition/incentive/inciting moment, emphasizes causes and de-emphasizes effects. Aristotle called the ensuing cause-and-effect *desis,* or tying up, today called complication(s) which occur during the rising action. These culminate in a crisis/climax/reversal/turning point, Aristotle's *peripateia.* This occurs at the plot's middle, where cause and effect are both emphasized. The falling action, which Aristotle called the *lusis* or unraveling, is today called the dénouement. The resolution comes at the catastrophe/outcome or end, when causes are emphasized and effects de-emphasized.

Story vs. discourse

In terms of plot, "story" is the characters, places, and events originating in the author's mind, while "discourse" is how the author arranges and sequences events—which may be chronological or not. Story is imaginary; discourse is words on the page. Discourse allows story to be told in different ways. One element of plot structure is relating events differently from the order in which they occurred. This is easily done with cause-and-effect; for example, in the sentence, "He died following a long illness," we know the illness preceded the death, but the death precedes the illness in words. In Kate Chopin's short story "The Story of an Hour" (1894), she tells some of the events out of chronological order, which has the effect of amplifying the surprise of the ending for the reader. Another element of plot structure is selection. Chopin omits some details, such as Mr. Mallard's trip home; this allows readers to be as surprised at his arrival as Mrs. Mallard is.

Analysis of plot structures through recurring patterns in actions or events

Authors of fiction select characters, places, and events from their imaginations and arrange them in ways that will affect their readers. One way to analyze plot structure is to compare and contrast different events in a story. For example, in Kate Chopin's "The Story of an Hour," a very simple but key pattern of repetition is the husband's leaving and then returning. Such patterns fulfill the symmetrical aspect that Aristotle said was required of sound plot structure. In James Baldwin's short story, "Sonny's Blues," the narrator is Sonny's brother. In an encounter with one of Sonny's old friends early in the story, the brother initially disregards his communication. In a subsequent flashback, Baldwin informs us that this was the same way he had treated Sonny. In Nathaniel Hawthorne's "Young Goodman Brown," a pattern is created by the protagonist's recurrent efforts not to go farther into the wood; in Herman Melville's "Bartleby the Scrivener," by Bartleby's repeated refusals; and in William Faulkner's "Barn Burning," by the history of barn-burning episodes.

Conflict

A conflict is a problem to be solved. Literary plots typically include one conflict or more. Characters' attempts to resolve conflicts drive the narrative's forward movement. Conflict resolution is often the protagonist's primary occupation. Physical conflicts like exploring, wars, and/or escapes tend to make plots most suspenseful and exciting. Emotional, mental, and/or moral conflicts tend to make stories more personally gratifying or rewarding for many audiences. Conflicts can be external or internal. A major type of internal conflict is some inner personal battle, or "man against himself." Major types of external conflicts include "man against nature," "man against man," and "man against society." Readers can identify conflicts in literary plots by asking themselves who the protagonist is, who or what the antagonist is, why the antagonist is an antagonist, why the protagonist and antagonist conflict, what events develop the conflict, which event is the climax, what the outcome tells them about the protagonist, and whether they sympathized or identified with the protagonist or antagonist and why.

Mood and tone

Mood is a story's atmosphere, or the feelings the reader gets from reading it. The way authors set the mood in writing is comparable to the way filmmakers use music to set the mood in movies. Instead of music, though, writers judiciously select evocative or descriptive words to evoke certain moods. The mood of a work may convey joy, anger, bitterness, hope, gloom, fear, an ominous feeling, or any other emotion the author wants the reader to feel. In addition to vocabulary choices, authors also use figurative expressions, particular sentence structures, and choices of diction that project and reinforce the moods they want to create. Whereas mood is the reader's emotions evoked by reading what is written, tone is the emotions and attitudes of the writer that s/he expresses in the writing. Authors use the same literary techniques to establish tone as they do to establish mood. An author may use a humorous tone, an angry or sad tone, a sentimental or unsentimental tone, or something else entirely.

Purposes of good dialogue

In literary fiction, effectively written dialogue serves at least one but usually several purposes. It advances the story and moves the plot. It develops the characters. It sheds light on the work's theme(s) or meaning(s). It can, often subtly, account for the passage of time not otherwise indicated. It can alter the direction that the plot is taking, typically by introducing some new conflict(s) or changing (an) existing one(s). Dialogue can establish a work's narrative voice and/or the characters' voices and set the tone of the story or of particular characters. When fictional characters display enlightenment or realization, dialogue can give readers an understanding of what those characters have discovered, and how. Dialogue can illuminate the motivations and wishes of the story's characters for its readers. By using consistent thoughts and syntax, dialogue can support character development. Skillfully created, it can also represent real-life speech rhythms in written form. Via conflicts and ensuing action, dialogue also provides drama.

In fictional literary works, effectively written dialogue should not have only the effect of breaking up or interrupting sections of narrative. Well-written dialogue does not reproduce verbatim things said in an author's real-life experiences. While dialogue may supply exposition for readers, it must nonetheless be believable. Dialogue should be dynamic, not static, and it should not resemble regular prose not representing conversation. Authors should not use dialogue as prose contexts for self-consciously "clever" similes or metaphors, which is unnatural and awkward. Dialogue should not slow down the movement of the plot or the story. When narrative would better establish a story's setting, authors should not substitute dialogue, which would be inappropriate. Authors should not express their own opinions in characters' dialogue. They should not try to imitate what real-life characters would say; dialogue must seem and sound natural, rather than actually duplicating natural speech. Dialogue should also not simply consist of conversations enclosed in quotation marks that do not serve the purpose of the story.

Effects of story events on works' meanings

Novelist E. M. Forster has made the distinction between story as relating a series of events, such as a king dying and then his queen dying, versus plot as establishing motivations for actions and causes for events, such as a king dying and then his queen dying from grief over his death. Thus plot fulfills the function of helping readers understand cause-and-effect in events and underlying motivations in characters' actions, which in turn helps them understand life. This affects a work's meaning by supporting its ability to explain why things happen, why people do things, and ultimately explain some of the meaning in life. Some authors find that while story events convey meaning, they do not tell readers there is any one meaning in life or way of living, but rather are mental experiments with various meanings and ways of life enabling readers to explore. Hence stories may not necessarily be constructed to impose one definitive meaning, but rather to find some shape, direction, and meaning within otherwise random events.

Analysis of character development

To understand the characters in a literary text, we can consider what kinds of observations the author makes about each character. We can look for contradictions in what a character thinks, says, and does. We can notice whether the author's observations about a character differ from what other characters in the story say about that character. We can note how the author describes each character. A character may be dynamic in that s/he changes in some significant way(s) during the story, or static in that s/he remains the same from the beginning of the story to the end. Characters may be perceived as "flat" or, in other words, not fully developed and/or without salient personality traits, or "round," as in more well developed, with characteristics that stand out vividly. Another thing to consider is whether characters in a story symbolize any universal properties. In addition, as readers we can think about whether we could compare and/or contrast the attributes of two characters in the same story to analyze how authors develop characters.

Figurative language

Figurative language is any language that extends past the literal meanings of the words. It serves the function of offering readers new insight into the people, things, events, and subjects covered in a work of literature. Figurative language also enables readers to feel they are sharing the authors' experiences. It can stimulate the reader's senses, make comparisons that readers find intriguing or even startling, and enable readers to view the world in different ways. Seven specific types of figurative language include: imagery, similes, metaphors, alliteration, personification, onomatopoeia, and hyperbole. Imagery is descriptive language that accesses the senses. Imagery can describe people, animals, or things. For example, the images T. S. Eliot uses in his poem "The Waste Land" of towers crumbling, wells dried up, and tombstones toppled over create mental images for the reader of the decay of a civilization.

Alliteration, personification, imagery, and simile

Alliteration is using a series of words containing the same sounds—assonance with vowels, and consonance with consonants. Personification is describing a thing or animal as a person. Imagery is description using sensory terms that create mental images for the reader of how people, animals, or things look, sound, feel, taste, and/or smell. This verse from Alfred Tennyson's poem "The Eagle" uses all of these types of figurative language: "He clasps the crag with crooked hands." Tennyson used alliteration, repeating /k/ and /kr/ sounds. These hard-sounding consonants reinforce the imagery giving visual and tactile impressions of the eagle. Tennyson also used personification, describing a bird as "he" and calling its talons "hands." Similes are stated comparisons using "like" or "as." William Wordsworth's poem about "Daffodils" begins, "I wandered lonely as a cloud." This simile compares his loneliness to that of a cloud. It is also personification, giving a cloud the human quality loneliness.

Metaphor and onomatopoeia

Metaphor is an implied comparison that does not use "like" or "as" the way a simile does. Henry Wadsworth Longfellow echoes the ancient Greeks in "O Ship of State": the metaphor compares the state and its government to a nautical ship and its sailing. Onomatopoeia uses words imitating the sounds of things they name/describe. For example, in his poem "Come Down, O Maid," Alfred Tennyson writes of "The moan of doves in immemorial elms, / And murmuring of innumerable bees." The word "moan" sounds like some sounds doves make, "murmuring" represents the sounds of bees buzzing, and "buzzing" is also an onomatopoetic word. And in his play *The Tempest,* in scene 2 of Act One, William Shakespeare's character Ariel says, "Hark, hark! / Bow-wow. / The watch-dogs bark! / Bow-wow. / Hark, hark! I hear/ The strain of strutting chanticleer / Cry, 'cock-adiddle-dow!'" Onomatopoetic words represent the sounds of a dog barking and a rooster crowing, respectively. ("Strain" is also imagery describing a rooster's crow as song; "strain" paired with "strutting" is alliteration.)

Hyperbole

Hyperbole is excessive exaggeration used for humor or emphasis rather than for literal meaning. For example, in *To Kill a Mockingbird*, Harper Lee narrated, "People moved slowly then. There was no hurry, for there was nowhere to go, nothing to buy and no money to buy it with, nothing to see outside the boundaries of Maycomb County." This was not literally true; Lee exaggerates the scarcity of these things for emphasis. In "Old Times on the Mississippi," Mark Twain wrote, "I... could have hung my hat on my eyes, they stuck out so far." This is not literal, but makes his description vivid and funny. In his poem "As I Walked Out One Evening", W. H. Auden wrote, "I'll love you, dear, I'll love you / Till China and Africa meet, / And the river jumps over the mountain / And the salmon sing in the street." He used things not literally possible to emphasize his meaning that he will love the person addressed forever.

Couplets and meter to enhance meaning in poetry

When a poet uses a couplet—a stanza of two lines, rhymed or unrhymed—it can function as the answer to a question asked earlier in the poem, or the solution to a problem or riddle. Couplets can also enhance the establishment of a poem's mood, or clarify the development of a poem's theme. Another device to enhance thematic development is irony, which also communicates the poet's tone and draws the reader's attention to a point the poet is making. The use of meter gives a poem a rhythmic context, contributes to the poem's flow, makes it more appealing to the reader, can represent natural speech rhythms, and produces specific effects. For example, in "The Song of Hiawatha," Henry Wadsworth Longfellow uses trochaic (/ ◡) tetrameter (four beats per line) to evoke for readers the rhythms of Native American chanting: "*By* the *shores* of *Gitche Gum*ee, / *By* the *shin*ing *Big*-Sea-*Wat*er / *Stood* the *wig*wam of No*ko*mis." (Italicized syllables are stressed; non-italicized syllables are unstressed.)

Effects of figurative devices on meaning in poetry

Through exaggeration, hyperbole communicates the strength of a poet's or persona's feelings and enhances the mood of the poem. Imagery appeals to the reader's senses, creating vivid mental pictures, evoking reader emotions and responses, and helping to develop themes. Irony also aids thematic development by drawing the reader's attention to the poet's point and communicating the poem's tone. Thematic development is additionally supported by the comparisons of metaphors and similes, which emphasize similarities among things compared, affect readers' perceptions of images and enhance the imagery, and are more creative than writing in only literal terms. The use of mood communicates the atmosphere of a poem, can build a sense of tension, and evokes the reader's emotions. Onomatopoeia appeals to the reader's auditory sense and enhances sound imagery even when the poem is visual (read silently) rather than auditory (read aloud). Rhyme connects and unites verses, gives the rhyming words emphasis, and makes poems more fluent. Symbolism communicates themes, develops imagery, and evokes readers' emotional and other responses.

Poetic structure to enhance meaning in poetry

The opening stanza of Romantic English poet, artist and printmaker William Blake's famous poem "The Tyger" demonstrates how a poet can enhance the meaning of the work through creating tension by using line length and punctuation independently of one another: "Tyger! Tyger! burning bright / In the forests of the night, / What immortal hand or eye / Could frame thy fearful symmetry?" The first three lines of this stanza are trochaic (/ ᴜ), with "masculine" endings—that is, strongly stressed syllables at the ends of each of the lines. But Blake's punctuation contradicts this rhythmic regularity by not providing any divisions between the words "bright" and "In" or between "eye" and "Could." This irregular punctuation foreshadows how Blake disrupts the meter at the end of this first stanza by using a contrasting dactyl (/ ᴜᴜ), with a "feminine" (unstressed) ending syllable in the last word, "symmetry." Thus Blake uses structural contrasts to heighten the intrigue of his work.

In enjambment, one sentence or clause in a poem does not end at the end of its line or verse, but runs over into the next line or verse. Clause endings coinciding with line endings give readers a feeling of completion, but enjambment influences readers to hurry to the next line to finish and understand the sentence. In his blank-verse epic religious poem "Paradise Lost," John Milton wrote: "Anon out of the earth a fabric huge / Rose like an exhalation, with the sound / Of dulcet symphonies and voices sweet, / Built like a temple, where pilasters round / Were set, and Doric pillars overlaid / With golden architrave." Only the third line is end-stopped. Milton, describing the palace of Pandemonium bursting from Hell up through the ground, reinforced this idea through phrases and clauses bursting through the boundaries of the lines. A caesura is a pause in mid-verse. Milton's commas in the third and fourth lines signal caesuras. They interrupt flow, making the narration jerky to imply that Satan's glorious-seeming palace has a shaky and unsound foundation.

Making predictions

When we read literature, making predictions about what will happen in the writing reinforces our purpose(s) for reading and prepares us mentally for beginning to read, and for continuing to read further. We can make predictions before we begin reading and during our reading. As we read on, we can test the accuracy of our predictions, revise them in light of additional reading, and confirm or refute our predictions. Some things that can help readers to make predictions about literary works include: thinking about the title of the book, poem, or play; looking at the illustrations when there are any; considering the structure of the text as we read; making use of our existing knowledge relative to the subject of the text; asking ourselves questions about the story, characters, and subject matter, particularly "why" and "who" questions; and then answering these questions for ourselves by referring to the text.

Making connections to enhance reading comprehension

Reading involves thinking. For good comprehension, readers make text-to-self, text-to-text, and text-to-world connections. Making connections helps readers understand text better and predict what might occur next based on what they already know, such as how characters in the story feel or what happened in another text. Text-to-self connections with the reader's life and experiences make literature more personally relevant and meaningful to readers. Readers can make connections before, during, and after reading—including whenever the text reminds them of something similar they have encountered in life or other texts. Knowing a work's genre (mystery, fantasy, or whatever it may be); common practices of a certain author; a story's geographical, historical, and social setting; characters that remind us of other people; familiar plot elements; literary structure and devices (such as flashbacks); themes encountered in other works; and similar use of language and tone to other works are all means for connections. Venn diagrams and other graphic organizers help visualize connections. Readers can also make double-entry notes: key content, ideas, events, words, and quotations on one side, and the connections with these on the other.

Summarizing literature to support comprehension

When reading literature, especially demanding works, summarizing helps readers identify important information and organize it in their minds; briefly monitor understanding; identify the main theme(s), problems and solutions; and sequence the story. Readers can summarize before, during, and after they read. They can refer to examples of other occasions in life for summarizing: giving others directions, generally describing our weekends or summers in limited time, and explaining news items/articles we read, to name a few. To summarize literary content, readers should use their own words. Previewing a text's organization before reading by examining the book cover, table of contents, and illustrations also aids summarizing. So does making notes of key words and ideas in a graphic organizer while reading. Graphic organizers can also be used after reading: readers skim the text, pick out the most important parts of three to five sentences, and determine what can be omitted with the aid of the organizer. Unimportant details should be omitted in summaries. Summaries of nonfiction can include description, problem-solution, comparison-contrast, sequence, main ideas, and cause-and-effect.

Evaluation of summaries of literary passages

A summary of a literary passage is a condensation in the reader's own words of the passage's main points. Some guidelines for evaluating a summary of a literary passage include: The summary should be complete yet concise. It should be accurate, balanced, fair, neutral, and objective, excluding the reader's own opinions or reactions. It should reflect in similar proportion how much each point summarized was covered in the original passage. Summary writers should include tags of attribution, like "Macaulay argues that" to reference the original author whose ideas are represented in the summary. Summary writers should not overuse quotations: they should only quote central concepts or phrases they cannot precisely convey in words other than those of the original author. Another aspect in evaluating a summary is whether it can stand alone as a coherent, unified composition, albeit a brief one. In addition, evaluation of a summary should include whether its writer has cited the original source of the passage so that readers of the summary can find it.

Textual evidence to evaluate predictions

Textual evidence to evaluate reader predictions about literature includes specific synopses of the work, paraphrases of the work or parts of it, and direct quotations from it. The best literary analysis shows special insight into a theme, character trait, or change. The best textual evidence supporting analysis is strong, relevant, and accurate. Analysis that is not best, but enough, shows reasonable understanding of theme, character trait, or change; contains supporting textual evidence that is relevant and accurate, if not strong; and shows a specific and clear response. Analysis that partially meets criteria also shows reasonable understanding, but the textual evidence is generalized, incomplete, only partly relevant or accurate, or connected only weakly. Or there may be only relevant, accurate textual evidence, but no analysis and a vague or unclear response. Analysis that is vague, too general or incorrect, with an unclear response and irrelevant or incomplete textual evidence; that only summarizes the plot; and/or that answers the wrong question, or answers no question, is not enough to be adequate.

Literary theories and criticism and interpretation

Literary theory gives a rationale for the literary subject matter of criticism, and also for the process of interpreting literature. For example, Aristotle's *Poetics'* requirement of unity underlies any discussion of unity in Sophocles' *Oedipus Rex.* Postcolonial theory, assuming historical racism and exploitation, informs Nigerian novelist and critic Chinua Achebe's contention that in *Heart of Darkness,* Joseph Conrad does not portray Africans with complete humanity. Gender and feminist theories support critics' interpretation of Edna Pontellier's drowning at the climax of Kate Chopin's novel *The Awakening* (1899) as suicide. Until the 19th century, critics largely believed literature referenced objective reality, holding "a mirror up to nature" as William Shakespeare wrote. Twentieth-century Structuralism and New Historicism were predated and influenced by radical, non-traditional, historicized, cross-cultural comparative interpretations of biblical text in 19th-century German "higher criticism." Literary critic Charles Augustin Saint-Beuve maintained that biography could completely explain literature; contrarily, Marcel Proust demonstrated in narrative that art completely transformed biography. A profound 19th-century influence on literary theory was Friedrich Nietzsche's idea that facts must be interpreted to become facts.

Geoffrey Chaucer's "The Parlement of Foules"

In his dream-vision, Cicero views the universe with his famous grandfather, learning philosophical principles of virtue during earthly, illusory, and deathlike life, toward Heaven's rewards in the afterlife's true life. Geoffrey Chaucer uses less grand designs in his dream-vision: Hoping to learn something from Cicero's work and influenced by it, he also dreams of Scipio Africanus. However, instead of touring the universe and Stoic philosophy, Africanus takes Chaucer to the temple of Venus—connecting with Chaucer's preface statement that he writes about love. This poem is noteworthy for the first known reference to St. Valentine's Day as being for lovers. Leaving Venus's temple, Chaucer witnesses Nature's comic "parliament" wherein birds, symbolizing human suitors, select mates. He alludes to sexual maturity at two years for male predator birds contrasting with one year for females: Nature grants the female eagle's request to defer choice for another year, but lets other birds form couples. Chaucer's awakening by morning birdsong celebrates summer, and illustrates the phenomenon that dreams often retroactively incorporate real sounds heard just before waking.

Aristotle's criteria for tragedy in drama

In his *Poetics,* Aristotle defined five critical terms relative to tragedy. (1) *Anagnorisis:* Meaning tragic insight or recognition, this is a moment of realization by a tragic hero(ine) when s/he suddenly understands how s/he has enmeshed himself/herself in a "web of fate." (2) *Hamartia:* This is often called a "tragic flaw," but is better described as a tragic error. *Hamartia* is an archery term meaning a shot missing the bull's eye, used here as a metaphor for a mistake—often a simple one—which results in catastrophe. (3) *Hubris:* While often called "pride," this is actually translated as "violent transgression," and signifies an arrogant overstepping of moral or cultural bounds—the sin of the tragic hero who over-presumes or over-aspires. (4) *Nemesis:* translated as "retribution," this represents the cosmic punishment or payback that the tragic hero ultimately receives for committing hubristic acts. (5) *Peripateia:* Literally "turning," this is a plot reversal consisting of a tragic hero's pivotal action, which changes his/her status from safe to endangered.

Theory of tragedy proposed by Hegel

Georg Wilhelm Friedrich Hegel (1770-1831) proposed a different theory of tragedy than Aristotle (384-322 BCE) which was also very influential. Whereas Aristotle's criteria involved character and plot, Hegel defined tragedy as a dynamic conflict of opposite forces or rights. For example, if an individual believes in the moral philosophy of the conscientious objector, i.e., that fighting in wars is morally wrong, but is confronted with being drafted into military service, this conflict would fit Hegel's definition of a tragic plot premise. Hegel theorized that a tragedy must involve some circumstance in which two values, or two rights, are fatally at odds with one another and conflict directly. Hegel did not view this as good triumphing over evil, or evil winning out over good, but rather as one good fighting against another good unto death. He saw this conflict of two goods as truly tragic. In ancient Greek author Sophocles' tragedy *Antigone,* the main character experiences this tragic conflict, between her public duties and her family and religious responsibilities.

Revenge tragedy

Along with Aristotelian definitions of comedy and tragedy, ancient Greece was the origin of the revenge tragedy. This genre became highly popular in Renaissance England, and is still popular today in contemporary movies. In a revenge tragedy, the protagonist has been done some serious wrong, such as the assault and murder of a family member. However, the wrongdoer has not been punished. In contemporary plots, this often occurs when some legal technicality has interfered with the miscreant's conviction and sentencing, or when authorities are unable to locate and apprehend the criminal. The protagonist then faces the conflict of suffering this injustice, or exacting his or her own justice by seeking revenge. Greek revenge tragedies include *Agamemnon* and *Medea.* Playwright Thomas Kyd's *The Spanish Tragedy* (1582-1592) is credited with beginning the Elizabethan genre of revenge tragedies. Shakespearean revenge tragedies include *Hamlet* (1599-1602) and *Titus Andronicus* (1588-1593). A Jacobean example is Thomas Middleton's *The Revenger's Tragedy* (1606, 1607). The 1974 movie *Death Wish* is a contemporary example.

Hamlet's "tragic flaw"

Despite virtually limitless interpretations, one way to view Hamlet's tragic error generally is as indecision: He suffers the classic revenge tragedy's conflict of whether to suffer with his knowledge of his mother's and uncle's assassination of his father, or to exact his own revenge and justice against Claudius, who has assumed the throne after his crime went unknown and unpunished. Hamlet's famous soliloquy, "To be or not to be" reflects this dilemma. Hamlet muses "Whether 'tis nobler in the mind to suffer the slings and arrows of outrageous fortune, / Or to take arms against a sea of troubles, / And by opposing end them?" He sees the final sleep of death as "the rub; / For in that sleep of death what dreams may come... Must give us pause... that the dread of something after death... makes us rather bear those ills we have / Than fly to others that we know not of? / Thus conscience does make cowards of us all." Hamlet's excessive conscience leads to paralyzing indecision, at least temporarily.

For much of William Shakespeare's tragedy, Hamlet suffers anxiety over what to do about his uncle Claudius's murdering his (Hamlet's) father, Hamlet. During this time, Hamlet's tragic error might be considered a lack of action, as he seems paralyzed by his quandary. But making matters worse, Hamlet attempts to kill Claudius surreptitiously by stabbing him through a tapestry, accidentally killing Polonius instead. However, he eventually becomes inspired with a solution to avoid direct confrontation: "The play's the thing / Wherein I'll catch the conscience of the king." He presents a play depicting a similar murder. By observing his reaction, Hamlet can confirm or deny Claudius's guilt (reported by the late King Hamlet's ghost, which Hamlet was unsure was a true ghost or the devil) to inform his decision. During the presentation, Gertrude fatally drinks wine that Claudius poisoned and intended for Hamlet. Then Laertes kills Hamlet, to avenge Hamlet's accidental murder of Laertes' father Polonius, and his sister Ophelia's madness and eventual suicide in reaction to Hamlet's behavior. Hamlet's indecision delays action, but his actions have more tragic outcomes.

Theme of overreaching

A popular theme throughout literature is the human trait of reaching too far or presuming too much. In Greek mythology, Daedalus constructed wings of feathers and wax that men might fly like birds. He permitted his son Icarus to try them, but cautioned the boy not to fly too close to the sun. The impetuous youth (in what psychologist David Elkind later named adolescence's myth of invincibility) ignored this, flying too close to the sun: the wax melted, the wings disintegrated, and Icarus fell into the sea and perished. In the Old Testament, God warned Adam and Eve not to eat fruit from the tree of knowledge of good and evil, that they might remain pure and innocent. Ignoring this banished them from Eden's eternal perfection, condemning them to mortality and suffering. The Romans were themselves examples of over-reachers in their conquest and assimilation of most of the then-known world and ultimate demise. In Christopher Marlowe's *Dr. Faustus* and Johann Wolfgang von Goethe's *Faust,* the protagonist sells his soul to the Devil for unlimited knowledge and success.

Carpe diem tradition in poetry

Carpe diem is Latin for "seize the day." A long poetic tradition, it advocates making the most of time because it passes swiftly and life is short. It is found in multiple languages, including Latin, Torquato Tasso's Italian, Pierre de Ronsard's French, and Edmund Spenser's English, and is often used in seduction to argue for indulging in earthly pleasures. Roman poet Horace's Ode 1.11 tells younger woman Leuconoe to enjoy the present, not worrying about inevitable aging. Two Renaissance Metaphysical Poets, Andrew Marvell and Robert Herrick, treated *carpe diem* more as a call to action. In "To His Coy Mistress," Marvell points out that time is fleeting, arguing for love, and concluding that because they cannot stop time, they may as well defy it, getting the most out of the short time they have. In "To the Virgins, to Make Much of Time," Herrick advises young women to take advantage of their good fortune in being young by getting married before they become too old to attract men and have babies.

"To His Coy Mistress" begins, "Had we but world enough, and time, / This coyness, lady, were no crime." Using imagery, Andrew Marvell describes leisure they could enjoy if time were unlimited. Arguing for seduction, he continues famously, "But at my back I always hear/Time's winged chariot hurrying near; / And yonder all before us lie / Deserts of vast eternity." He depicts time as turning beauty to death and decay. Contradictory images in "amorous birds of prey" and "tear our pleasures with rough strife / Thorough the iron gates of life" overshadow romance with impending death, linking present pleasure with mortality and spiritual values with moral considerations. Marvell's concluding couplet summarizes *carpe diem*: "Thus, though we cannot make our sun / Stand still, yet we will make him run." "To the Virgins, to Make Much of Time" begins with the famous "Gather ye rosebuds while ye may." Rather than seduction to live for the present, Robert Herrick's experienced persona advises young women's future planning: "Old time is still a-flying / And this same flower that smiles today, / Tomorrow will be dying."

Reflection of content through structure

Wallace Stevens' short yet profound poem "The Snow Man" is reductionist: the snow man is a figure without human biases or emotions. Stevens begins, "One must have a mind of winter," the criterion for realizing nature and life does not inherently possess subjective qualities; we only invest it with these. Things are not as we see them; they simply are. The entire poem is one long sentence of clauses connected by conjunctions and commas, and modified by relative clauses and phrases. The successive clauses and phrases lead readers continually to reconsider as they read. Stevens' construction of the poem mirrors the meaning he conveys. With a mind of winter, the snow man, Stevens concludes, "nothing himself, beholds nothing that is not there, and the nothing that is" (ultimate reductionism). Linguist and poetics expert Jay Keyser once remarked (NPR, 2005) that he wrote all the words of "The Snow Man" on white cards and made them into a mobile; it was "perfectly balanced, like an Alexander Calder creation." He said the mobile visually represented the poem's content.

Contrast of content and structure

Robert Frost's poem "Stopping by Woods on a Snowy Evening" (1923) is deceptively short and simple, with only four stanzas, each of only four lines, and short and simple words. Reinforcing this is Frost's use of regular rhyme and meter. The rhythm is iambic tetrameter throughout; the rhyme scheme is AABA in the first three stanzas and AAAA in the fourth. In an additional internal subtlety, B ending "here" in the first stanza is rhymed with A endings "queer," "near," and "year" of the second; B ending "lake" in the second is rhymed in A endings "shake", "mistake," and "flake" of the third. The final stanza's AAAA endings reinforce the ultimate darker theme. Though the first three stanzas seem to describe quietly watching snow fill the woods, the last stanza evokes the seductive pull of mysterious death: "The woods are lovely, dark and deep," countered by the obligations of living life: "But I have promises to keep, / And miles to go before I sleep, / And miles to go before I sleep." The last line's repetition strengthens Frost's message that despite death's temptation, life's course must precede it.

Aspects that combine to total effect in Theodore Roethke's "The Waking"

"The Waking" is a villanelle, with five tercets, one quatrain, and only two rhymes. Roethke alternately repeats two main lines: "I wake to sleep, and take my waking slow," and "I learn by going where I have to go" throughout, gradually revealing meaning. Continuous overall rhythm and revolving sound patterns of interconnected rhyming and assonance create perpetual motion, reflecting the life cycle. Roethke's use of villanelle form perfectly suits this cyclical effect: repetition, becoming hypnotically chant-like, reinforces the poem's mystical quality. Waking to sleep, learning by going, and "think[ing] by feeling" represent paradoxes: meaning, like form, becomes circular. These symbolize abandoning conscious rationalism to embrace spiritual vision. We wake from the vision to "Great Nature," and "take the lively air" in life's dance. "This shaking keeps me steady"— another paradox—juxtaposes and balances fear of mortality with ecstasy in embracing experience. The transcendent vision of all life's interrelationship demonstrates, "What falls away is always. And is near." Readers experience the poem holistically, like music, through Roethke's integration of theme, motion, and sound.

Sylvia Plath's use of villanelle form to convey meaning in "Mad Girl's Love Song"

Sylvia Plath wrote the poem "Mad Girl's Love Song" in college to exemplify young love. The two repeated lines, "I shut my eyes and all the world drops dead" and "(I think I made you up inside my head.)" reflect the existential viewpoint that nothing exists in any absolute reality outside of our own perceptions. In the first stanza, the middle line, "I lift my lids and all is born again," in its recreating the world, bridges between the repeated refrain statements—one of obliterating reality, the other of having constructed her lover's existence. Unlike other villanelles wherein key lines are subtly altered in their repetitions, Plath repeats these exactly each time. This reflects the young woman's love, also not changing throughout the poem. The final quatrain expresses some regret: "I should have loved a thunderbird instead; / At least when spring comes they roar back again." Plath contrasts the thunderbirds' rebirth with the unchanging love she depicts, and reinforces it. The unchanging repeated lines mirror the lack of progress in her love.

Ted Hughes' animal metaphors

Hughes frequently used animal metaphors, as in "Crow" and collected poems about the mythic creature-character Crow. In "The Thought Fox," a model of concise, structured beauty, Hughes characterizes the poet's creative process with succinct, striking imagery of an idea as a fox entering his head. Repeating "loneliness" in the first two stanzas emphasizes the poet's lonely work: "Something else is alive / Beside the clock's loneliness." He treats an idea's arrival as separate from himself. Three stanzas detail in vivid images a fox's approach from the outside winter forest at starless midnight —its nose, "Cold, delicately" touching twigs and leaves; "neat" paw prints in snow; "bold" body; wide, deep, brilliant green eyes; and self-contained, focused progress—"Till, with a sudden sharp hot stink of fox," he metaphorically depicts poetic inspiration as the fox's physical entry into "the dark hole of the head." Hughes ends by summarizing his vision of poet as an interior, passive idea recipient, with the outside world unchanged: "The window is starless still; the clock ticks, / The page is printed."

Literary examples of metaphor

A metaphor is an implied comparison, i.e. it compares something to something else without using "like", "as", or other comparative words. For example, in "The Tyger" (1794), William Blake writes, "Tyger Tyger, burning bright, / In the forests of the night;" this is a metaphor as Blake compares the tiger to a flame not by saying it is like a fire, but by simply describing it as "burning." Henry Wadsworth Longfellow's poem "O Ship of State" (1850) uses an extended metaphor by referring consistently throughout the entire poem to the state, union, or republic as a seagoing vessel, referring to its keel, mast, sail, rope, anchors, and to its braving waves, rocks, gale, tempest, and "false lights on the shore". Within the extended metaphor, Wordsworth uses a specific metaphor: "...the anchors of thy hope!" This is a metaphor because, like Blake (above), Wordsworth does not say the state's hope is like a ship's anchors; he equates them without using comparative words.

Literary examples of similes

A simile is a directly stated comparison of one thing to another thing, often using "like" or "as". In his novel *Lord Jim* (1900), Joseph Conrad writes in Chapter 33, "I would have given anything for the power to soothe her frail soul, tormenting itself in its invincible ignorance like a small bird beating about the cruel wires of a cage." Conrad uses the word "like" to compare the girl's soul to a small bird. His description of the bird beating at the cage shows the similar helplessness of the girl's soul to gain freedom. In his poetic Scots song "A Red, Red Rose" (1794), Robert Burns writes, "O my Luve's like a red, red rose, / That's newly sprung in June: / O my Luve's like the melodie, / That's sweetly play'd in tune." Burns uses "like" to compare his beloved to a beautiful, freshly blooming flower. In a second simile, he compares her to a beautiful musical melody. In the poem *The Daffodils*

(1888), Wordsworth writes, "I wandered lonely as a cloud / that floats on high o'er vales and hills," comparing his persona's loneliness to that of a single cloud in the sky.

When an author uses similes to compare one thing to another, this gets readers' attention; stimulates readers' imaginations; and appeals to readers' senses by describing sensations of sight, sound, touch, smell, and/or taste. Similes lend more lifelike characteristics to fictional and poetic characters. Readers can more easily relate emotions expressed by authors to their own personal experiences when they read similes authors use. Consequently, readers can better understand literary subject matter when authors compare things to other things using similes. Additionally, similes offer readers ways to introduce more variety into the way they think, and show them different/new perspectives for perceiving reality. In his "Sonnet 18" (1609), Shakespeare writes, "Shall I compare thee to a summer's day? / Thou art more lovely and more temperate". This simile does not use "like" or "as" the way many similes do, yet it does directly state a comparison by using the verb "compare".

Literary examples of personification

Personification is the device of attributing human qualities and/or behaviors/actions to something that is not human. While personification is the literary term for this, a synonym used in the social sciences is anthropomorphism. In his romantic tragedy *Romeo and Juliet* (1597), Shakespeare writes dialogue spoken by Capulet (Act 1, Scene 2): "When well-appareled April on the heel / Of limping winter treads..." This contains three instances of personification: (1) April is a month, not a lady, yet he describes April as being well-dressed and as (2) treading (walking); (3) winter is a season, does not have a physical heel, and cannot limp. In his poem "Loveliest of Trees" (1896), A. E. Housman describes the cherry tree as "Wearing white for Eastertide." He personifies the tree's white flowers as white clothing, as a human would wear for Easter. In her short story, "How Pearl Button Was Kidnapped" (1912), Katherine Mansfield describes "...little winds playing hide-and-seek..." She personifies breezes as playing children.

Personification, i.e. attributing human qualities and actions to inanimate objects, non-human living things, or abstract concepts, imbues text with more profound meanings. We humans tend to be anthrocentric; i.e., we view the world from our human perspective, seeing non-human entities in a human light as well. When authors and poets use personification, they bring inanimate objects to life and characterize plants, animals, and ideas with human traits. Readers can better understand the nature and behaviors of non-human things/creatures by reading about them through the lens of personification. We can more easily relate to human beings, qualities, traits, and behaviors than non-human ones. Moreover, author use of personification opens up new, divergent, varied, and creative perspectives for readers. As an example, in his poem "Ode: Intimations of Immortality from Recollections of Early Childhood" (1807), William Wordsworth writes, "The Moon doth with delight / Look round her when the heavens are bare". He personifies the inanimate object of the moon as a human female looking around "her", creating a vivid visual image and investing the scene with emotional mood and tone.

Figurative vs. literal language, denotation vs. connotation, and technical language

As in fictional literature, informational text also uses both literal language, which means just what it says, and figurative language, which imparts more than literal meaning. For example, an informational text author might use a simile or direct comparison, such as writing that a racehorse "ran like the wind." Informational text authors also use metaphors or implied comparisons, like describing "the cloud of the Great Depression." Similar to literal and figurative, denotation is the literal meaning or dictionary definition of a word whereas connotation is feelings or thoughts associated with a word not included in its literal definition. For example, "politician" and "statesman" have the same denotation, but in context, "politician" may have a negative connotation while "statesman" may have a positive connotation. "Inexpensive" and "cheap" both denote "not costly," but the former has a neutral connotation while the latter can have a negative one. Technical language is vocabulary related to a specific discipline, activity, or process. For example, in closet-organizing instructions, "itemize" is technical language; in fire-building instructions, "kindling" is technical language.

Making inferences about informational text

With informational text, reader comprehension depends not only on recalling important statements and details, but also on reader inferences based on examples and details. Readers add the information they have read in the text to what they already know to draw inferences about the text. These inferences help the reader to fill in the information that the text does not explicitly state, enabling them to understand the text better and answer more questions about it. When reading a nonfictional autobiography or biography, for example, the most appropriate inferences for the reader to make might concern the events in the book, the actions of the subject of the autobiography or biography, and the message the author means to convey. When reading a nonfictional expository (informational) text, the reader would best draw inferences about problems and their solutions, and causes and their effects. When reading a nonfictional persuasive text, the reader will want to infer ideas supporting the author's message and what the author is trying to convince the intended audience.

Standards for citing textual evidence for grade levels 6-12

Reading standards for informational texts expect sixth-graders to cite textual evidence to support their inferences and analyses. Seventh-graders are expected additionally to identify several specific pieces of textual evidence to defend each of their conclusions. Eighth-graders are expected to differentiate strong from weak textual evidence. Ninth- and 10th-graders are expected to be able to cite thorough evidence as well as strong evidence from text. Eleventh- and 12th-graders are expected, in combination with the previous grade-level standards, to determine which things are left unclear in a text. Students must be able to connect text to their background knowledge and make inferences to understand text, judge it critically, draw conclusions about it, and make their own interpretations of it. Therefore, they must be able to organize and differentiate between main ideas and details in a text to make inferences about them. They must also be able to locate evidence in the text.

Paired reading strategy to identify main ideas and details

Students can support one another's comprehension of informational text by working in pairs. Each of the two students silently reads a portion of text. One student summarizes the text's main point, and then the other must agree or disagree and explain why. The pair will then develop an agreement as to what the text's main idea is. Then each of the students in the pair takes a turn at identifying details in the text portion that support the main idea that they have identified. After this, the pair of students silently reads the next portion of the text. Then they go through the same steps as before, but with their roles reversed this time. Each pair of students can keep track of the central ideas and supporting details by taking notes in two columns: one for main ideas and the other for the details that support those main ideas.

Text coding

Some experts (cf. Harvey and Daniels, 2009) recommend text coding or text monitoring as an active reading strategy to support student comprehension of informational texts. As they read short independent reading selections that their teachers assign them according to their reading levels, students make text code notations on Post-it Notes or in the margins of the text. Teachers should model text coding for students one or two codes at a time until they have demonstrated all eight codes: A check mark means "I know this." An X means "This is not what I expected." An asterisk (*) means "This is important." A question mark means "I have a question about this." Two question marks mean "I am really confused about this." An exclamation point means "I am surprised at this." An L means "I have learned something new from this." And an RR means "I need to reread this part."

Two-column notes

When students read or listen to an informational text, it can help them find and note its main ideas and supporting details by using the "two-column notes" strategy. Teachers should first introduce this strategy to students, model it, and have them practice using it. As students use two-column notes, they can better organize textual information, find data in text supporting conclusions, and evaluate whether textual evidence supports author claims. For example, in analyzing Abraham Lincoln's Gettysburg Address, students put in the Main Ideas column, "Our founding fathers created the U.S." Next to it in the Details column, they place "Conceived in liberty" and "Dedicated to all men being created equal." Under Main Ideas: "Now the U.S. is in a Civil War." Under Details: "Testing whether our nation as conceived can survive." Main Ideas: "We are here to dedicate the Gettysburg battlefield." Details: "The dedication is to those who died in the war," "This is their final resting place," and "This is a fitting and proper thing to do."

Structures or organizational patterns in informational texts

Some informational text is descriptive: It uses sensory imagery that helps readers to see, hear, feel, taste, and smell its information and/or it informs readers about what, who, when, where, and why related to the text's subject or topic. Another structure or pattern of informational text is sequence and order: Chronological texts relate events in the sequence that they occurred, from start to finish, while how-to texts organize information into a series of instructions in the sequence in which the steps should be followed. Comparison-contrast structures of informational text describe various ideas to their readers by pointing out how things or ideas are similar and how they are different. Cause and effect structures of informational text describe events that occurred, and identify the causes or reasons that those events occurred. Problem and solution structures of informational text introduce and describe problems, and then offer one or more solutions for each problem described.

Connections and distictions among elements in text

One of the Common Core State Standards in English Language Arts for reading informational texts is for students to be able to analyze how an informational text makes connections and distinctions among ideas, events, or individuals, such as by comparing them or contrasting them, making analogies between them, or dividing them into categories to show similarities and differences. For example, teachers can help eighth-graders analyze how a biology text author divides animals into categories of carnivores, which eat only meat; herbivores, which eat only plants; and omnivores, which eat both meat and plants. Teachers and students can identify the author's comparisons and contrasts of groups. Teachers can help students analyze these processes by supplying sentence frames. For example, "A _____ is a _____, so" and "A _____ is a _____ which means." The students fill these empty spaces in, such as, "A frog is a carnivore, so it eats only meat," and "A rabbit is an herbivore, which means it eats only plants."

Text features in informational texts

The title of a text gives readers some idea of its content. An appendix, at the back of the book or document, adds important information not in the main text. Captions, below or beside illustrations or photos, explain what those images show or contain. Charts and tables are visual forms of information that making something easier and faster to understand. Diagrams are drawings that show relationships between things or explain how they work. Glossaries, usually found at the backs of books, list technical terms alphabetically with their definitions to aid vocabulary learning and comprehension. Graphs visually show relationships of multiple sets of information plotted along vertical and horizontal axes. Headings separate sections of text and show the topic of each. An index, at the back of a book, lists the book's important topics alphabetically with their page numbers to help students find them easily. Maps show geographical information visually to help students understand the relative locations of places covered in the text.

Illustrations and photographs are pictures visually emphasizing important points in text, helping to make it more interesting. Boldface print is used to emphasize certain words, often identifying words included in the text's glossary where readers can look up their definitions. The table of contents is a list near the beginning of a text, showing the book's sections and chapters and their coinciding page numbers. This gives readers an overview of the whole text, and helps them find specific chapters easily. A timeline is a visual graphic showing historical events in chronological order to help readers see their sequence. A subheading divides subject headings into smaller, more specific categories to help readers organize information. Footnotes, at page bottoms, give readers more information, such as citations, links, or further details and discussions of statements or references in main text. Bullet points list items separately, making facts and ideas easier to see and understand. A sidebar is a box of information to one side of the main text giving additional information, often on a more focused or in-depth example of a topic.

Connotation and denotation

While denotation is a word's definition/literal meaning, its connotation is an implied meaning that readers infer. Teachers can help students understand positive or negative connotations of words depending on their sentence contexts. For example, the word "challenge" has a positive connotation in this sentence: "Although I finished last, I still accomplished the challenge of running the race." Teachers can give students a multiple-choice game wherein they choose whether "challenge" here means (A) easy, (B) hard, (C) fun, or (D) taking work to overcome. The word "difficult" has a negative connotation in this sentence: "I finished last in the race because it was difficult." Students choose whether "difficult" here means (A) easy, (B) hard, (C) fun, or (D) lengthy. Positive and negative connotations for the same word can also be taught. Consider the following sentence: "When the teacher asked Johnny why he was in the restroom so long, he gave a *smart* answer." In this context, "smart" means disrespectful and carries a negative connotation. But in the sentence, "Johnny was *smart* to return to class from the restroom right away," the same word means wise and carries a positive connotation.

Technical language

Technical language, like what is found in scientific texts, is more impersonal than literary and vernacular language. Passive voice tone makes tone impersonal. For example, instead of writing, "We found this a central component of protein metabolism," scientists write, "This was found a central component of protein metabolism." While science professors traditionally instructed students to avoid active voice because it leads to first-person ("I" and "we") usage, science editors today find passive voice dull and weak. Many journal articles combine both. Tone in technical science writing should be detached, concise, and professional. While one writes in the vernacular, "This chemical has to be available for proteins to be digested," professionals write technically, "The presence of this chemical is required for the enzyme to break the covalent bonds of proteins." Science writers also must achieve balance in mood between self-deprecating and grandiose. For instance, self-deprecating: "With fewer than ten reproducible assays, our findings are insignificant." Grandiose: "From our findings, we conclude everybody needs these supplements." And balanced: "We conclude more research is needed to isolate the mechanism this chemical initiates."

Explicit and implicit information

When informational text states something explicitly, the reader is told by the author exactly what is meant, which can include the author's interpretation or perspective of events. For example, a professor writes, "I have seen students go into an absolute panic just because they weren't able to finish administering the Peabody [Picture Vocabulary Test] in the time they were allotted." This explicitly tells the reader that the students were afraid, and by using the words "just because," the writer indicates their fear was exaggerated out of proportion relative to what happened. However, another professor writes, "I have had students come to me, their faces drained of all color, saying 'We weren't able to finish the Peabody.'" This is an example of implicit meaning: the second writer did not state explicitly that the students were panicked. Instead, he wrote a description of their faces being "drained of all color." From this description, the reader can infer the students were so frightened that their faces paled.

Identifying author's point of view or purpose

In some informational texts, readers find it easy to identify the author's point of view and/or purpose, as when the author explicitly states his or her position and/or reason for writing. But in other texts which are difficult, and/or whose authors give neutral or balanced viewpoints, it is harder. This is particularly true in scientific texts, wherein authors may state the purpose of their research in the report, but never state their point of view except by interpreting evidence or data. To analyze text and identify point of view or purpose, readers should ask themselves the following four questions: (1) With what main point or idea does this author want to persuade readers to agree? (2) How do this author's choices of words affect the way that readers consider this subject? (3) How do this author's choices of examples and/or facts affect the way that readers consider this subject? And (4) What is it that this author wants to accomplish by writing this text?

Use of rhetoric

There are many ways authors can support their claims, arguments, beliefs, ideas, and reasons for writing informational texts. For example, authors can appeal to readers' sense of logic by communicating their reasoning through carefully sequenced series of logical steps to help "prove" the points made. Authors can appeal to readers' emotions by using descriptions and words that evoke feelings of sympathy, sadness, anger, righteous indignation, hope, happiness, or any other emotion to reinforce what they express and share with their audience. Authors may appeal to the moral or ethical values of readers by using words and descriptions that can convince readers of the idea that something is right or wrong. By relating personal anecdotes, authors can supply readers with more accessible, realistic examples of points they make, as well as appealing to their emotions. They can provide supporting evidence by reporting case studies. They can also illustrate and illuminate their points by making analogies to which readers can better relate.

<u>Rhetorical devices</u>
An anecdote is a brief story authors may relate, which can illustrate their point(s) in a more real and relatable way. Aphorisms concisely state common beliefs and may rhyme. For example, Benjamin Franklin's "Early to bed and early to rise / Make a man healthy, wealthy, and wise" is one. Allusions refer to literary or historical figures to impart symbolism to a thing or person, and/or create reader resonance. A literary example is that in John Steinbeck's *Of Mice and Men,* protagonist George's last name is Milton, alluding to John Milton who wrote *Paradise Lost,* to symbolize George's eventual loss of his dream. Satire is a writing style that ridicules or pokes fun at human foibles or ideas. Jonathan Swift and Mark Twain are two examples of authors who wrote satirically. A parody is a form of satire that imitates another work to ridicule its topic and/or style. Paradox is a statement that is true despite appearing contradictory. Hyperbole is overstatement using exaggerated language. Oxymoron combines seeming contradictions, such as "deafening silence" or "jumbo shrimp."

Analogies compare two things sharing some common elements. Similes (stated comparisons using the words "like" or "as") and metaphors (implied comparisons) are considered forms of analogy. When using logic to reason with audiences, syllogism refers either to deductive reasoning or a deceptive, very sophisticated, or subtle argument. Deductive reasoning moves from general to specific, inductive reasoning from specific to general. Diction is author word choice establishing tone and effects. Understatement achieves effects like contrast or irony by downplaying or describing something more subtly than warranted. Chiasmus uses parallel clauses, the second reversing the order of the first. Examples include T. S. Eliot's "Has the Church failed mankind, or has mankind failed the Church?" and John F. Kennedy's "Ask not what your country can do for you; ask what you can do for your country." Anaphora regularly repeats a word or phrase at the beginnings of consecutive clauses or phrases to add emphasis to an idea. A classic example of anaphora was Winston Churchill's emphasis of determination: "We shall fight in the trenches. We shall fight on the oceans. We shall fight in the sky."

Language Use and Vocabulary

Dialect

Dialect is the form of a language spoken by people according to their geographical region, social class, cultural group, or any distinctive group. It includes pronunciation, grammar, and spelling. Literary authors often use dialect when writing dialogue to illustrate the social and geographical backgrounds of specific characters, which supports character development. For example, in *The Adventures of Huckleberry Finn* (1885), Mark Twain's novel is told in the first person by protagonist Huck in the dialect of the young and uneducated white Southern character, opening with this sentence: "You don't know about me without you have read a book by the name of The Adventures of Tom Sawyer, but that ain't no matter." Twain uses a different and exaggerated dialect to represent the speech of the African-American slave Jim: "We's safe, Huck, we's safe! Jump up and crack yo' heels. Dat's de good ole Cairo at las', I jis knows it."

In *To Kill a Mockingbird,* author Harper Lee used dialect in the characters' dialogue to portray the speech of uneducated Southern American people: "Reckon I have. Almost died the first year I come to school and et them pecans—folks say he pizened 'em." She also uses many Southern regional expressions, such as "right stove up," "What in the sam holy hill...?", "sit a spell," "fess" (meaning "confess"), "jim-dandy," and "hush your fussing." These contribute to Lee's characterization of the people she describes, who live in a small town in Alabama circa the 1930s. In *Wuthering Heights* (1847), Emily Bronte reproduces Britain's 18th-19th-century Yorkshire dialect in the speech of servant Joseph: "Running after t'lads, as usuald!... If I war yah, maister, I'd just slam t'boards i' their faces all on 'em, gentle and simple! Never a day ut yah're off, but yon cat o' Linton comes sneaking hither; and Miss Nelly, shoo's a fine lass!" Emily's sister Charlotte also used this dialect in *Jane Eyre* for a farm woman: "T'pig don't want it."

In addition to using dialects to support character development in novels, plays, poems, and other literary works, authors also manipulate dialects to accomplish various purposes with their intended reading audiences. For example, in an English Language Arts lesson plan for eighth graders (Groome and Gibbs, 2008), teachers point out author Frances O'Roark Dowell from Boone, North Carolina, set her Edgar Allan Poe and William Allen White Award-winning teen novel *Dovey Coe* (2000) in the Western North Carolina mountains of 1928. Dowell writes protagonist Dovey's narration in the regional Appalachian Mountain dialect to remind readers of the significance of the novel's setting. This lesson plan further includes two poems by African-American author Paul Laurence Dunbar: "When Malindy Sings" and "We Wear the Mask." Students are asked why Dunbar wrote the former poem in Southern slave dialect and the latter in Standard English. Exercises include identifying dialect/Standard English features, rewriting dialect in Standard English, identifying audiences, and identifying how author choices of dialects or Standard English affect readers and accomplish author purposes.

Dialect vs. diction

When written as characters' dialogue in literary works, dialect represents the particular pronunciation, grammar, and figurative expressions used by certain groups of people based on their geographic region, social class, and cultural background. For example, when a character says, "There's gold up in them thar hills," the author is using dialect to add to the characterization of that individual. Diction is more related to individual characters than to groups of people. The way in which a specific character speaks, including his or her choice of words, manner of expressing himself or herself, and use of grammar all represent individual types of diction. For example, two characters in the same novel might describe the same action or event using different diction: One says "I'm heading uptown for the evening," and the other says "I'm going out for a night on the town." These convey the same literal meaning, but due to their variations in diction they are expressed in different ways.

<u>Simple survey research into linguistic dialects</u>
To learn about different dialects spoken in different geographic regions, social classes, and cultural groups, students can undertake simple surveys of small groups of informants. Students should first make a list of words they have heard used in certain dialects. Then they can ask their respondents to identify the words in the list whose meanings they know. Students can also ask respondents which words they have heard of before, but whose meanings are unfamiliar to them. Using their lists of dialect words, students can ask informants to identify which of the words they personally still use in their day-to-day conversations. They might want to ask respondents a combination in the same survey, of both which words they know and which they still use in their speech. For a more multidimensional survey, a student can ask the sampled informants all three—words that they know, those that they have heard of but do not know the meanings, and those that they use in their speech.

<u>Influences on regional dialect</u>
Linguistic researchers have identified regional variations in vocabulary choices, which have evolved because of differences in local climates and how they influence human behaviors. For example, in the Southern United States, the Linguistic Atlas of the Gulf States (LAGS) Project by Dr. Lee Pederson of Emory University discovered and documented that people living in the northern or Upland section of the Piedmont plateau region call the fungal infection commonly known as athlete's foot "toe itch," but people living in the southern or Lowland section call it "ground itch." The explanation for this difference is that in the north, temperatures are cooler and people accordingly wear shoes, so they associate the itching with the feet in their description, but in the south, temperatures are hotter and people traditionally went barefoot, so they associated the itching with the ground wherefrom they presumably contracted the infection. Additional variations identified between northern and southern parts of the Gulf States include "chigger" versus "red bug," "dragonfly" versus "snake doctor," and "wishbone" versus "pullybone."

Parts of speech

Nouns are words for persons, places, or things. The words *girl, town*, and *house* are all nouns. Nouns are frequently the sentence subjects. Proper nouns are names. Pronouns replace nouns, including personal pronouns specifying person, number, gender, or case. Some common pronouns are *I, you, he, she, it, none,* and *which*. Personal pronouns may be subjective, such as sentence/clause subjects, or objective, like the objects of verbs or prepositions. Verbs are words for actions or states of being. Verbs are often sentence predicates. Adjectives are descriptive words modifying nouns, for example, *big* girl, *red* house, or other adjectives, such as *great* big house. Adverbs are descriptive words modifying verbs, adjectives, or other adverbs (including clauses), often ending in *–ly*. Examples include running *quickly* and *patiently* waiting. Conjunctive adverbs connect two clauses. The words *also, finally, however, furthermore, consequently, instead, meanwhile, next, still, then, therefore, indeed, incidentally,* and *likewise* are all conjunctive adverbs. Prepositions connect nouns/pronouns/phrases to other words in sentences, such as *on, in, behind, under, beside, against, beneath, over,* and *during*. Prepositional phrases include prepositions, their objects, and associated adjectives/adverbs. Conjunctions connect words/phrases/clauses. Common conjunctions include *and, when, but, or/nor, for, so,* and *yet*.

Fragments and run-on sentences

A sentence fragment is missing some essential component: a subject, predicate, or a dependent clause with no independent clause. An example of the latter is: "Although I knew that." This is incomplete because "although" makes it a dependent clause with no independent clause to complete the thought. By adding an independent clause, the sentence becomes complete: "Although I knew that, I forgot it." The statement "Going to dinner" has a subject (the gerund "going," a verbal functioning as a noun) and a prepositional phrase ("to dinner") but it does not have a proper subject. Again, adding a subject solves the problem: "We are going to dinner." To repair the statement "The friendly woman Mary," simply add a verb: "The friendly woman is Mary." Run-on sentences lack necessary punctuation and/or connecting words: "We went to their party we had a very good time we plan to go again." This can be corrected several ways: "We went to their party. We had a very good time. We plan to go again." Or, less choppily: "We went to their party; we had a very good time, and we plan to go again."

Inconsistent verb tenses and non-parallel structure

While changing verb tenses in writing can indicate temporal relationships, switching tenses in a sentence if both or all verbs represent the same time frame is incorrect. For example, "The professor explained the theory to students who ask questions" uses inconsistent verb tenses. The verbs should be either "explained" and "asked" or "explains" and "asks." It is also incorrect to maintain the same verb tense when the time frame shifts among actions. The sentence, "Before they even saw the evidence, they decided" should actually read, "Before they even saw the evidence, they *had* decided" because "decided" occurred prior to "saw." "Susie loves the puppy she adopted" is correct: present-tense "loves" is true currently, while past-tense "adopted" is something Susie did previously and is not doing currently. An example of non-parallel structure is: "She enjoys skating, skiing, swimming, and to sail a boat." Because the first three objects are all gerunds ("-ing" participles used as nouns), the fourth should be "sailing" to be consistent, not the inconsistent infinitive "to sail."

Colons vs. semicolons, its vs. it's, and saw vs. seen

Semicolons separate independent clauses, such as "She likes music; she likes to dance." Colons separate clauses when the second explains or illustrates the first: "She likes music: she likes to dance to it." People often misuse semicolons. For example, business letter salutations should use colons. "Dear Mr. Johnson:" for example. Semicolons are never correct here ("Dear Mr. Johnson;"). Another common error is inserting an apostrophe into "its" to indicate possession. For example, the sentence, "The house is old; *its* paint is peeling" is correct. People often incorrectly spell this possessive personal pronoun as "it's." Their error is because some possessive nouns/pronouns use apostrophes, such as "Barbara's idea" or "the man's hat." But "its," along with "yours," "hers," and "theirs" (without noun objects) do not. The only correct usage of "it's" is as a contraction of "it" and "is," as in "It's raining outside." "Saw" is the past tense of "to see." "Seen" is the perfect tense, used with auxiliary verbs to form present perfect "have seen," or past perfect, "had seen." This is why "I seen you" and "I have saw" are both incorrect.

Phrases, clauses, and independent and dependent clauses

A clause has a subject and a predicate and the other elements of a sentence. An independent clause can stand on its own as a sentence. A dependent clause has a subject and a predicate, but it also has a subordinating conjunction, a relative pronoun, or some other connecting word or phrase that makes it unable to stand alone without an accompanying independent clause. For example, "I knew she was not at home" is an independent clause that can be a sentence on its own. But "because I saw her leave" is a dependent clause due to the subordinating conjunction "because," which makes it depend on the independent clause. The two clauses, joined together, form the complex sentence, "I knew she was not at home because I saw her leave." A phrase is neither a complete sentence nor a clause. It lacks a subject, or a predicate, or both. For example, "late at night" is an adverb phrase; "into the house" is a prepositional phrase. Phrases modify other sentence parts.

Simple, compound, and complex sentences

A simple sentence is the same thing as an independent clause. It states a complete thought and includes a subject and predicate/verb. An example is, "Some students cram before tests." "Students" is the subject; "some" is a modifying adjective. "Cram" is the verb; "before tests" is a modifying prepositional phrase. A compound sentence includes two independent clauses connected by a coordinator (*for, and, nor, but, or, yet, so*). For example, "Andrew likes history, but Cynthia prefers math" is a compound sentence. Independent clauses can also be joined by a semicolon instead of a coordinator: "Andrew likes history; Cynthia prefers math." A complex sentence has an independent clause and dependent clause, joined by a subordinator: "While Andrew likes history, Cynthia prefers math." The subordinating conjunction "while" makes the first clause dependent on the second. In the complex sentence, "Students are tired on exam day when they have crammed all night," the second clause, made subordinate by "when," depends on the independent clause that came first.

Compound, complex, and compound-complex sentences

Compound sentences consist of two independent clauses, joined by a coordinating conjunction or punctuation like a semicolon, a colon, or sometimes a comma (for example, "He likes coffee, she likes tea"). Complex sentences consist of an independent clause and a dependent clause, connected by a subordinating word, making one clause subordinate to/dependent on the other. A compound-complex sentence includes two independent clauses, plus one or more dependent clauses. "Susan likes art, and Emily prefers science" is a compound sentence. "Although Susan likes art, Emily prefers science" is a complex sentence. An example of a compound-complex sentence is, "Susan, who draws well, likes art, but Emily, who is very methodical, prefers science." "Susan likes art" is an independent clause. "Who draws well" is a dependent clause with subordinator "who" modifying subject "Susan." "Emily prefers science" is another independent clause. "Who is very methodical" is another dependent clause with subordinator "who" modifying subject "Emily." "But" is the coordinating conjunction joining the two independent clauses.

Lie vs. lay

"To lie" is the infinitive form of the verb, as in "It is restful to lie down on a bed." Many people incorrectly use "lay down" instead. "To lay" is always a transitive verb, which means that it requires an object, and it means to make something lie down or to set something down, as in, "Lay that book on the table." The non-infinitive "lay" is the past tense of "to lie," e.g., "Yesterday I lay down." But the past tense of the transitive verb "to lay" is "laid," as in, "Yesterday I laid the book on the table." The present perfect and past perfect tenses of the intransitive verb "to lie" are both "lain," as in "I have lain here a long time" or "I had lain there all day before they came." However, the present and past perfect tenses of the transitive verb "to lay" are both "laid," as in "I have laid this book down for now" and "I had laid this book down last week."

Compound words

Compound words are words that consist of two single words that are used together to give a more specific meaning so commonly or often that they have been combined to form one word. These may be any part of speech, but are often nouns or adjectives. Some examples of nouns are *footsteps*, *heartbeat*, *countertop*, *gunshot*, *housewife*, *household*, *bookshelf*, *songbook*, *storybook*, *timetable*, *halfway*, *aftermath*, and *upkeep*. Some examples among adjectives include *paint-chipped*, *two-person* or *four-person* (as in *four-person* table or *two-person* serving), *beat-up*, *pock-marked*, *war-torn*, *world-weary*, and *evidence-based*. Compound adjectives may be hyphenated while compound nouns may not, but the reverse can also be true, as it is the compound adjective *bloodstained*. Also, authors may create compound adjectives when writing descriptively, as in *acne-scarred*, *hail-pitted*, and *flower-adorned*, to name a few. Some inexperienced writers make errors in spelling compound words as two words, such as *up keep*, *foot steps*, *after math*, and *half way*, among others.

Dangling participles and squinting modifiers

Dangling participles are common writing errors. They occur when someone writes a participial ("-ing") phrase followed by a clause, but the syntax makes the participle seemingly modify that clause when it really modifies something else that is unstated. Consider the following sentence, "Always getting into trouble, her life changes." The participle "getting" should modify an absent "she," but it incorrectly modifies "her life" instead. Her life is not always getting into trouble, she is. Or another example, "After eating his lunch, we left the restaurant." The dangling participle makes it sound as if we both ate his lunch. If the writer meant to indicate he ate, it should read, "After he ate his lunch, we left the restaurant." "Joanne's mother left when she was young" has a squinting modifier, making unclear who was young when the mother left—Joanne, her mother, or both. Possible corrections include: "Her mother left when Joanne was young," "Joanne's mother left as a young woman," or "Her young mother left when Joanne was a young child."

Misplaced modifiers

Misplaced modifiers are in the wrong part of a sentence, appearing to modify the wrong thing. For example, "This author creates a drama revolving around one character's journey in his new publication." This sounds like the new publication is a part of the character's journey, not the author's creation. Correction involves moving the prepositional phrase: "In his new publication, this author creates a drama revolving around one character's journey." Some other simple examples of how modifier placement affects meaning include: "She ate only fruit" versus "She only ate fruit." The first sentence means she ate nothing except fruit; the second means she did not plant, pick, wash, or cook fruit, but only ate it. Or, "He failed nearly every class he took" versus "He nearly failed every class he took." The former means he actually failed most of the classes he took, while the latter means he passed every class he took, but just barely. "Covered with flowers, she admired the field" means she was covered with flowers; "She admired the field covered with flowers" is correct.

Inconsistent verb tense

A narrative includes the following: "Anticipating the explosion, the insurgent watched the Humvees drive out of range. He frowned. Impatiently he jerks at the wire connected to the grenade's pin. But the handle was caught on something and had not detonated the grenade. Staring incredulously at the pin, he reaches over to turn off the radio. But another part of his mind thought it was better that the grenade did not explode. His survival instinct was being triggered. He gets out of the car and shuts the door." This narrative switches tenses. To correct this, the verbs should be consistent in tense. They should then read as one of the following. The verb tenses should be "watched... frowned... jerked... was (caught)... had not detonated... reached... thought... had not exploded... was being triggered... got out... shut." Conversely, they could also be "watches... jerks... is (caught)... has not detonated... reaches... thinks... did not explode... is being triggered... gets out... shuts." When the main narrative is in the past tense, the reference to something occurring earlier should be in the past perfect tense; when narrative is in the present tense, the reference should be in the present perfect tense.

Phrases vs. clauses and transitive vs. intransitive verbs

A clause makes a complete sentence, which can be just a subject and verb. However, the verb must be intransitive—one that does not require an object—for the sentence to be complete. For example, "I am," "I live," and "I love" are all complete sentences, but "I like" (or "I hate") is not because "like" needs an object—I like what? "I like it," "I like this," "I like you," "I like food," "I like to eat," and "I like eating" are all examples of complete sentences and independent clauses. A phrase lacks either a subject or a verb. For example, while "I like to go swimming" is a clause/sentence, "to go swimming" is a phrase: it has a verb but no subject. "You understood" is an example of an acceptable unstated subject. The imperative "Go now" is a complete sentence wherein the subject "you" is understood; the meaning is "[You] go now."

Punctuation errors in possessive pronouns

Many people make the error of misspelling the possessive pronoun "its" as "it's" when the apostrophe is only ever used in the contraction of "it is," and never in the possessive. Another common error is misspelling other possessive pronouns by using apostrophes, such as "your's" and "her's." These are always incorrect. A possessive pronoun taking a noun as its object, such as "his hat," "your hat," or "her hat" is not complicated by any –s ending. However, when the possessive pronoun does not have any noun object, the –s ending is added: "It is hers," "That hat is yours," or "She is a friend of theirs." Just like other possessive pronouns without –s endings ("That hat is his" or "This is mine"), the possessive pronouns ending with –s never include an apostrophe. With the proliferation of websites with large amounts of text written and typed by people not expert or even basically educated in grammar, errors such as these are more frequently visible than ever.

Drawbacks to wordprocessing spell checkers

Microsoft Word is one of the most popular word processing programs. It has many excellent features facilitating composition. However, students and other writers must realize that its spell checkers, and those of similar programs, are far from perfect. One cannot rely on them without paying attention to what they do. For example, a college student writing a paper on Sophocles' *Oedipus Rex* correctly typed the name of key character Laius, king of Thebes and father of Oedipus, throughout his paper. However, his spell checker, not recognizing the name, "corrected" it to Louis. The student only realized this at the last minute while on his way to class, paper in hand, without a computer or printer nearby, and he had to rewrite every instance of the name by hand. Spell checkers commonly fail to recognize proper names and foreign language words. To eliminate the red zigzag underline that Word uses to indicate a misspelling, simply right-click and select "Add to dictionary" from the drop-down menu. Students and writers must consciously proofread everything they write, rather than assume spell checkers are always correct.

Microsoft Word's grammar check identifies many common errors, but is often incorrect. It does not recognize reflexive verbs, such as "assess themselves" or "do it for themselves," and suggests changing "themselves" to "them." Many writers and students get perplexed when writing a complete sentence to find Word underlining it with a green zigzag, labeling it a "fragment." Sometimes this reflects a true error, like leaving the verb out of a clause. But other times, it makes no sense by current writing standards. Sometimes one simply reverses the order of two clauses and the markup disappears. Microsoft Word's grammar check also inexplicably mistakes things like subject-verb agreement with number. For example, a writer can type, "A given number of posters costs" and grammar check will incorrectly suggest changing "costs" to "cost." The subject is the singular "number," not plural object "posters." Right-clicking, selecting "Grammar" from the drop-down menu, and selecting "Ignore rule" eliminates such wrong "corrections." (Another option is to simply ignore the markups.) If their grammatical knowledge is insufficient, writers and students can consult reputable grammar experts' websites about suspect "corrections."

The grammar checkers in popular word processing software programs like Microsoft Word can catch many inadvertent errors often caused by hurried typing and/or careless writing. However, these programs are not always correct, and in fact are often incorrect. Not only will Word's grammar checker incorrectly label some constructions incorrect when they are not, but it will also fail to identify other errors. For example, Noam Chomsky's famous sample sentence, "Colorless green ideas sleep furiously" is grammatically, morphologically, and syntactically correct in its construction, but makes no sense semantically—which was Chomsky's point. Grammar checkers are not people who can think, reason, and understand; they are simply programmed to identify certain things categorized as errors. So the grammar checker has no problem with Chomsky's sentence and does not flag anything in it as wrong. This is an example of how grammar checkers not only over-correct by identifying correct usages as incorrect, but also under-correct by not identifying incorrect usages. Writers and students must use their own judgment and knowledge and consult grammatical experts and/or their websites when needed.

Affixes

Affixes in the English language are morphemes that are added to words to create related but different words. Derivational affixes form new words based on and related to the original words. For example, the affix *–ness* added to the end of the adjective *happy* forms the noun *happiness.* Inflectional affixes form different grammatical versions of words. For example, the plural affix *–s* changes the singular noun *book* to the plural noun *books*, and the past tense affix *–ed* changes the infinitive or present tense verb *look* to the past tense *looked.* Prefixes are affixes placed in front of words. For example, *heat* means to make hot; *preheat*, using the prefix *pre-*, means to heat in advance. Suffixes are affixes placed at the ends of words. The *happiness* example above contains the suffix *–ness.* Circumfixes add parts both before and after words, such as how *light* becomes *enlighten* with the prefix *en-* and the suffix *–en.* Interfixes compound words via central affixes: *speed* and *meter* become *speedometer* via the interfix *–o–.*

Word roots, prefixes, and suffixes to help determine meanings of words

Many English words were formed from combining multiple sources. For example, the Latin *habēre* means "to have," and the prefixes *in-* and *im-* mean a lack or prevention of something, as in *insufficient, inordinate, intemperate,* and *imperfect.* Latin combined *in-* with *habēre* to form *inhibēre*, whose past participle was *inhibitus.* This is the origin of the English word *inhibit,* meaning to prevent from having. Hence by knowing the meanings of both the prefix and the root, one can decipher the word meaning. In Greek, the root *enkephalo-* refers to the brain. This informs the meanings of many medical terms used in English: *encephalitis, hydrocephalus, electroencephalogram, anencephaly,* and so on. And knowing prefix and suffix meanings, like *–itis* meaning inflammation, *hydro-* meaning water, *electro-* meaning electrical, *–gram* meaning writing/drawing/record, and *an*-meaning not/without, informs the rest of the words' meanings: brain inflammation, water/fluid on the brain, an electrical brain record, and the condition of not having a brain.

Prefixes

While knowing prefix meanings helps ESL and beginning readers learn new words, other readers take for granted the meanings of known words. However, prefix knowledge will also benefit them for determining meanings or definitions of unfamiliar words. For example, native English speakers and readers familiar with recipes know what *preheat* means. Knowing that *pre-* means in advance can also inform them that *presume* means to assume in advance, that *prejudice* means advance judgment, and that this understanding can be applied to many other words beginning with *pre-.* Knowing that the prefix *dis-* indicates opposition informs the meanings of words like *disbar, disagree, disestablish,* and many more. Knowing *dys-* means bad, impaired, abnormal, or difficult informs *dyslogistic, dysfunctional, dysphagia,* and *dysplasia.* With technical terminology, as in medicine, specific prefixes can indicate organs and systems: knowing *hepat(o)-* refers to the liver and *splen(o)* to the spleen informs *hepatitis* and *hepatosplenic.* Knowing *macro-* means large and *micro-* means small informs terms like *macroglossia, microglossia, macrocephaly,* and *microcephaly.* Knowing *hydro-* refers to water informs *hydrocephalus, hydration,* and *anhydrous.*

Suffixes

In English, certain suffixes generally indicate both that a word is a noun, and that the noun represents a state of being or quality. For example, *-ness* is commonly used to change an adjective into its noun form, as with *happy* and *happiness, nice* and *niceness, sturdy* and *sturdiness, quick* and *quickness,* and so on. The suffix *–tion* is commonly used to transform a verb into its noun form, as with *converse* and *conversation, convene* and *convention, move* and *motion,* and *locomote* and *locomotion.* Thus, if readers are unfamiliar with the second form of a word, knowing the meaning of the transforming suffix can help them determine meaning, especially if they know the meaning of the first form (which knowledge of word roots will help). With medical terminology, knowing that the suffix *–osis* can mean a diseased/abnormal condition can help them define many words, such as *sclerosis, leukosis, cirrhosis,* and *arthrosis,* to name a few. And knowing that *–itis* means inflammation informs many word meanings like *appendicitis, bronchitis, laryngitis, arthritis, pneumonitis,* and many more.

Context clues to help determine meanings of words

If readers simply bypass unknown words in reading, they can reach unclear conclusions about what they read. However, if they look for the definition of every unfamiliar word in the dictionary, it can slow down their reading progress. Moreover, the dictionary may list multiple definitions for one word; then readers must still examine surrounding context to determine which definition is the one that applies. Hence context is important to new vocabulary regardless of reader methods. Four types of context clues are examples, definitions, descriptive words, and opposites. Authors may use a certain word, and then follow it with several different examples of what it describes. Sometimes authors actually supply a definition of a word they use, which is especially true in informational and technical texts. Authors may use descriptive words that elaborate upon a vocabulary word they just used. While this may be done to make their prose colorful or memorable, it nonetheless affords context clues for readers. Authors may also use opposites with negation that help define meaning.

Examples and appositives

An author may use a word and then give examples that illustrate its meaning. Consider this text: "For students who are deaf or hard of hearing, teachers who do not know how to use sign language can help them understand certain instructions by using gestures instead, like pointing their fingers to indicate which direction to look or go; holding up a hand, palm outward, to indicate stopping; holding the hand(s) flat, palm(s) up, curling a finger toward oneself in a beckoning motion to indicate 'come here'; or curling all fingers toward oneself repeatedly to indicate 'come on', 'more', or 'continue.'" The author of this text has used the word "gestures" and then followed it with examples of gestures. A reader unfamiliar with the word "gestures" can deduce from the examples given that this word means hand motions in this context. Readers can find examples by looking for signal words "for example," "for instance," "like" (as in the text presented above), "such as," and "e.g."

While readers sometimes have to look for definitions of unfamiliar words in a dictionary and/or do some work to determine a word's meaning from its surrounding context, at other times an author may make it easier for readers by defining certain words they use. For example, an author may write, "The company did not have sufficient capital, that is, available money, to continue operations." The author defined "capital" as "available money," and heralded the definition with the phrase "that is." Another way that authors supply word definitions is with appositives. Rather than being introduced by a signal phrase like "that is," "namely," or "meaning," an appositive comes after the vocabulary word it defines and is enclosed within two commas. For example, an author may write, "The Indians introduced the Pilgrims to pemmican, cakes they made of lean meat dried and mixed with fat, which proved greatly beneficial to keep settlers from starving while trapping." In this example, the appositive phrase following "pemmican" and preceding "which" defines the word "pemmican."

Descriptions

When readers encounter a word they do not recognize in a text, the author may expand on that word to illustrate it better. While the author may do this to make the prose more picturesque and vivid, the reader can also take advantage of this description to provide context clues to the meaning of the unfamiliar word. For example, an author may write, "The man sitting next to me on the airplane was obese. His shirt stretched across his vast expanse of flesh, strained almost to bursting." The descriptive second sentence elaborates on and helps to define the previous sentence's word "obese" to mean extremely fat. One author described someone who was obese simply, yet very descriptively, as "an epic in bloat." A reader unfamiliar with the word "repugnant" can decipher its meaning through an author's accompanying description: "The way the child grimaced and shuddered as he swallowed the medicine showed that its taste was particularly repugnant."

Opposites with negation to determine meanings of words

Text authors sometimes introduce a contrasting or opposing idea before or after a concept they present. They may do this to emphasize or heighten the idea they present by contrasting it with something that is the reverse. However, readers can also use this author's technique to help themselves with comprehension of new vocabulary words. For example, an author may write, "Our conversation was not cheery. We sat and talked very solemnly about his experience, and a number of similar events." The reader who is not familiar with the word "solemnly" can deduce by the author's preceding use of "not cheery" that "solemn" means the opposite of cheery or happy, so it must mean serious or sad. Or if someone writes, "Don't condemn his entire project because you couldn't find anything good to say about it," readers unfamiliar with "condemn" can understand from the sentence structure that it means the opposite of saying anything good, so it must mean reject, dismiss, or disapprove. "Entire" adds another context clue, meaning total or complete rejection.

Syntax to determine part of speech and meanings of words

Syntax is sentence structure and word order. Suppose that a reader encounters an unfamiliar word when reading a text. To illustrate, consider an invented word like "splunch." If this word is used in a sentence like "Please splunch that ball to me," the reader can assume from syntactic context that "splunch" is a verb. We would not use a noun, adjective, adverb, or preposition with the object "that ball," and the prepositional phrase "to me" further indicates "splunch" represents an action. However, in the sentence, "Please hand that splunch to me," the reader can assume that "splunch" is a noun. Demonstrative adjectives like "that" modify nouns. Also, we hand someone some*thing*—a thing being a noun; we do not hand someone a verb, adjective, or adverb. Some sentences contain further clues. For example, from the sentence, "The princess wore the glittering splunch on her head," the reader can deduce that it is a crown, tiara, or something similar from the syntactic context, without knowing the word.

Syntax to indicate different meanings of similar sentences

The syntax, or structure, of a sentence affords grammatical cues that aid readers in comprehending the meanings of words, phrases, and sentences in the texts that they read. Seemingly minor differences in how the words or phrases in a sentence are ordered can make major differences in what that sentence means. For example, here are two sentences that use exactly the same words, with the only difference being their order; one phrase is located in a different place in each sentence, with the result being that they have different meanings: (1) "The man with a broken arm sat in a chair." (2) "The man sat in a chair with a broken arm." The first sentence means the man had a broken arm and sat in a chair. The second sentence means the man sat in a chair that had a broken arm. While both indicate a man sat in a chair, differing syntax indicates whether the man's or chair's arm was broken.

Nuances of word meaning relative to connotation, denotation, diction, and usage

A word's denotation is simply its objective dictionary definition. However, its connotation(s) refer(s) to the subjective associations, often emotional, that specific words evoke in listeners and readers hearing and seeing them. Two or more words can have the same dictionary meaning, but very different connotations. Writers use diction (a style element) to convey various nuances of thought and emotion by selecting synonyms for other words that best communicate the associations they want to trigger for readers. For example, a car engine is naturally greasy; in this sense, "greasy" is a neutral term. But when a person's smile, appearance, or clothing is described as "greasy," it has a pejorative connotation. Because of usages that have occurred in recent times, many words have gained additional and/or different meanings. The word "gay" used to have only the meaning of happy, or festive as in the Christmas carol "Deck the Halls" lyrics "Don we now our gay apparel," but by the 20th century, it had also come to indicate a sexual preference.

Figures of speech

A figure of speech is a verbal expression, used not only in speech but also in writing, whose meaning is figurative rather than matching the literal meanings of the words in it. For example, the figure of speech "butterflies in the stomach" does not literally mean someone has actual butterflies in his or her stomach; it is a metaphor representing the fluttery feelings some people get in their stomachs when they are nervous or excited—or when they "fall in love"—another figure of speech so common we take it for granted, but which does not mean physically falling. "Hitting a sales target" does not mean physically hitting a target with arrows as in archery; it is a metaphor for meeting a sales quota. "Climbing the ladder of success" does not involve physically climbing an actual ladder; it metaphorically likens advancing in one's career to ascending ladder rungs. Similes, such as "light as a feather" (meaning very light, not a feather's actual weight), and hyperbole, like "I'm starving/freezing/roasting," are also figures of speech.

In English, a very common idiomatic expression meaning it is raining very hard is "raining cats and dogs." Foreigners have difficulty translating or understanding such non-literal expressions. The origin of this figure of speech is in Teutonic mythology. Circa 100 B.C., some Celtic or Germanic people living in Jutland believed in the Old Norse religion wherein Odin was the god of war, wisdom, and the main god in charge of the world. The Teutonic belief then was that Odin's dog took the form of the wind, and a cat assumed the form of the rain. During rainstorms, they believed Odin's dog—the wind—was chasing a cat—the rain. When rain poured down, they attributed it to Odin dropping cats and dogs from the sky. Over 2,000 years later, although modern peoples do not believe Odin is responsible or that wind and rain are in dog and cat form, they have still preserved this ancient expression calling a heavy downpour "raining cats and dogs."

The figure of speech "in hot water" is familiar to most native English-language speakers. In the Middle Ages, many countries were governed via feudal systems wherein lords owned land and serfs worked that land. In those days, legal court systems and jury trials had not yet been developed. To determine someone's guilt or innocence, officials often used "trials by ordeal." A crime deemed worthy of the death penalty was tried by an ordeal of fire or hot water. With a hot water trial, the suspect was placed into a large pot of boiling water. If the suspect survived, s/he was judged innocent. If the accused person died from being in the boiling water, s/he was found guilty. Such trials were used to try many crimes, including witchcraft. The original term "in hot water" dates back to when someone accused of a capital crime was literally placed in hot water. Although this practice has long since become obsolete, the expression "in hot water" persists to describe discomfort, difficulty, or danger.

While the meaning of the saying, "Leave no stone unturned" is obvious—to look everywhere when searching for something, and/or to spare no effort in doing work thoroughly—we tend to take this common expression for granted and may not know its original source. The saying actually dates back to ancient Greek mythology. Many ancient Greek myths, plays, poems, popular stories, and other literature include references to consulting the Oracle at Delphi, who they believed could communicate with the gods and thus predict the future and answer all questions. For example, the Oracle at Delphi predicted the eventual fate of Oedipus in Sophocles' tragedy *Oedipus Rex*. Socrates, Homer, and others referred to this Oracle. Tragedian Euripides once related a story that a general, defeated in battle, buried his treasure before fleeing the area. Someone asked the Oracle at Delphi where this treasure was. The reply was that to find the treasure, one should "leave no stone unturned"—in other words, to look everywhere possible.

While "tying the knot" is figurative today, it was done literally in many ancient traditions. For example, in early Hindu tradition, at the end of the wedding ceremony the groom placed a colored ribbon around the neck of the bride. The father of the bride could demand a higher price of the groom for his daughter before this ribbon was tied, but once it was knotted, he could not, and the marriage was permanent (early Hinduism prohibited separations or divorces). Early Parsees, Indian Zoroastrians descended from Persians, bound grooms at wedding ceremonies with seven-stranded cords. This was both to assure tight bonds, and to show the Parsee belief in seven as a lucky and sacred number. In the ancient Phoenician city-state of Carthage, at weddings the bride and groom were tied together with leather laces around their thumbs. And in Roman weddings, the bride's girdle was tied with a knot so tight it was called a Herculean knot, which the groom had to loosen or untie.

In the 18th and 19th centuries, well-dressed ladies wore corsets, dresses, and shoes, all of which had to be pulled together to fasten them. Corsets, which were early girdles, were very tight: their laces had to be pulled strenuously together. Dresses featured many hooks and eyes to be fastened, which also required pulling the two sides together. Even shoes and boots had leather thongs that had to be pulled together before buckling the outer buckles. Rich women had female assistants to help with this, but other women relied on their husbands for assistance. The phrase "making ends meet" originally referred to the physical efforts required for ladies to dress properly. But over time, innovations in apparel manufacturing made clothes easier to put on and fasten, while fashionable clothing still became more expensive. Accordingly, the meaning of the expression evolved to signify not physical struggles, but the economic struggle of financing a lady's fashionable wardrobe. Eventually this generalized to mean any financial struggle.

Before industrial developments enabled maritime and aerial warfare, wars were fought only on land. Troops were accompanied by musicians—fifes and drums at the least, and often entire bands. In preparation for battle, as soldiers were forming lines, the bands headed up the lines, playing martial music to alert, support, and inspire the troops, who had to "face the music." Before giving the "forward march" command, the first command was "face the music." Another military practice to which this phrase is attributed is the history of the dishonorable discharge, wherein a soldier was literally drummed out of service: the company stood at attention, and the drum and fife bands accompanying the troops played a tune called "Rogue's March," popular with the American army during the Revolutionary War, including drum rolls to "drum out" the disgraced one who had to "face the music." A theatrical application of this figure of speech is the test of an actor's courage when in the spotlight onstage, facing musicians in the orchestra pit.

Writing, Speaking, and Listening

Persuasive techniques

To appeal using reason, writers present logical arguments, such as using "If... then... because" statements. To appeal to emotions, authors ask readers how they would feel about something or to put themselves in another's place, present their point as making them feel best, and tell readers how they should feel. To appeal to character, morality, or ethics, authors present their points to readers as the right or most moral choices. Authors cite expert opinions to show readers that someone very knowledgeable about the subject or viewpoint agrees. Testimonials, via anecdotes about and/or quotations from someone who agrees, add support. Bandwagon appeals persuade readers that everybody else agrees with author views. Authors appeal to greed by presenting their choice as cheaper, free, and/or more valuable for less cost. They appeal to laziness by presenting their views as more convenient, easy, or relaxing. Authors also anticipate potential objections and argue against them before audiences think of them, thereby depicting those objections as weak.

Authors can use comparisons like analogies, similes, and metaphors to persuade audiences. For example, a writer might represent excessive expenses as "hemorrhaging" money, which the author's recommended solution will stop. Authors can use negative word connotations to make some choices unappealing to readers, and positive word connotations to make others more appealing. Using humor can relax readers and garner their agreement. However, writers must take care: ridiculing opponents works with readers who already agree, but otherwise can backfire by angering other readers. Rhetorical questions need no answer, but create effect that can force agreement, such as asking the question, "Wouldn't you rather be paid more than less?" Generalizations persuade readers by being impossible to disagree with; writers can make these appear to support their viewpoints, like saying, "We all want peace, not war" regarding more specific political arguments. Transfer and association persuade by example: if advertisements show attractive actors enjoying their products, audiences imagine they will experience the same. Repetition, which is repeating certain statements frequently, can also sometimes effectively persuade audiences.

Critical evaluation of effectiveness of persuasive methods

First, readers should identify the author's thesis—what s/he argues for or against. They should consider the argument's content and why the author saw a need to present it. Does the author offer solutions to problems raised? If so, are they realistic? Note all central ideas and evidence supporting the author's thesis. Research any unfamiliar subjects or vocabulary. Readers should then outline or summarize the work in their own words. Identify which type(s) of appeal(s) the author uses. Readers should evaluate how well the author communicated meaning from the reader's perspective: Did they respond emotionally to emotional appeals with anger, upset, happiness, etc.? If so, why? Decide if the author's reasoning sufficed for changing the reader's mind. Determine whether the content and presentation were accurate, cohesive, and clear. Readers should also ask themselves whether they found the author believable or not, and why or why not they did.

Classical author appeals

In his *On Rhetoric,* ancient Greek philosopher Aristotle defined three basic types of appeal used in writing. He called these pathos, ethos, and logos in Greek. *Pathos* means suffering or experience and refers to appeals to the emotions (the English word "pathetic" comes from this root). Writing that is meant to entertain audiences, by making them either happy, as with comedy, or sad, as with tragedy, uses pathos. Among criteria for writing tragedy in his *Poetics*, Aristotle included its evoking the emotions of terror and pity. *Ethos* means character and connotes ideology (the English word "ethics" comes from this root). Writing that appeals to credibility, based on academic, professional, or personal merit uses ethos. *Logos* means "I say" and refers to a plea, opinion, expectation, word or speech, account, opinion, or reason. (The English word "logic" comes from this root.) Aristotle used it to mean persuasion that appeals to the audience through reasoning and logic to influence their opinions.

Technical material for non-technical readers

Writing about technical subjects for non-technical readers differs from writing for colleagues in that authors begin with a different goal: it may be more important to deliver a critical message than to impart the maximum technical content possible. Technical authors also must assume that non-technical audiences do not have the expertise to comprehend extremely scientific or technical messages, concepts, and terminology. They must resist the temptation to impress audiences with their scientific knowledge and expertise, and remember that their primary purpose is to communicate a message that non-technical readers will understand, feel the impact of, and respond to by changing their attitudes and/or taking appropriate actions. Similarities in non-technical and technical styles include: both should formally cite references when used, and acknowledge other authors' work utilized. Both must follow intellectual property and copyright regulations. This includes the author's protecting his/her own rights, or a public domain statement, as s/he chooses.

Writers of technical or scientific material may need to write for many non-technical audiences. Some readers have no technical or scientific background; others do, but not in the same field as the authors. Government and corporate policymakers and budget managers need technical information they can understand for decision-making. Citizens affected by technology and/or science are another audience. Non-governmental organizations can encompass many of the preceding groups. Elementary and secondary school programs also need non-technical language for presenting technical subject matter. Reasons that technical authors need to write using non-technical language include: for communicating messages as opposed to denser content; for informing colleagues, both within and without one's field; for obtaining support for a budget or project; and for better informing a wider range of citizens who have the right to know important information without being stymied by the barrier of jargon or unfamiliar terminology and vocabulary.

Authors in technical fields may write using non-technical language to serve the purpose of collecting consumer responses to surveys of public comprehension, perceptions of, and views toward technology and science. They may use non-technical language in popular representations of science, or to present scientific or para-scientific belief systems. They will need to use it to support school instruction in the sciences. They will also need it for writing about the history of science education and the history of popular science. If they write about science and the media, they will need to use non-technical language. Authors with scientific backgrounds who also write science fiction must be equally able to use non-technical language to reach this reading audience. They must use it for scientific lobbying. Reporting studies they may conduct evaluating interactive science centers and science exhibits also requires non-technical language, as do public scientific information services. Popular "anti-science" protests are another purpose. Writing about science and applicable technologies in developing countries also needs non-technical wording.

When authors of technical information must write about their subjects using non-technical language that readers outside their disciplinary fields can comprehend, they should not only use non-technical terms, they should also use normal, everyday language to accommodate non-native-language readers. For example, instead of writing that "eustatic changes" like "thermal expansion" causing "hazardous conditions" in the "littoral zone," an author would do better to write that a "rising sea level" is "threatening the coast." When technical terms cannot be avoided, authors should also define and/or explain them using non-technical language. Although authors must cite references and acknowledge others' work they use, they should avoid the kinds of references or citations that they would use in scientific journals—unless they reinforce author messages. They should not use endnotes, footnotes, or any other complicated referential techniques because non-technical journal publishers usually do not accept them. Including high-resolution illustrations, photos, maps, or satellite images and incorporating multimedia into digital publications will enhance public non-technical writing about technical subjects. Technical authors may publish using non-technical language in e-journals, trade journals, specialty newsletters, and daily newspapers.

Evaluating arguments made by informational text writers

First, identify an argument's conclusion. Then identify premises the author states supporting the conclusion. How readers word conclusions they identify can affect their identification of premises; they may want to reword or even redefine the conclusion. Try to paraphrase premises for clarification and make the conclusion and premises fit. List all premises first, sequentially numbered, then finish with the conclusion. Identify any premises or assumptions not stated by the author but required for stated premises to support the conclusion. Read word assumptions sympathetically, as the author might. Evaluate whether premises reasonably support the conclusion: For inductive reasoning, the reader should ask if the premises are true, and if they support the conclusion. If so, how strongly? For deductive reasoning, the reader should ask if the argument valid or invalid. If all premises are true, the argument is valid if the conclusion cannot be false. But if it can, then the argument is invalid. Alter an invalid argument to become valid, adding any premises needed. Are premises true, false, or questionable? How might the author defend them? Optional recursion: Start again, this time using significant premises as conclusions, and find and evaluate more supporting arguments.

Determining an informational author's purpose

Informational authors' purposes are why they wrote texts. Readers must determine authors' motivations and goals. Readers gain greater insight into text by considering what motivated the author. This develops critical reading skills. Readers perceive writing as a person's voice, not simply printed words. Uncovering author motivations and purposes empowers readers to know what to expect from text, read for relevant details, evaluate authors and their work critically, and respond effectively to the motivations and persuasions of the text. The main idea of a text is what the reader is supposed to understand from reading it; the purpose of the text is why the author has written it and what the author wants readers to do with its information. Authors state some purposes clearly, while others may be unstated but equally significant. When purposes stated contradict other parts of text, authors may have hidden agendas. Readers can better evaluate a text's effectiveness, whether they agree or disagree with it, and why they agree or disagree through identifying unstated author purposes.

Logical fallacies

Post hoc ergo propter hoc is Latin for "After this, therefore because of this." This equates to reasoning that because X happened before Y, X must have caused Y. But just as correlation does not imply causation, neither does chronological sequence. For example, one cannot assume that because most rapists read pornography as teenagers that pornography causes rape. A red herring is irrelevant information introduced to distract others from the pertinent issue. For example, one author claims that welfare dependence raises crime rates, while another argues plausibly that some increase in crime is justified in addressing poverty. However, if the second author argued instead, "But how can the poor survive without help?" that would be a red herring. Slippery slopes, when fallacious, are arguments that one thing will cause others without demonstrating any cause-and-effect relationship—hence non-sequiturs. For example, arguing that legalizing one drug will cause all drugs to be legalized is obviously false. Straw man is refuting an exaggeration or caricature of someone's argument, not the real argument.

Rationales for knowing logical fallacies
For writing persuasion and argumentation, logic is necessary, but so are supporting facts, insights, and the plausibility of an argument. Although logic by itself may show that the answer to a question discussed is unknown, the most plausible argument can still convince audiences. One reason for knowing the names of, and processes involved in, logical fallacies is enabling writers to identify flawed reasoning by those presenting opposing viewpoints—and identify them precisely by supplying a Latin name for each. This also indicates an author may better understand the opposite position than its presenter does. Another reason is that by identifying logical fallacies, the author does not simply make an opponent's argument weaker or less convincing, but s/he actually eliminates it from the discussion/debate instead. Rather than counterarguments—allowing opponents' rhetoric proving their arguments' importance—this makes audiences question the validity, even existence, of the opposing argument. If the other author cannot justify it strongly, that argument can be negated, and so the audience does not even consider it.

Steps or strategies to draw attention to logical fallacies in opposing arguments
The writer should first restate the targeted opposing argument. Then s/he points out this argument is a logical fallacy, providing the Latin name for the fallacy identified. The writer then explains the meaning of this logical fallacy, and why it involves erroneous reasoning. Writers must not let their language become pompous or pedantic in tone during this explanation. Instead, they appeal more to audiences by stating the meaning of the fallacy as though their perceptive readers and listeners already know it, and they recognize this audience knowledge. For example, if a writer identifies an opposing writer's use of an appeal to public opinion, s/he defines this by pointing out that majority agreement with a position does not make it right. Writers then give overt examples of a fallacy's incorrectness—such as historical beliefs that the world was flat or that slavery was acceptable did not make such beliefs correct. Lastly, writers state the erroneous argument should be ruled out entirely, leaving opponents only (an) inadequate remaining argument(s) and an untenable position.

Argumentum ad antiquitatem means an argument to tradition or antiquity. We have often read or heard this used when people write or say, "We have always done it this way." An example might be that the governments of all major societies have always supplied state funding for cultural pursuits and the arts. However, it is not logical that the fact of people always having done something intrinsically warrants continuing to do it. An inherent weakness of this argument is that others can refute it easily just by drawing attention to it. Therefore, it should not be a writer's first choice. If one feels the need to use this argument, one way to provide it with more support than simply presenting it by itself is offering a reason for respecting the tradition cited. One might support arguing for a tradition with the evolutionary principle of natural selection—such as saying that the reason all known civilizations practice this tradition is because those that ignored it failed to survive.

Argumentum ad hominem is against the person, not the person's statements/ideas. The arguer attacks a person's motives or character, not what s/he wrote or said. This is less often by name-calling, such as "He is a communist/fascist/greedy capitalist," but more common by attacking the person as information source. If one cites ending the Vietnam War, signing environmental laws, and opening China as positive accomplishments of Richard Nixon, and quotes him regarding free trade, then the *ad hominem* arguer might cite the Watergate scandal as evidence Nixon was a "crook" and liar, so nobody can believe anything he said. Arguments *ad hominem* also are used against people arguing for anything that would benefit them and against anything that would disadvantage them—like owners of corporate conglomerates arguing against anti-trust laws—shifting focus away from the argument's validity to focus on who makes it. *Ad hominem* is not fallacious against statements by those with vested interests in deception. Many *ad hominem* arguments may be restated about ideas versus people—such as not claiming someone is a fascist, but his/her position is.

Argumentum ad ignorantiam is an argument appealing to ignorance. In other words, the arguer presumes the truth of something based on its not being proven untrue. For example, one would do better by presenting actual data to prove climate change than by arguing it is true because nobody has proven it false. The burden of proof is a key factor for determining whether this argument is fallacious or not. As an analogy, in the United States legal system, a defendant is innocent until proven guilty—rather than guilty until proven innocent as in some other court systems. Thus defense attorneys can argue that their client is not guilty because the prosecution has not proven him/her guilty. However, prosecuting attorneys cannot argue that the defendant must be guilty of committing a crime because s/he has no alibi. Both arguments constitute *ad ignorantiam*, but in the American legal system, the burden of proof is on the prosecution rather than the defense. Similarly, in rhetoric, the proposer typically has the burden of proof.

The logical fallacy *argumentum ad logicam*, or argument/appeal to logic, presumes something is untrue based on somebody's invalid argument or proof. It is fallacious to deem a proposal false just because of unsound reasoning defending it. There could exist other, valid arguments or proofs for the proposal. The *argumentum ad logicam* frequently occurs within the context of the *straw man* fallacy, which argues against a distortion or exaggeration of a position, not the actual position. The *ad logicam* appeal is determined as fallacious or not through the burden of proof: If the proposer of the original position does not prove it, s/he loses the debate even though other arguments not presented could have proven it. Also, if one side disproves another's point as invalid, it will be judged invalid, regardless whether the proposer could have proven it with a better argument because s/he did not do so; the burden of proof is on the proposer. This determination of fallacy or validity via burden of proof is comparable to that used with *argumentum ad ignorantiam*.

Argumentum ad misericordiam means argument/appeal to pity. This is often employed by those pleading to others for donations and other assistance to help starving children, abused animals, and poor people. Of course many pity such victims and want to help, but what makes this appeal illogical is that by itself, it cannot make expenses free, make true something untrue, or render something possible that is impossible. It is valid, however, to emphasize a problem's significance as a way of supporting one's proposing a particular solution to that problem. The proposer of the solution must then be able to address such objections as whether that solution is possible or feasible; what negative impacts it could have on others, even while providing positive impacts on those it would help; and its expenses and how to provide for those. Appealing to pity is acceptable to support arguments that a proposal's benefits justify its costs, but unacceptable as the sole response to objections without otherwise addressing them.

Argumentum ad nauseam translates literally as argument to the point of nausea. In other words, this tactic involves repeating one's point over and over until listeners are so disgusted at hearing it that they cannot tolerate hearing it any longer. Reiterating a true statement over and over is not fallacious in itself, but expecting such repetition to replace actual logic is. Despite the absence of reasoning, repetition has a powerful effect of making one's listeners remember the statements repeated. This makes *argumentum ad nauseam* very popular. When one side in a spoken or written debate or controversy has used this technique of constant repetition without supplying any evidence to support or document the assertion, this is an opportunity for the other side to point out the use of repetition alone, and moreover, to call attention to the fact that the other has not presented any information to substantiate the repeated statement. Making clear that the other person has repeatedly stated a point without proving it will refute it.

Argumentum ad numerum, translated as argument or appeal to numbers, is a rhetorical device of citing mathematical figures as "proof" that something is true. For example, one might argue, "80 percent of the public supports this legislation." The fallacy here is that the agreement of the majority does not make something true. The 80 percent of the public that supports a law could be wrong in doing so—like in the antebellum Southern United States, where the majority of the public supported slavery. They had considerable incentive to take this position to preserve the entire foundation of their economy and way of life, but they were not morally justified in doing so. *Argumentum ad numerum* resembles *argumentum ad populum*—appeal to popularity or to the people. Their minor difference is that arguing to the people appeals directly to the nearby public, while appealing to numbers attempts to persuade others based on citing how many other people agree. These are similar enough to be often used interchangeably in rhetoric.

The meaning of *argumentum ad verecundiam* is arguing or appealing to authority. This is attempting to prove one's position by citing the opinion of someone who is not an expert in the specific subject at issue. For example, Enrico Fermi and Albert Einstein were both pacifists, and objected strenuously to having their science applied for building bombs. While some agree and some do not, the fact is that Fermi and Einstein were experts in nuclear physics, but not in politics or foreign policy. Citing or quoting authorities in the subject under discussion, though, is not fallacious. It is also acceptable to quote a non-expert who nevertheless made an eloquent statement appropriate to one's argument. Unacceptable uses of the appeal to authority, which opponents are justified in calling out and criticizing, include using unqualified sources to verify facts unaccompanied by any other sources that are qualified, and/or implying that a given position has to be correct just because somebody thought that it was.

Circulus in demonstrando is Latin for a circular argument. This means that by trying to use the assertion or idea they want to prove is itself a part of their proof, people using circular argumentation are actually "talking in circles." As an example, someone argues, "X is illegal. Because it is illegal, one should not do it. Because one shouldn't do it, the government should prevent people from doing it. This is why it is illegal." In this example, the circular nature of the argument is obvious. However, some arguments are circular but less easily recognized. Some politicians and political commentators can be notorious for using circular arguments. To refute the fallacy of *circulus in demonstrando,* one can summarize the arguer's statement as "You are saying that X is true because X is true," and then additionally point out that the arguer has not provided any information as to why X is true—in other words, they have provided no actual proof.

"Complex question" refers to a rhetorical tactic wherein a speaker or writer forms a question to presume implicitly something not established as true. An obvious example is when reporters or lawyers ask someone, "Have you stopped embezzling?" when there is no proof that the person questioned ever embezzled. This tactic is employed to trick people into admitting things they would not admit in direct questioning. A less obvious example is asking someone, "Since most African-Americans are poor, do you believe the measures proposed would be effective?" The first clause is not true, but the person questioned could be so focused on the second clause and how to answer it as to overlook the falsehood. This is more effective in spoken than written language: in real-time spoken interactions, it can confuse someone; in a written piece, the reader has time to reconsider it and realize it is untrue. A major drawback is that if the person questioned notices the falsehood and confronts the questioner, it makes the questioner appear foolish.

Cum hoc ergo propter hoc means in Latin, "With this, therefore because of this." In other words, because these occur together, one causes the other. A parallel fallacy in scientific research is assuming that correlation indicates causation. Things can occur together out of coincidence: people may attribute economic improvement to a certain president's administration when it may be more due to technological advances. Things can occur together, but one is an effect of prior causes: an improved economy during one president's administration can be the result of an earlier president's actions. Things can occur together and be unrelated to each other, but both related to a common reason: as an economic remedy, one president enacts downsizing measures, which many voters dislike, so they consequently elect a different president, and benefits of the previous president's downsizing appear after the election of the subsequent president. Whereas correlation can never mean causation in scientific research, in rhetoric one may attribute causation to correlation if one can provide sufficiently convincing reasons for it.

The Latin *dicto simpliciter* literally means "spoken simply," a figuratively sweeping generalization. When people make sweeping proclamations they presume are always true, they are stereotyping—which is another term for this. An example is generalizing that as a group, women are not as strong physically as men and assuming that therefore, they cannot serve equally in the military. While the first statement is true in general, it is not always true of specific individuals: some women are far stronger than the average of women as a group. In rhetoric, it is typically sufficient simply to state why a sweeping generalization does not prove someone's point without using the official terminology or pointing out its logical fallacy. Sweeping generalizations are understood by the public without instruction in rhetorical devices. Hence, experts also advise that naming the fallacy in Latin in this case seems condescending. Non-fallacious generalizations are always true individually, such as "Normal human females have two X chromosomes; normal human males have an X and a Y chromosome."

The appeal to nature assumes that anything natural or part of nature is good, and/or that anything not natural is bad. For example, some people may argue that birth control or homosexuality is wrong because these are not natural. In addition to the problem of defining the meaning of "natural," it is also illogical to equate "unnatural" or non-natural with wrong. Human beings use fire, construct and use tools, wear clothing, and farm the soil; these can be deemed not "natural," yet they are both common and beneficial. Because of these inherent weaknesses, this argument is not effective. For instance, defending environmentalism only on the basis of preserving natural resources or wildernesses does not provide strong enough reasons. However, this important cause can be defended more strongly by appealing to humans on the basis of their own survival by arguing that humans live within a complex ecosystem that is easily damaged by certain human activities which could destroy both the ecosystem and thus humanity as a part of it.

In the naturalistic fallacy, one draws conclusions regarding values—in other words, right and wrong or good and bad—based only on factual statements. This is fallacious because any logical inferences based on facts alone will constitute simply more statements of fact, rather than statements of value. In order to come to conclusions related to values, the axioms, principles, premises, or assumptions that one states must include a statement(s) of value as well. Having given an axiom of value rather than of fact, then one can use it together with facts to make conclusions about values. For instance, the statement, "This medication will keep you from dying" might seem to connect to a conclusion, "You should take this medication." However, the former is a statement of fact, the latter one of value. For the conclusion to be logically valid, an additional premise is needed, "You should do what you need to do to stay alive."

Argumentum ad antiquitatem, or appeal to tradition—that is, something is right because it has always been done, and the appeal to nature—or that something is right because it is natural, are forms of the naturalistic fallacy: they draw conclusions about values using statements of fact without any statement(s) of value to connect logically with conclusions. Facts represent what is; values represent what ought to be. Philosopher David Hume described these fallacies as attempts to bridge the "is-ought gap." Initial axioms of value are not necessarily justifiable via pure logic. However, rhetoric is not limited to pure logic. Three ways to rebut an axiom of value, such as "Anything natural is good," are: (1) Ask if anybody—yourself, the judge of a debate, or even your opponent who stated it—truly believes this; (2) present another value axiom that competes with it, like "Anything that improves people's lives is good," so the judge is forced to choose between the two; and (3) cite logical ramifications of the statement's contradiction of basic morality.

In Latin, *non sequitur* means "It does not follow." If someone says, for instance, "Racism is wrong; thus affirmative action is necessary," this conclusion does not logically follow the initial premise. If one says instead, "Racism is wrong; affirmative action would decrease racism; thus affirmative action is needed," the logical connection is supplied. Some rhetoricians include *non sequiturs* in their opening arguments strategically—to avoid giving away to their opponents a counterargument they anticipate. Except in the cases of significant, obvious counterarguments that should be anticipated and answered early, it is more strategic to wait for an opponent to raise an argument to rebut, rather than waste time and energy answering unstated objections. It is inadvisable to claim *non sequitur* whenever an opponent does not anticipate each of one's counterarguments. The best application for pointing out this fallacy is when an opponent attempts to show a causal chain without proving each link. Identifying each unsubstantiated step ultimately reveals such attempted chains as weak and implausible.

Petitio principii means "begging the question": when attempting to prove something, one assumes the same thing one wants to prove. In terms of logical structure, this is the same as using a circular argument. Although the meaning of "begging the question" is quite specific, many people misuse this term in rhetorical arguments. A question is begged if it is asked during a conversation but never answered, and meanwhile the parties in the discussion come to a conclusion about a related issue. For example, someone might argue, "Some people campaign for legalizing pornography because it is a medium for freedom of expression. However, this 'begs the question' of what freedom of expression means." This uses the term incorrectly. Some issues and discussions motivate questions rather than begging them. A more correct example of "begging the question" would be if someone argued, "Because we believe that pornography should be legalized, this means it constitutes a valid medium of free expression. Being free expression, it therefore should not be banned."

Translated from Latin, *tu quoque* means "you too." The old saying "Two wrongs don't make a right" addresses this fallacy. In rhetoric, one commits an error in logic—for example, making unproven claims—and defends it by rejoining that the opposition did the same. That both sides made the same error does not excuse either one. Though *tu quoque* is an obvious fallacy, it is often used to significant advantage in rhetoric: Disregarding whether any proposition is true or false, debaters can show which side made the better performance in arguing. For example, if both sides have equally appealed to audience pity (*argumentum ad misericordiam*), or both have used equal *ad hominem* arguments (attacking the person, not what s/he says), then to be fair a judge must penalize both equally, not just one. Additionally, it is not fallacious to show that "non-unique" advantages or disadvantages that apply equally to both sides cannot warrant preferring either position. *Tu quoque* can ensure that judging is only according to differentiating factors between sides.

Author's argument in argumentative writing

When an author writes in argumentative mode, the argument is a belief, position, or opinion that the author wants to convince readers to believe as well. For the first step, readers should identify the issue the author discusses. Some issues are controversial, meaning people disagree about them. For example, gun control, foreign policy, and the death penalty are all controversial issues. Readers should consider whether the author's selected issue is controversial. The next step is to ask oneself what the author's position about the chosen issue is. That position or viewpoint constitutes the author's argument. Readers should then identify the author's assumptions: things s/he accepts, believes, or takes for granted without needing proof. Inaccurate or illogical assumptions produce flawed arguments, causing readers not identifying author assumptions to be misled. Readers should identify what kinds of supporting evidence the author offers—research results, personal observations or experiences, case studies, facts, examples, expert testimony and opinions, and comparisons. Readers should decide how relevant or directly related this support is to the argument.

The first three reader steps to evaluate an author's argument are to identify the assumptions the author makes about the issue discussed in the writing, identify what kinds of evidence the author gives to support the argument, and decide how relevant the supporting evidence is. For example, if an author is not an expert on a particular topic, then that author's personal experience or opinion might not be very relevant. The fourth step in evaluating an author's argument is to assess how objective the author is. For example, consider whether the author introduces clear, understandable supporting evidence and facts to support the argument. The fifth step is evaluating whether the author's argument is complete or not. When authors give sufficient support for their arguments and also anticipate and respond effectively to opposing arguments or objections to their points, their arguments are complete. However, some authors omit information that could detract from their arguments. If instead they stated this information and refuted it, it would strengthen their arguments.

In order, readers should identify the author's assumptions about the issue s/he writes about, then identify what supporting evidence the author presents, assess the relevance of that evidence, evaluate the author's objectivity, and consider the completeness of the author's argument. Authors may omit detracting information rather than presenting and refuting it. Authors may also not present enough supporting information. The sixth step in evaluating an author's argumentative writing is to assess whether the argument is valid. Providing clear, logical reasoning makes an author's argument valid. Readers should ask themselves whether the author's points follow a sequence that makes sense, and whether each point leads to the next. The seventh step is to determine whether the author's argument is credible, meaning that it is convincing and believable. Arguments that are not valid are not credible, so step seven depends on step six. Readers should not feel overwhelmed at several steps; be mindful of their own biases during evaluation; and not expect authors to prove their arguments conclusively, but rather to reason and support arguments effectively.

Literature, body of literature, research question, problem statement, and review of literature

In research, literature refers to writing on a research topic. The body of literature is all writing and supporting data published on a given topic or research question. A research question or problem is what a researcher wants to find an answer to or resolve. In a research paper, the problem statement clearly identifies the issue, tells why the researcher cares about this issue, defines the scope of the research by focusing on specific variables, and shows why those variables matter. The problem statement follows the title and abstract in the research paper, supplying context for the rest and getting reader attention. Whether professionals or students, when researchers conduct academic research projects, their literature reviews, which thoroughly examine the extant body of literature on their chosen research topic, form a necessary component of the project by showing what work has already been done toward answering the research question that they have chosen to investigate.

Primary and secondary sources

When one conducts research and then writes a research paper reporting the results of that investigation, an essential part of the paper is a literature review. In reviewing the literature, one may examine both primary and secondary sources. Primary sources contain original information, like reports other researchers have made of their findings and other first-hand accounts written by experimenters or witnesses of discoveries or events. They may be found in academic books, journals and other periodicals, and authoritative databases. Secondary sources refer to information originally given by other people or found in other places. They may be cited, quoted, or described in books, magazines, newspapers, films, audio and video materials, databases, and websites. Accounts of research and its results are always informed and directed by reviews of the pertinent literature. These depict the present research as a cumulative process integral to the scientific method. Literature reviews also test the research question one wants to answer relative to the existing knowledge about the topic.

Addressing research questions

When asking a research question, the researcher may find through making a careful review of the existing literature that the question s/he has chosen has already been answered definitively. In this case, the researcher should modify the question or ask a different one. If their research question has not been answered in the literature, researchers should consider the following: What knowledge exists about the topic, in what chronological sequence the knowledge about this topic has been developed, whether there are any gaps in the knowledge about this topic, what needs and opportunities for additional research other researchers and writers have identified, and how one plans to fill in these gaps. Researchers should also consider whether consensus or controversy exists about pertinent matters and, with the latter, which positions exist. Research trajectories suggested by others' work, and the most productive direction for one's research the literature indicates are also considerations. Researchers should realize there are no absolute answers: they must decide in the context of their work what is important.

Literature review

One main part of a literature review is searching through the existing literature. The other is actually writing the review. Most voluntary researchers enjoy knowledge, so they must take care not to get lost among all the data available without making any progress in their literature review. A remedy is to prepare by writing or printing one's research question and keeping it nearby when searching, and by making a search plan and establishing a time limit in advance. Finding a seemingly endless number of references indicates a need to revisit the research question because it is too broad. Finding too little material means the research question and/or topic is too narrow, in which case one should reconsider the area to investigate. With cutting-edge research, one may find that nobody has ever investigated their question and/or area of interest. This requires systematic searching: with abstracts in periodicals for an overview of available literature; research papers or other specific sources to explore its references; and books and general sources, using their references to find a specific topic.

When searching published literature on a research topic, one must take plenty of thorough notes. We often happen upon references we are not ready for at the time but could use later, without making notes, it becomes frustrating when we want to read the entire reference we saw before but cannot find it again. It is easy to start a word processing document along with the Internet browser to take running notes while searching. Practicing online resource use helps: researchers and students should connect to the Internet regularly, view resources for their research often, learn how to use resources correctly and efficiently, experiment with resources available within the discipline(s), open and examine databases, become familiar with reference desk materials, find publications with abstracts of articles and books on one's topic, use papers' references to locate the most utile journals and important authors, identify keywords for refining and narrowing database searches, and peruse library catalogues online for available sources—all while taking complete notes.

As one searches the literature available about a given subject, one will gradually develop an overview of the body of literature. This signals the time to prepare for writing the literature review. The researcher should assemble the documents with all the notes s/he has taken while searching, copies of all the journal articles made, and all the books acquired. Then one should again write the research question at the top of a page, and list below it all of the author names and keywords discovered while searching. It is also helpful to observe whether any groups or pairs of these stand out when viewing the list. These activities are parts of structuring one's literature review—the first step for writing a thesis, dissertation, or research paper. Writers should rewrite as necessary rather than expecting to make only one draft. However, they should also not become stuck in rewriting any portion, which impedes momentum; skipping to a less problematic portion and revisiting the earlier part later is better.

Editing and revising

After composing a rough draft of a research paper, the writer should edit and rewrite it. The purpose of the paper is to communicate the answer to one's research question in an efficient and effective manner. The writer should edit the draft to make it as concise and clear as possible. This is often easier to do after writing the first draft than during it, as writers get some distance and objectivity when reviewing their first efforts. If the paper will include an abstract and an introduction, the writer should compose these after writing the rest. Because the point is to communicate ideas and information, writing should have consistency as well as succinctness and clarity. Not all readers understand technical terminology or long words: whenever possible, writers should use these only sparingly, and otherwise replace them with shorter, simpler words that do not change the meaning. Many writing and style guides exist for researchers lacking writing experience and/or confidence to consult.

Writing bodies and conclusions of literature review papers

Writers should first write a rough draft of their literature review paper. Then they should edit it to increase its clarity, eliminate verbiage and make the writing more concise, and change wording and terminology that could confuse some readers to simpler and more understandable language with the same meanings. Writers should always reread what they write. They should also ask others to read it and give them honest feedback. Additionally, the writer should read the paper aloud to hear how it sounds. Then s/he should rewrite and revise the paper based on the information gleaned. Throughout a literature review, the writer should not only summarize and comment on each source reviewed and what s/he has learned from it, s/he should also relate these findings to the original research question. The writer should explicitly state in the conclusion how the research question and pertinent literature interaction is a learning process devloped throughout the body, reflecting on insights gained through the process.

Citing sources

Formal research paper writers must cite all sources used—books, articles, interviews, conversations, and anything else that contributed to the research. One reason is to give others credit for their ideas and words. Otherwise, writers can be accused of stealing others' ideas; using others' words without quoting and citing sources is plagiarism. Another reason is to help readers find more information about the paper subject to read and research further. An additional reason is to make one's paper academically authoritative. To prepare, research writers should keep a running list of sources consulted, in an electronic file or on file cards. This prevents frantic last-minute searches for missing source information. For every source used, the writer needs the following: Author and/or editor name, title, publication date, city, and publisher name for books; author name, title, journal (or magazine or newspaper) name, volume and issue number, publication date, and page numbers for articles; and in addition to the information for articles, the URL, database name, name of the database's publisher, and the date of access for electronic resources.

Three common reference styles are MLA (Modern Language Association), APA (American Psychological Association), and Turabian (by expert author Kate Turabian). Each style formats citation information differently. Professors and instructors often specify that students use one of these in their syllabus. If not, students can ask them. Sometimes it is obvious: APA style is used in psychology and sociology papers, and MLA style is used in English literature papers and similar scholarly projects. Historically, book titles were underlined to differentiate them from articles and other titles. However, today, underlines frequently signal hyperlinks to Internet documents and pages. To eliminate confusion, book, journal, magazine, newspaper and other titles formerly underlined are now italicized instead. Poem and short story titles are enclosed in quotation marks. Article titles are neither underlined nor italicized in the three major styles, but titles of journals where they appear are italicized. Article titles are enclosed in quotation marks in MLA and Turabian style, but not APA style. Government document titles are italicized in all three, while their sources (like the U.S. Congress and the Senate) are italicized in APA and Turabian, but not MLA.

MLA uses quotation marks around magazine article titles, but APA and Turabian do not. All three italicize magazine names. The manuals differ in ordering issue number, publication year, and page numbers. APA places (year) after article title, then magazine name, month, and page numbers. MLA follows article title with magazine title, then (year), number, month, and page numbers. Turabian puts magazine name after article title, then issue number, month, year, and page numbers. MLA and Turabian use quotation marks around print journal article titles, APA does not. APA puts publication year after author name(s); MLA and Turabian after journal name, issue, and volume numbers, but before page numbers. Turabian and APA put city and publisher after page numbers, MLA before. APA places (year, month, date) of print, microfilm, or microfiche newspaper articles after author name(s); MLA and Turabian place date, month, and year after newspaper name. Journal and newspaper articles from databases are cited similarly to print, microfilm, and microfiche, but with database name, retrieval date, and URL added. Websites need not be in bibliographies, but URLs and access dates should be included in the text.

When citing articles or chapters in books, APA style follows article title with a comma and book title; MLA uses a period, then book title. Turabian uses a period, then "In" followed by book title. When citing books, APA style uses authors' first initials; joins author names with an ampersand (&); follows with publication year in parentheses, period; title, period; city, colon; and publisher name. MLA and Turabian spell out authors' first names, join author names with "and," separate parts with periods like APA, and follow publisher names with publication year. For citing government documents, APA separates with commas, starting with title, government body name, Congress, its number, session number, year, page number. MLA separates with periods; starts with government body/division names; continues with title, Congress and session numbers when applicable; adds resolution number; and finishes with publication city, colon, publisher, comma, year. Turabian is separated by periods and includes government body/division names,title, comma, Congress number when applying, and date. Sequencing within titles (such as committees/hearings) differ among manuals.

Citations of whole websites need only the URL (web address) in the body of the paper's text and enclosed within parentheses. Websites need not be included in the paper's bibliography, references, or works cited page. APA provides additional information about this at the following web address: http://www.apastyle.org/elecsource.html. For citing single documents found on websites, APA uses this format: Author last name, comma; author first initial, period; (year, month, date); title without quotation marks, period; publication city, colon, publisher/website owner, period; "Retrieved" month, date, year "from the World Wide Web:" URL on a separate line. MLA uses this format: Author last name, comma; author first name, period; title in quotation marks, period; italicized title, period; publisher/website owner, period; and date, month, year, period; URL on a separate line. Turabian uses this format: Author last name, comma; author first name, period; title in quotation marks, period; title, without italics or quotation marks, period; "Available from" and URL in the same line, period; and "Accessed" date, month, year.

To refer to authoritative sources for citing more complicated or specialized resources used in research, such as legislative publications, audiovisual resources, or manuscripts, at http://library.csudh.edu/cyberlib/research.htm is the section on Research and Writing Resources of California State University Dominguez Hills (CSUDH) University Library's website. The APA Manual is available in print: *Publication Manual of the American Psychological Association,* 6th ed., July 2009, and electronically in a Kindle edition. (The sixth is the latest edition as of February 2014.) APA has also adapted from this edition the *APA Style Guide to Electronic References,* and a pocket guide, *Concise Rules of APA Style.* Garner and Smith's *The Complete Guide to Citing Government Information Resources: A Manual for Writers and Librarians,* June 1993 (revised edition) is available in paperback on Amazon.com. *MLA Handbook for Writers of Research Papers* (7th edition, 2009) is available at MLA Bookstore's website. Turabian's *A Manual for Writers of Research Papers, Theses, and Dissertations* (8th edition, revised, 2013) is available from the University of Chicago Press website.

Integrating references and quotations

In research papers, one can make an argument and, without disrupting it, mention studies whose conclusions agree with one's position (Reed 284; Becker and Fagen 93), and those disagreeing (Limbaugh 442, Beck 69) by including parenthetical citations (for example, in this sentence). Quotations should be selective: writers should compose an original sentence and incorporate only a few words from a research source. If students cannot write more, or at least the same number of words as are in the quotation to analyze and concur with or rebut it, they are likely padding their compositions. When quoting sources, students and other writers should work to include quotations and references seamlessly into their sentences, instead of interrupting the flow of their own argument by summarizing the import of a source. Summarizing others' content is often a student ploy to bolster papers' word counts, a technique that is not intellectually original or engaging. Writing that analyzes the content, evaluates it, and synthesizes material from various sources demonstrates critical thinking skills and is thus more valuable.

Incorporating outside sources

Writers do better to include shorter quotations rather than longer ones. For example, six to eight long passages quoted within a 10-page paper are excessive. It is also better to avoid wording like "This quotation shows," "As you can see from this quotation," or "It talks about." These are amateurish, feeble efforts to interact with other authors' ideas. Also, writing about sources and quotations wastes words more effectively used to develop one's own ideas. Quotations should stimulate discussion, not quash it. Ending a paragraph, section, or paper with a quotation is not incorrect per se, but using it to prove a point, without anything more in one's own words regarding the point or subject, is avoiding thinking critically about the topic and considering multiple alternatives. It can also be a tactic to dissuade readers from challenging one's propositions. Writers should include references and quotations that disagree as well as agree with their thesis. Presenting evidence on both sides of an issue makes it easier for reasonably skeptical readers to agree with a writer's viewpoint.

Informative/explanatory vs. argumentative writing

Informative/explanatory writing begins on the basis that something is true or factual, while argumentative writing strives to prove something that may or may not be true or factual. Whereas argument is intended to convince readers that something is true or persuade readers to agree with the author's position, informative/explanatory text is instead intended to provide information and insight to readers. Rather than persuading readers, informative/explanatory writing concentrates on informing readers about why or how something is as it is. This includes offering new information to readers, explaining how a process works to readers, and/or developing a concept for readers. In accomplishing these objectives, the writing may emphasize such naming and differentiating various kinds of things within a category; providing definitions of things; providing details about the parts of something; explaining a particular function or behavior; and giving readers explanations for why a fact, object, event, or process exists or occurs.

Necessary skills for informative/explanatory writing

For students to write in informative/explanatory mode, they must be able to locate and select information pertinent to their topic from primary and secondary sources. They must also combine their own experiences and existing knowledge with this new information they find. They must not only select facts, details, and examples relevant to their topics, but also learn to incorporate this information into their writing. Students need at the same time to develop their skills in using various writing techniques, such as comparing and contrasting, making transitions between topics/points, citing scenarios and anecdotes related to their topics, and other strategies in the craft of writing. In instruction of explanatory/informative writing, teachers must "read like writers" to use mentor texts to consider author craft and technique. They can find mentor texts in blogs, websites, newspapers, novels, plays, picture books, and many more. Teachers should know the grade-level writing standards for informative/explanatory writing to select classroom-specific, appropriate mentor texts.

Narrative writing

Put simply, narrative writing tells a story. The most common examples of literary narratives are fictional novels. Non-fictional biographies, autobiographies, memoirs, and histories also use narrative. Narratives should tell stories in such a way that the readers learn something, or gain insight or understanding. Students can write more interesting narratives by relating events or experiences that were meaningful to them. Narratives should not begin with long descriptions or introductions, but start with the action(s) or event(s). Students should ensure that there is a point to their story by describing what they learned from the experience they narrate. To write effective description, students should include sensory details. They can access these by reviewing all five senses, asking themselves what they saw, heard, felt/touched, smelled, and tasted during the experiences they describe. In narrative writing, the details supplied should be concrete rather than abstract. Using concrete details enables readers to imagine everything that the writer describes.

Sensory details and concrete vs. abstract descriptions

Students need vivid description to write descriptive essays. When writing narratives, they must also include description—of characters, things, and events. Students should remember to describe not only the visual detail of what someone or something looks like, but details from all senses— how people and things sound, feel, smell, and taste. For example, they can contrast the feelings of a sea breeze versus a mountain breeze, describe how they think something inedible would taste, and sounds they hear in the same location at different times of day and night. Readers have trouble visualizing images or imagining sensory impressions and feelings from abstract descriptions, so concrete descriptions clarify and make these more real to readers. Concrete language provides information that readers can grasp and may empathize with, while abstract language can leave readers feeling disconnected, empty, even confused. "It was a lovely day" is abstract, but "The sun shone brightly, the sky was blue, the air felt warm, and a gentle breeze wafted across my skin" is concrete.

Students should avoid abstract language in description because it will not help readers understand what they want to express. Concrete language conveys to readers impressions, images, and feelings they want to experience. Abstract language is more general, concrete language more specific. For example, "Ms. Couch was a good teacher" uses abstract language. It gives only a general idea of the writer's opinion. But "Ms. Couch could really help us take our ideas and turn them into good essays and stories" uses concrete language, giving more specific examples of what Ms. Couch did that made her a good teacher. "I like writing poems but not essays" gives readers a general idea that the student prefers one genre over another, but not why. But by saying, "I like writing short poems with rhythm and rhyme, but I hate writing five-page essays that go on and on about the same ideas," readers understand that the student prefers the brevity, rhyme, and meter of short poetry over the length and redundancy of longer prose.

Journals

A journal is typically an individual's personal account of events, experiences, feelings, and thoughts in that individual's life. Many people write journals to confide their feelings and thoughts and/or help them process experiences they have had. When people write such journals as private documents not meant for sharing with others, they may not be concerned with grammar, spelling, or other writing mechanics. However, authors may write journals that they expect or hope to publish someday; in this case, they not only express their thoughts and feelings and process their experiences, but they additionally attend to their craft in writing them. Some authors compose journals to document particular time periods or series of related events, such as cancer diagnosis, treatment, surviving the disease, and how these experiences have changed/affected them; experiences in recovering from addiction; journeys of spiritual exploration and discovery; trips to or time spent in another country; or anything else someone wants to personally document. Journaling can also be therapeutic: some people use them to work through feelings of grief over loss.

Books written in diary form

The Diary of a Young Girl by Dutch Jewish Anne Frank (1947) contains her life-affirming, nonfictional diary entries from 1942-1944 while her family hid in an attic from World War II's genocidal Nazis. *Go Ask Alice* (1971) by Beatrice Sparks is a cautionary, fictional novel in the form of diary entries by an unhappy, rebellious teen who takes LSD, runs away from home and lives with hippies, and eventually returns home. The title quotes lyrics from the Jefferson Airplane song *White Rabbit* (1967), written and sung by Grace Slick, comparing the effects of LSD via extended metaphor to Lewis Carroll's (1865) depiction of *Alice's Adventures in Wonderland*. Frank's writing reveals an intelligent, sensitive, insightful girl, raised by intellectual European parents, who believes in the goodness of human nature despite surrounding atrocities. Character Alice, influenced by early 1970s counterculture, becomes less optimistic. However, adolescent searches for personal identity are evident in both books. Frank died in a Nazi concentration camp; the fictitious Alice died in a drug overdose.

Letters

Letters are typically messages written to communicate with other people. In addition to letters written between individuals, some writers compose letters to the editor of newspapers, magazines, and other publications; some write "Open Letters" to be published and read by the general public. Open letters, while intended for everyone to read, may also identify a group of people or a single person whom the letter directly addresses—or not. In everyday use, the most-used forms are business letters and personal or friendly letters. Both kinds share common elements, like business or personal letterhead stationery; the writer's return address at the top; the addressee's address next; a salutation, such as "Dear [name]" or some similar opening greeting, followed by a colon (:) in business letters or a comma (,) in personal letters; "To Whom it May Concern:" in business letters without specific individual addressees; the body of the letter, with paragraphs as indicated; and a closing, like "Sincerely/Cordially/Best regards/etc." or "Love," in intimate personal letters.

The Greek word for "letter" is *epistolē*, wherefrom English derives the word "epistle." The earliest literary letters were called epistles, including the New Testament's Epistles from the Apostles to the Christians. In ancient Egypt, the writing curriculum in scribal schools included the epistolary genre. Epistolary novels frame a story in the form of letters. For example, 18th-century English novelist Samuel Richardson wrote the popular epistolary novels *Pamela* (1740) and *Clarissa* (1749). Henry Fielding's satire of *Pamela,* entitled *Shamela* (1741) mocked epistolary writing. French author Montesquieu wrote *Lettres persanes* (1721); Jean-Jacques Rousseau wrote *Julie, ou la nouvelle Héloïse* (1761); and Pierre Choderlos de Laclos penned *Les Liaisons dangereuses* (1782), which was adapted into a screenplay for the multiple Oscar-winning 1988 English-language movie *Dangerous Liaisons*. German author Johann Wolfgang von Goethe wrote *The Sorrows of Young Werther* in epistolary form. Frances Brooke also wrote the first North American novel, *The History of Emily Montague* (1769) using epistolary form. In the 19th century, epistolary novels included Honoré de Balzac's *Letters of Two Brides* (1842) and Mary Shelley's *Frankenstein* (1818).

Essays

The basic format of an essay can be said to have three major parts: the introduction, the body, and the conclusion. Further, the essay's body can be divided into the writer's main points. Short and simple essays may have three main points, while essays covering broader ranges and going into more depth can have almost any number of main points, depending on length. An essay's introduction should answer three questions: (1) What is the subject of the essay? For example, if a student writes an essay about a book, the answer would include the title and author of the book and any additional information needed—such as what the book is about if the title does not indicate this. (2) How does the essay address the subject? To answer this, the writer identifies the essay's organization by briefly summarizing main points and/or evidence supporting them. (3) What will the essay prove? This is the thesis statement, usually the first paragraph's last sentence, clearly stating the writer's message.

An essay consists of an introduction, a body, and a conclusion. The introduction gives the essay's topic, previews its organization by summarizing its main points and supporting evidence, and introduces the thesis statement—the writer's major point. The body elaborates on all the main points related to the thesis and evidence supporting them. The conclusion restates the content of the introduction, and may also summarize the argument or description contained in the body. In the essay's body, the writer should introduce one main point; explain the meaning of this point; make quotations, cite facts, and offer other evidence to support the point; and then explain how this point and the evidence given to support it are related to the thesis. The writer should then repeat this procedure in a new paragraph with each of the additional main points. In addition to relating each point to the thesis, clearly restating the thesis in at least one sentence of each paragraph is also advisable.

An essay's basic parts are its introduction, body, and conclusion. The introduction tells essay's subject, how the essay's structure addresses this subject, and the author's major point or thesis statement. The body is where the writer introduces a series of main points related to the thesis, and provides evidence to support each of these points. The last part, the conclusion, reiterates the content of the introduction, including the thesis, to review them for the reader. The essay writer may also summarize the highlights of the argument or description contained in the body of the essay, following the same sequence originally used in the body. For example, a conclusion might look like Point 1 + Point 2 + Point 3 = Thesis, or Point 1 → Point 2 → Point 3 → Thesis Proof. Good organization makes essays easier for writers to compose, and provides a guide for readers to follow in reading them. Well-organized essays hold reader attention better, and are more likely to get readers to accept their theses as valid.

Speeches

Speeches are compositions written to be delivered or read in spoken language in public, to various groups of people, at formal or informal events. Some generic types include welcome speeches, thank-you speeches, keynote addresses, position papers, commemorative and dedication speeches, and farewell speeches. Speeches are commonly written in present tense. Speeches begin with an introduction, wherein the speaker greets the audience. At official functions, specific audience members are named ("Chairperson [name]," "Principal [name], teachers, and students") and when audiences include a distinguished guest, s/he is named as well. Then the speaker introduces himself/herself by name, position, and department/organization as applicable. The speaker then introduces the topic. Then s/he states the purpose of the speech. The body of the speech follows, similarly to the body of an essay, stating its main points, their elaboration, and supporting evidence. Finally, in the conclusion, the speaker states his/her hope for accomplishing the speech's purpose and thanks the audience for attending and listening to the speech.

Blogs

The word "blog" derives from "web log" and refers to writing done exclusively on the Internet. Readers of reputable newspapers expect quality content and layouts that enable easy reading. These expectations also apply to blogs. For example, readers can easily move visually from line to line when columns are narrow; overly wide columns cause readers to lose their places. Blogs must also be posted with layouts enabling online readers to follow them easily. However, because the way people read on computer, tablet, and smartphone screens differs from how they read print on paper, formatting and writing blog content is more complex than writing newspaper articles. Two major principles are the bases for blog-writing rules: (1) Whereas readers skim print articles to estimate their length, online they must scroll down to scan; therefore, blog layouts need more subheadings, graphics, and other indications of what information follows. (2) Onscreen reading is harder than reading printed paper; therefore, legibility is crucial in blogs.

Writing forms

When authors write narrative, their purpose is telling a story. Even when they mean to teach lessons or provide insight through relating events and experiences, they still do so by telling stories. Descriptive writing aims to recreate a moment, scene, event, or experience by conveying details vividly to appeal to readers' senses, imaginations, and emotions. Expository writing aims to provide information, explain ideas and processes, and/or give step-by-step directions how to do something. Persuasive/argumentative writing aims to convince readers to agree with the author's viewpoint, opinion, or position, by both providing supporting evidence, and using subjective/expressive language to sway readers' opinions and influence their feelings and beliefs. Speculative writing, rather than informing or explaining as expository/informational writing does, aims to explore ideas and, rather than convincing readers to agree, aims to encourage readers also to consider ideas and various potential thoughts and reactions associated with them. Points are less clear and definitive, and structures looser, in speculative writing than in exposition or argumentation.

Considerations to teach students about occasions, purposes, and audiences

Teachers can explain to students that organizing their ideas, providing evidence to support the points they make in their writing, and correcting their grammar and mechanics are not simply for following writing rules or correctness for its own sake, but rather for ensuring that specific reader audiences understand what they intend to communicate. For example, upper-elementary-grade students writing for lower-elementary-grade students should write in printing rather than script, use simpler vocabulary, and avoid writing in long, complex, compound, or complex-compound sentences. The purpose for writing guides word choice, such as encouraging readers to question opposing viewpoints or stimulate empathy and/or sympathy. It also influences narrative, descriptive, expository, or persuasive/argumentative format. For instance, business letters require different form and language than parent thank-you notes. Persuasive techniques, like words that evoke certain reader emotions, description that appeals to reader beliefs, and supporting information can all affect reader opinions.

Questions to ask to determine content and format

When student writers have chosen a viewpoint or idea about which to write, teachers can help them select content to include and the writing format(s) most appropriate to their subject. They should have students ask themselves what their readers need to know to enable them to agree with the viewpoint in the writing, and/or to believe what the writer is saying. Students can imagine another person hearing them say what they will write about, responding, "Oh, yeah? Prove that!" Teachers should have students ask themselves what kinds of evidence they should supply to prove their positions/ideas to skeptical readers. They should have students consider what points they will make in writing with which readers might disagree. Students should consider what knowledge their reading audience shares in common with them. They should also consider what information they need to share with their readers. Teachers can have students adapt various writing formats, organizing techniques, and writing styles to different purposes and audiences to practice with choosing writing modes and language.

Appropriate kinds of writing for different tasks, purposes, and audiences

Students who are writing to persuade their parents to grant them some additional privilege, such as permission for a more independent activity, should use more sophisticated vocabulary and diction that sounds more mature and serious to appeal to the parental audience. Students who are writing for younger children, however, should use simpler vocabulary and sentence structure, as well as choosing words that are more vivid and entertaining. They should treat their topics more lightly, and include some humor as is appropriate. Students who are writing for their classmates, regardless whether they are writing in expository, argumentative, narrative, or speculative form, might use language that is more informal, as well as age-appropriate. Students wanting to convince others to agree with them should use persuasive/argumentative form. Those wanting to share an experience with readers should use descriptive writing. Those wanting to relate a story and what can be learned from it should write narratives. Students can use speculative writing to invite others to join them in exploring ideas.

Main ideas, supporting details, and outlining a topic

Writers often begin their first paragraph by stating their main idea or point, also known as their topic sentence. In the rest of the paragraph, they supply particular details that develop and support the main point. One way to visualize the relationship between the main point and supporting information is as a table: the tabletop is the main point, and each of the table's legs is a supporting detail or group of details. Both professional authors and writing students can benefit in planning their writing by first making an outline of the topic. Outlines facilitate quick identification of the main point and supporting details without having to wade through the intervening language that will exist in the fully developed essay, article, or paper. Outlining can also help readers to analyze a piece of existing writing for the same reason. The outline first summarizes the main idea in one sentence. Then, below that, it summarizes the supporting details in a numbered list, also of one sentence each.

Words that signal introduction of successive details

When someone writes a paragraph beginning with the topic sentence, the second sentence may begin with a phrase like "First of all," introducing the first supporting detail/example. The writer may introduce the second supporting item with words or phrases like "Also," "In addition," and "Besides," among others. The writer might introduce succeeding pieces of support with wording like, "Another thing," "Moreover" "Furthermore," or "Not only that, but…" The writer may introduce the last piece of support with "Lastly," "Finally," or "Last but not least." Writers get off the point by presenting "off-target" items not supporting the main point. For example, a main point "My dog is not smart" is supported by the statement, "He's six years old and still doesn't answer to his name." But "He cries when I leave for school" is not supportive, as it does not indicate lack of intelligence. Writers stay on the point by presenting only supportive statements that are directly relevant to and illustrative of their main point.

Paragraph

A paragraph is generally a group of sentences that forms a unit separate from (but connected to) other paragraphs. Typically, all of one paragraph's sentences relate to one main idea or point. Two major properties that make paragraphs effective or ineffective are focus and development, or lack thereof. Paragraphs with poor focus impede comprehension because the sentences they contain seem unrelated. When writers attempt to include too many ideas in a paragraph rather than focusing on the most important idea, or fail to supply transitions between ideas, they produce unfocused or at least inadequately-focused paragraphs. Undeveloped or inadequately-developed paragraphs may use good writing, but are still not convincing or effective. When writers misunderstand their reading audience, depend overly upon generalization, and fail to offer specific details, their paragraph development is poor. They may omit key term definitions, supporting evidence, setting description, context for others' ideas, background, and other important details because they assume that readers already know these things and think they would bore readers by repeating them.

Writing effective paragraphs
The first thing a writer should do to write good paragraphs is to focus upon one main idea as a paragraph's subject or topic. Writers may introduce a paragraph by stating this main idea in a topic sentence. However, the main idea may be so obvious that writers can imply it rather than state it overtly and readers can easily infer it. Another thing writers should do is to use specific details to develop the main idea. Details should capture readers' attention and also explain author ideas. Insufficient detail makes a paragraph too abstract, which readers find boring and even confusing. Excessive detail makes a paragraph unfocused, which readers find overwhelming, and again, even confusing. A third thing writers should do is to develop paragraphs using structural patterns. Paragraphs have a nearly limitless range of structures, but certain patterns appear more often,

including narration, description, definition, example and illustration, division and classification, comparison and contrast, analogy, cause and effect, and process.

Structural patterns

Narration, description, definition, example and illustration, and division and classification: In narration, a paragraph develops its main idea by using a story or a portion of a story. Writers may use stories as anecdotal evidence to support the main point. In description, the writer helps readers to construct a clear image of a scene or event by including specific, sensory and other details that depict a person, thing, place, and/or time. Description shows readers instead of telling them. In definition, the writer uses a paragraph to provide readers with a detailed definition of a term that is central to the piece of writing. In example and illustration, the writer provides the readers with one or more examples that illustrate the point that the writer wants to make. Paragraphs using division divide one whole thing into its component parts according to some particular principle—for example, body parts or experiment steps. Paragraphs using classification group separate things into categories by their similarities or commonalities, also according to some particular principle—such as mammals and insects, tragedies and comedies, and so on.

Analogy, cause and effect, and process: Paragraphs that compare two or more things make note of their similarities, i.e., all or many of the characteristics that those things share in common. Paragraphs that contrast two or more things make note of how they differ from one another. Another common paragraph technique is both comparing and contrasting two or more items within the same paragraph, showing both similarities and differences. Analogy compares two things in a way that they are not usually compared, often because they are things belonging to very different categories. This can afford new reader insight. Writers may use analogies to develop their ideas. Writers also develop their ideas in paragraphs through cause and effect, which either explains what caused some event or result, or shows the effects that something produced. Paragraphs may start with cause(s) and proceed to effect(s), or begin with effect(s) and then give cause(s). Process paragraphs describe and/or explain some process. They often sequence the stages, phases, or steps of the process using chronological order.

Coherence

When a paragraph is coherent, its parts or details fit together such that readers clearly perceive it, and its parts flow well from each to the next. Writers produce more coherent paragraphs when they select structural patterns appropriate to the conceptual content. There are several techniques writers can use to make paragraphs more coherent. Repetition connects sentences by repeating key words, phrases, and/or pronouns referring to these. This not only helps sentences flow together, it also signals to readers the significance of the ideas these words and phrases communicate. Parallelism uses parallel structure, within and also between and among sentences. Humorist Bill Maher once said, "We're feeding animals too sick to stand to people too fat to walk." His parallelism emphasized and connected two issues: using downed cows as food, and the obesity epidemic. Consistency keeps the viewpoint, tone, and linguistic register consistent within the paragraph or piece. Finally, transitions via connective words and phrases aid coherence immensely.

Transitions

Transitions between sentences and paragraphs help guide readers from idea to idea. They also indicate relationships between sentences and paragraphs. Writers should use transitions judiciously: they should not overuse these, and should take care to select the right transition for their purpose. For example, transitional words and phrases indicating time include: thereafter, afterward, immediately, earlier, meanwhile, recently, lately, later (on), now, (ever) since, soon, as soon as, when, then, until, before, in the past, presently, simultaneously, so far, thus far, previously, at that time, and at last. Transitions indicating sequence include: too, first, second, third, further, furthermore, moreover, also, again, and, and then, next, still, too, besides, and finally. Transitions specifying comparison include: similarly, in the same way, likewise, also, again, and once more. Transitions that indicate contrast include: but, even so, even though, although, despite, however, instead, in spite of, nonetheless, nevertheless, on the one hand... on the other hand, regardless, irrespective, though, still, yet, contrastingly, differently, and in contrast.

Transitional words and phrases
Transitions indicating examples include: for example, for instance, the following example, such as, to illustrate, indeed, in fact, of course, namely, specifically, and after all. Transitions indicating cause and effect include: because, consequently, hence, thus, therefore, thereupon, then, to this end, since, so, as a result, if... then, and accordingly. Transitions indicating place include: near, nearby, far, faraway, here, there, to the left, to the right, next to, above, below, adjacent to, beyond, opposite, across from, beside, alongside, at the back, in the front, in front of, behind, to the side, and abreast of. Transitions expressing concession include: granted that, naturally, of course, I admit that, it may seem that, it may appear, and although it is true that. Transitions showing repetition, summary, or conclusion include: as mentioned earlier, as we have seen, as noted, in other words, in any event, in short, on the whole, to summarize, therefore, as a result, to conclude, and in conclusion. These tell readers how a sentence relates to the previous one(s), and directs their thinking across ideas.

Coherence vs. cohesion

Cohesive writing flows, making readers feel ease in moving from sentence to sentence and that all sentences hold together. Coherent writing contains sentences that are not only clear individually, but also combine into a unified paragraph or passage focusing on a group of ideas that fit together. While we are often warned against using passive voice, sometimes a paragraph or passage is more cohesive using a passive construction when it allows sentences to flow together better. For example, "Scientists are studying black holes. A black hole is made when a dead star collapses..." The passive voice allows repetition of "black hole" from the end of the first sentence to the beginning of the second, connecting this idea. Making one sentence follow from the previous one is the "old-to-new" technique. If the second sentence in active voice read, "When a dead star collapses, it becomes a black hole..." The term "black hole" would be further away from the first sentence and they would not connect or flow as well.

Writers can make text cohesive with the old-to-new principle: starting sentences with information familiar to readers, and ending them with information unexpected to readers. Someone can write a cohesive paragraph because sentences flow together well: each new sentence refers to a word or idea in the previous one. However, a cohesive paragraph may still not be coherent, as when the writer connects words or ideas between sentences, but changes the subject with each new sentence. When writing is coherent, readers can make sense of paragraphs or passages because sentence ideas integrate into a unified whole with interrelated concepts. Coherent writing enables readers to recognize individual sentence topics readily, and realize how they combine into a group of connected ideas. Readers feel more comfortable when sentence topics appear earlier in sentences, and when a sequence of sentences indicates the import of the entire paragraph or passage. Beginning sentences with familiar information in short and simple phrases, keeping topics consistent, and making movement between ideas obvious will help produce cohesive and coherent writing.

Writing style and linguistic form

Linguistic form comes from the phonological, morphological, syntactic, and semantic parts of a language. It encodes the literal meanings of words and sentences. Writing style consists of different ways of encoding that meaning, and indicating figurative and stylistic meanings. The stylistic choices that writers make accomplish three basic effects upon their reading or listening audiences: (1) they communicate meanings beyond linguistically dictated meanings; (2) they communicate the author's attitude, such as persuasive/argumentative effects accomplished through style; and (3) they communicate or express feelings. Within style, component areas include: narrative structure; viewpoint; focus; sound patterns; meter and rhythm; lexical and syntactic repetition and parallelism; writing genre; representational, realistic, and mimetic effects; representation of thought and speech; meta-representation (representing representation); irony; metaphor and other indirect meanings; representation and use of historical and dialectal variations; gender-specific and other group-specific speech styles, both real and fictitious; and analysis of the processes whereby readers infer meanings from writing.

Introduction

Because readers encounter the introduction first, writers should design introductory paragraphs to capture reader interest. Introductions should state the main point, thesis, or topic sentence soon and logically. Writers should use introductions to prepare readers for the content of the body of the essay or piece. To do this, writers should narrow their topics to a main idea. They should determine which main points support the main idea, and then decide in what sequence to order those points. Then they should list all of the details that support each of those main points, and organize these details in sequential order. Some techniques for sequencing include strongest-to-weakest and weakest-to-strongest, logical progression, or sequencing by association. Writers should compose a thesis statement, which may contain their plan for the piece's structure and organization. Then they make a first draft of the body of the document, including transitions between sentences and paragraphs. Finally, they write the introduction, focusing on getting the reader's attention and engaging his/her interest, integrating the thesis into the introduction, and maintaining the document's organization and structure.

Body

In the introduction to an essay, a writer has established the thesis or main idea, and may have indicated how the rest of the piece will be structured. In the body of the piece, the writer elaborates upon, illustrates, and explains the thesis statement. How writers sequence supporting details and their choices of paragraph types are development techniques. Writers may give examples of the concept introduced in the thesis statement. If the subject includes a cause-and-effect relationship, the author may explain its nature and causality. A writer may explain and/or analyze the main idea of the piece. Authors will often present arguments for the veracity or credibility of their thesis statement. If they use ambiguous terms, writers may use development to define or clarify them. Writers may organize paragraphs within the body using natural sequences, like space and/or time. They may employ inductive reasoning, using multiple details to establish a generalization or causal relationship, or deductive reasoning, proving a generalized hypothesis or proposition through a specific example/case.

Conclusion

Two important principles to consider when writing the conclusion of a written piece are strength and closure. When a conclusion is strong, it gives the reader the sense that the main points made by the author were meaningful and important, and that the facts and arguments that the author presented to prove or support those main points were convincing, solid, and well-developed. When a conclusion achieves closure, it gives the reader the sense that the writer has stated what needed stating and the work is complete, rather than that the writer simply stopped writing upon reaching the number of words specified. Some things to avoid when writing concluding paragraphs include: introducing a completely new idea in the conclusion; beginning with "In conclusion" or "To summarize," which is overly obvious and unoriginal; apologizing for one's opinions and/or writing; repeating the thesis word for word, rather than rephrasing it; and believing that the conclusion must always summarize the piece.

Effectively delivering speeches

Speakers should deliver speeches in the natural manner of a conversation rather than being rigidly formal or theatrical. Effective delivery is also supported by speaker confidence. Speakers should be direct, building audience rapport through personal connection. Using vivid imagery activates listeners' feelings. Speakers should be mindful of the occasion, subject, and audience of their speeches and take care to use appropriate language for these. Good speakers learn vocal control, including loudness, speed, pitch, use of pauses, variety among vocal tones, pronunciation of words, and clear articulation. They employ their voices to express enthusiasm and emphasize important points. Nonverbal behaviors, such as eye contact with all listeners, facial expressions, gestures, and body movements clarify communication, stress important ideas, and influence listener perceptions that the speaker is trustworthy, competent, of good character, and hence credible. Nonverbal communications should seem as spontaneous and natural as vocal or verbal ones. Good posture is important. Speakers should know their speeches well and practice copiously. They should avoid tapping pencils or their feet, eye- or face-rubbing, pacing, hair-twirling, or other random or irrelevant movements.

Media and format choices

Experts consider effective communication strategies to combine two or three different media types. Media and format choices are influenced by the target audience; the presenters' budget; the best channels of communicating for specific audiences; the duration of the communication; and, with communication intended to promote social change, the relative importance of inducing meaningful audience participation. Two media types are TV and radio. Both are high-status mass media that reaches many people. TV reaches the general public but also can be customized for specialized target audiences, while radio reaches specific target audiences. TV has a broad reach, radio broad-to-medium. TV has the advantage of video plus audio, while audio only is one radio disadvantage. Both are useful for communicating simple slogans and messages, and both can generate awareness, interest, and excitement. A disadvantage is that TV is more expensive than radio, while radio is more expensive than other media. TV and radio audiences cannot interact directly except during call-in programs. Programming times may be inconvenient, but tape, digital sound, and digital video recording (DVR) can remedy this.

Newspapers

Except for the occasional community columns, news releases, and letters to the editor, newspaper pages and features afford little opportunity for audience input or participation. However, they reach and appeal to the literate public, though the general public is unlikely to read them. Cost is an advantage: those producing their own news releases and photographs can do so for free. Hiring a PR writer costs money, but not as much as radio or TV spots do. Additional advantages include that newspaper features are high-status, and that audiences can reread and review them as often as they like. Disadvantages include that they do not reach audiences in as much depth as TV and radio, that they require literacy of audiences, and that their publication is subject to editors' whims and biases. Newspaper pieces combining advertising and editorial—"advertorials"—afford inclusion of paid material, but are viewed as medium-status. They share other disadvantages with newspaper features and pages, but they cost more.

Internet websites and blogs, and mobile phones and text messaging

Computer literacy is required for online material, but participation potential is high via websites, e-networking, list-serves, and blogging. Mobile phones and text messaging have potential for enormous direct, public, two-way and one-on-one communication, timely information and reminders. Web media need a literate public. They can be designed for specific audiences. Mobile and text media are ubiquitously popular, but also appeal especially to certain demographics like teens and young adults. Web media afford global information, are accessible by increasingly technology-literate populations, and are high-status. List-serves can be inexpensive. Links to related websites and pages within existing sites are also advantages. Mobile and text media are increasing in reach, especially in rural regions; are decreasing in cost; and are very popular. Web media disadvantages include requiring computers, people to design and manage them and supply content, and technical support. Mobile and text media disadvantages include required brevity in texts, provider messaging charges, and working best when connected to other communications.

Public presentations and PowerPoint presentations

Public presentations allow great potential for audience participation and interaction. Feedback can also be incorporated in PowerPoint presentations. Public presentations can directly target various audiences. PowerPoint presentations are best for sophisticated audiences like professionals, civil servants, and service organizations. Public presentations can encourage the establishment of partnerships and groups, stimulate local ownership of issues and projects, and make information public. Well-designed PowerPoint presentations are good for stimulating audience interest, selling ideas, and marketing purposes. Also, they are accessible online by many more computer users in addition to the in-person presentations' audiences. Public presentations' drawbacks include only being useful for moments in a process rather than throughout; being limited to nights, weekends, or when audiences are available; and not always attracting the intended audiences. PowerPoint disadvantages include requiring projectors and equipment, electricity, and computer skills to show them, and being limited to communicating more general points, outlines, and summaries rather than conveying a lot of information in more detail.

Evaluating speeches for concise information

To convince or persuade listeners and/or reinforce a message, speeches must be succinct. Audiences become confused if speakers include excessive anecdotes and details. If a speaker takes three minutes or more to get to the point when making a statement and/or answering a question, audience attention will flag, and will only get worse when details get off the subject. With answers, the asker and speaker may both even forget what the question was. Speakers should practice not only rehearsing written speeches, but also to develop skill for spontaneous question-and-answer sessions after speeches. Speakers should differentiate necessary from simply interesting information because audience members' brains stop processing input beyond their limits to prevent overload. Speakers should know what point(s) they wish to make. They should not fear pausing before responding to questions, which indicates thoughtfulness and control. Restating questions increases comprehension, appropriate responses, and allows time to form answers mentally.

Clearly written prose and speeches

To achieve clarity, a writer or speaker must first define his or her purpose carefully. The speech or piece must be organized logically, so that sentences make sense and follow each other in an understandable order. Sentences must also be constructed well, and the writer should choose the words used with precision. Organizing a speech in advance using an outline provides the writer/speaker with a blueprint, directing and focusing the composition to meet its intended purpose. Organized speeches enable audiences to comprehend and retain the presented information more easily. Humans naturally seek to impose order on the world by seeking patterns. Hence, when ideas in a speech are well-organized and adhere to a consistent pattern, the speaker communicates better with listeners. Speechwriters can use chronological patterns to organize events, sequential patterns to organize processes by their steps, and spatial patterns to help audiences visualize geographical locations and movements or physical scenarios. Comparison-contrast patterns give audiences insight about similarities and differences between and among topics, especially when listeners are more familiar with one than the other.

Attributes and benefits of certain organizational patterns

When a speechwriter uses an advantages-disadvantages pattern of organization, s/he presents audiences with the pros and cons of a topic. This aids writers in discussing two sides of an issue objectively without an argumentative position, enabling listeners also to weigh both aspects. When a speechwriter uses a cause-and-effect pattern, it can help to persuade audiences to agree with an action or solution the speaker advocates by showing significant relationships between and among factors. Writers may separate an outline into two main "cause" and "effect" sections, or separate it into sections, one for each cause, that includes its effect(s). Persuasive writing also benefits from problem-solution patterns: by establishing the existence of a problem, writers induce audiences to realize a need for change. By supplying a solution and supporting its superiority above other solutions, the writer convinces audiences of the value of that solution. When none of these patterns—or chronological, sequential, spatial, or comparison-contrast patterns—applies, writers often use topical patterns. These organize information by various subtopics and types within the main topic or category.

Techniques to ensure active listening and productive participation

When assigning students to participate in cooperative learning projects and/or discussions, teachers should consider their cognitive, emotional, behavioral, and social developmental levels. If a teacher assigns a topic for age levels younger than the class, students will be bored and unengaged. If the topic assigned is for age levels older than the students, they will be confused, overwhelmed, or lost. Before initiating class or group discussions, teachers should model and explain appropriate behaviors for discussions—particularly for students unfamiliar or inexperienced with these. For example, teachers can model by demonstrating active listening, including eye contact, affirming or confirming the speaker's message, and restating the speaker's message for confirmation or correction. Teachers should establish clear ground rules, such as not interrupting others when they are speaking; not monopolizing the conversation; not engaging in cross-talk; not insulting classmates verbally; taking turns; waiting for appropriate openings in the conversation to make comments; and, for young children and students with behavioral issues, not engaging in physical contact like hitting, kicking, and biting.

Posters and brochures

Both posters and brochures share in common the lack of potential feedback—unless they have been broadly tested, or if their publication is accompanied by workshops and other participatory events at the community level or higher. Both can target audiences of the general public and more specific public sectors. Posters are better for communicating simple slogans and messages, while brochures can include more detail and are better for printing instructional information. Both can be inexpensive to produce. Posters particularly can often be printed in-house without using outside printing companies. Disadvantages of posters include the simplicity required of their messages, and the requirement of literacy in written language and visual elements to understand them. Disadvantages of brochures include their limitations of distribution to specific groups or areas and, like posters, also requiring literacy to read and understand them. Because of their size, a given number of posters costs more than the same number of brochures. Moreover, if brochures are printed only as needed and in-house, they can cost even less.

Flyers and fact sheets

Flyers and fact sheets have one-way communication potential because readers cannot give feedback. Their target audiences are general. Some advantages of using this form of media include flexibility: people can distribute them following various community meetings; put them on car windshields in parking lots or in supermarkets and other stores; on bulletin boards at community agencies and organizations, public and private elementary and secondary schools, colleges, and universities; hand them out at community events and from convention booths and other displays; and also mail them out to recipients. When printed on colored paper using black ink, they can be very inexpensive. They afford recipients the convenience of being able to review them at their leisure. Organizations and individuals can produce flyers and fact sheets in-house, or even at home with desktop publishing software. Disadvantages include their limitation to single facts or tips, and specific information on specified topics. They cost the same as printing brochures, but fact sheets printed in black and white cost half what full-color brochures do.

English Language Arts Instruction

Evaluating information sources in various media forms

With the wealth of media in different formats available today, users are more likely to take media on their face value with less questioning. However, to understand the content of media, consumers must act as educated consumers by critically evaluating each source. Users should ask themselves about media sources: Who is delivering this message, and why? What methods do a media source's publishers employ to gain and maintain users' attention? Which points of view is the media source representing? What are the various ways in which a reader of a media source could interpret the message that the source is delivering? And what information is missing from the message conveyed by a media source? Is the source scholarly, i.e., peer-reviewed? Does it include author names and their credentials pertinent to the information? Who publishes it, and why? Who is the target audience? Is the language technically specific or non-technical/public? Are sources cited, research claims documented, conclusions based on furnished evidence, and references provided? Is the publication current? All of these questions and more can and should be asked of media sources.

For books, consider whether information is up-to-date, and whether historical perspectives apply. Content is more likely to be scholarly if publishers are universities, government, or professional organizations. Looking for book reviews also informs users. For articles, look for biographical author information; publisher name; frequency of periodical publication; and whether advertising is included and, if so, whether for certain occupations/disciplines. For web pages, check their domain names, publishers or sponsors (strip back URLs to uncover), look for author/publisher contact information, check dates of most recent page updates, and be alert to biases and verify information's validity. Quality and accuracy of web pages located through search engines rather than library databases ranges widely, indicating careful user inspection. Web page recommendations from reliable sources like university faculties can help indicate quality and accuracy. Citations of websites by credible or scholarly sources also show reliability, as do links from other reputable sites. Authors' names, relevant credentials, affiliations, and contact information support their authority. Site functionality, such as ease of navigation, ability to search, site maps and/or indexes, are also criteria to consider.

Persuasive media

Some media using persuasion are advertising, public relations, and advocacy. Advertisers use persuasion to get consumers to purchase goods and services. The public relations field uses persuasion to give consumers good impressions of companies, governments, or organizations. Advocacy groups use persuasion to garner support or votes. Sources use commercials, public service announcements, speeches, websites, and newsletters, among others. Activists, lobbyists, government officials, and politicians use political rhetoric involving persuasive techniques. Basic techniques include using celebrity spokespersons, whom consumers admire or aspire to resemble; or, conversely, "everyday people" (albeit often portrayed by actors) with whom consumers identify. Using expert testimonials lends credibility. Explicit claims of content, effectiveness, quality, and reliability—which often cannot be proven or disproven—are used to persuade. While news and advocacy messages mostly eschew humor for credibility's sake (except in political satire), advertising often persuades via humor, which gets consumer attention and associates its pleasure with advertised products and services. "Weasel words," such as qualifiers, are often combined with

- 78 -

exaggerated claims. Intensifiers—hyperbole, superlatives, and repetition—within and of messages, and sentimental appeals are also persuasive.

Intermediate techniques

Dangerous propagandist Adolf Hitler said people suspect little lies more than big ones; hence the "Big Lie" is a persuasion method requiring consumers' keen critical thinking to identify. A related method is charisma, which can induce people even to believe messages they would otherwise reject. *Euphemism* substitutes abstract, vague, or bland terms for more graphic, clear, and unpleasant ones. For example, the terms "layoffs" and "firing" are replaced by "downsizing," and "torture" is replaced with "intensive interrogation techniques." Extrapolation bases sweeping conclusions on small amounts of minor information to appeal to what consumers wish or hope to be so. Flattery appeals to consumer self-esteem needs, such as the McDonald's slogan, "You deserve a break today" or L'Oreal's "You're worth it." Flattery is sometimes accomplished through contrast, like ads showing stupid actions by others to make consumers feel superior and smarter. "Glittering generalities" are "virtue" concepts, such as beauty, love, health, democracy, freedom, and science. Persuaders hope these gain consumer acceptance without questioning what they mean, whether their use is applicable, or investigating evidence. The opposite is name-calling to persuade rejecting someone or something.

American citizens love new ideas and technology. Persuaders exploit this by emphasizing the newness of products, services, and candidates. Conversely, they also use nostalgia to evoke consumers' happy memories, which they often remember more than unhappy ones. Citing "scientific evidence" is an intermediate version of the basic technique of expert testimonials. Consumers may accept this as proof, but some advertisers, politicians, and other persuaders may present inaccurate or misleading "evidence." Another intermediate technique is the "simple solution." Although the natures of people and life are complex, when consumers feel overwhelmed by complexity, persuaders exploit this by offering policies, products, or services they claim will solve complicated problems with simple means. Persuaders also use symbols—images, words, and names we associate with more general, emotional concepts like lifestyle, country, family, religion, and gender. While symbols have power, their significance also varies across individuals: for example, some consumers regard the Hummer SUV as a prestigious status symbol, while others regard it as environmentally harmful and irresponsible.

Advanced techniques

Ad hominem, Latin for "against the man"—also called "shoot the messenger"—attacks someone delivering a message, not the message itself. It operates by association: problems with the messenger must indicate problems with the message. "Stacking the deck" misleads by presenting not complete information, but only selected information supporting persuader positions. Denial evades responsibility, either directly or indirectly, for controversial or unpopular subjects: A politician saying, "I won't mention my opponent's tax evasion issues" manages to mention them while seeming less accusatory. Persuaders use majority belief, such as "Four out of five dentists recommend this brand" or the ubiquitous "[insert number] people can't be wrong." In an intensified version, persuaders exploit group dynamics at rallies, speeches, and other live-audience events where people are vulnerable to surrounding crowd influences. Scapegoating—blaming one person or group for complex problems, is a form of the intermediate "simple solution" technique, a practice common in politics. Timing also persuades, like advertising flowers and candy preceding Valentine's Day, ad campaigns preceding new technology rollouts, and politician speeches following big news events.

Rules and rationales for writing blogs

Expert web designer, copywriter, and blogger Annabel Cady (http://www.successfulblogging.com/) shares the following blog-posting rules: Format all posts considering page layout and for easy scanning. Column width should be a maximum of 80 characters, including spaces, for easier reading. Headings and subheadings separate text visually, enable scanning or skimming, and encourage continued reading. Bullet-pointed or numbered lists enable quick information location and scanning. Punctuation is critical, so beginners should use shorter sentences until confident. Blog paragraphs should be far shorter—two to six sentences each—than paragraphs written on paper to enable "chunking" because reading onscreen is more difficult. Sans serif fonts are usually clearer than serif fonts, and larger font sizes are better. Highlight important material and draw attention with **boldface**, but avoid overuse. Avoid hard-to-read *italics* and ALL CAPITALS. Include enough blank spaces: overly busy blogs tire eyes and brains. Images not only break up text, but also emphasize and enhance text, and can attract initial reader attention. Use background colors judiciously. Be consistent throughout posts: people read them in different orders. Tell a story with a beginning, middle, and end.

Educational benefits of digital media

Digital media are powerful by being flexible, versatile, and able to be transformed, marked, and networked. For example, printed ink on paper and paint on canvas are permanent. However, digital images of these—while they sacrifice physical texture and some visual depth, tone, and subtlety in the latter case—have the advantage that they can be displayed on anything from a giant public video screen, to a desktop or laptop monitor, to a palm device or smartphone screen in multiple global locations. Digital images can also be manipulated to sharpen, blur, darken, or lighten them, or remove, transpose, duplicate, recombine, and restore portions. Images, text, and voice can be saved exactly and reliably over time periods, and also adapted or changed to the benefit of teachers of diverse classrooms. Digital media are not limited to text and pictures as books are: they also include video and audio, and combine video and sound with text. Students can interact with multiple media at once, choose preferred formats, and compensate for or adapt to learning difficulties.

Unlike hard copies, digitally-saved materials can be linked to each other. Embedded hyperlinks afford many learning supports to students, such as dictionaries, thesauruses, encyclopedias; reading comprehension prompts; supplementary materials to build student background knowledge; visual graphic organizers; and electronic notepads for keeping running notes. Students can rapidly navigate between words in a text and their dictionary definitions; images and their descriptions; videos and their captions; or a passage of text by an author and an audio file of it being read aloud, or an audio file of related sounds. Another advantage for teachers and students is that websites and pages are often constantly updated in real time. Educators and learners can access information and opinions contributed by a wide variety of peers, experts, and mentors—not just locally, but globally. Multimedia packages enable multisensory, multimodal experiences rather than simply reading print. Access is almost instantaneous. Networking affords teachers and students interconnected communication and information, plus formats and experiences more similar in their diversity to the diversity of individual learners.

extends the classroom

Transforming and marking digital media

Students can use within-media transformations to change how website content is displayed by turning graphics or sound on or off, adjust volume, and change text and image appearance by using different computers, different browsers, adjusting browser settings, and so on. Cross-media transformations can convert speech to text or text to speech via software, and can do so automatically by embedding into other software and browsers. This helps students with vision and hearing problems, auditory processing deficits, and reading or learning disabilities. HTML (Hypertext Markup Language) and XML (Extensible Markup Language), both used in web design, enable text choices like certain fonts for certain parts of web pages. With minimal training, teachers and students can use these tools to change and mark online text to accommodate different learning needs. For example, students can underline all summary sentences in detailed texts, and teachers can italicize all English words in a text having Greek or Latin roots, or boldface all metaphors. Unlike highlighter pens, digital markups can be hidden, displayed, expanded, deleted, and changed as student needs change.

Instructional videos

Instructional videos have great two-way communication potential because whoever produces a video can build opportunities for questions and feedback into its format and presentation. Videos can be made to target particular audiences interested in their subject matter. Advantages include that videos can be paused for discussion, and replayed whenever needed to see or hear parts again. They also enable their producers to record processes, including "before," "during," and "after" phases. They can be played back immediately after recording. They are accessible, because most communities have at least one DVD player or computers. Even the video producer's own laptop can be used to play video files. Videos also have the advantage of high status. Moreover, video players and computers are continually becoming less expensive to buy and use. Disadvantages include needing editing software and equipment in some cases, needing support from other print materials, the danger of overuse if other media or methods could be more appropriate, and higher up-front costs. Producers must account for the costs of script development and hiring local performers as needed.

DVDs or CDs

DVDs and CDs are often passively received by audiences (except those designed to be interactive games), which gives viewers the potential to participate, and are becoming increasingly prevalent and popular. They are commonly used to target specific audiences; younger people are especially attracted to them. Compared to many other media formats, discs are comparatively inexpensive to make, and are easy to transport due to their small size and weight. They enjoy high status, and people tend to perceive them as "professional" in nature. They are more resistant to damage and aging than older videotape technology, making them more durable. Some disadvantages include needing computer access to produce and play, and certain software programs to produce, especially if the producer wants to include video animation and audio commentary—as is common today on movie DVDs, for example. If a DVD includes video animation, this alone can cost at least a couple thousand dollars. Producers must also consider the time of paid staff, and production and labeling expenses.

Active student listening

Active listening is described as having multiple dimensions. It involves listening processes required of people for their engagement in constructing meaning out of what they hear; being agile, reflective, and creative in considering and manipulating information they receive; and making competent decisions rich in ideas. The natural properties of speech and thought are conducive to active listening: the typical speed of speaking is roughly 125 words a minute, whereas the estimated speed of thinking is roughly 500 words a minute. Therefore, students have around 375 words a minute of spare time to think about the speech they hear. As an educator (Carbone, in TILT Posts 2013-2014) points out, students' minds can wander during this extra time, so teachers can instruct them to use the time instead to summarize lecture information mentally—a form of active listening. Listening and learning share common characteristics of being social and reciprocal. They also both allow and require students to process and consider speech they hear and stimulate their curiosity about subsequent information.

Whole-class learning circles

Forming whole classes into learning circles requires student application of skills for listening to teacher lessons/lectures; synthesizing information they heard, read, reviewed, and studied; and summarizing information received. Teachers can prepare students by articulating central discussion points; identifying next steps in thought, question forming, analysis, and action; guiding student analysis and construction of meaning from what they have read, observed, and experienced; and asking students questions beginning with "What...? So What? and Now What?" Basic ground rules for learning circles include: (1) No student interrupts another. (2) Students may skip a turn until others have taken turns, but no student speaks out of turn. (3) Each student has a certain length of time for speaking. (4) Each student starts by restating what was said previously by another/several other students (e.g., summarizing shared points, differing points, missed points, or points not discussed fully). (5) After every student has had one turn, general discussion is open, possibly guided by teacher-provided questions.

Procedures and ground rules for smaller groups

Teachers can develop student discussion skills integrating listening, reading, and speaking skills by assigning small discussion groups to tackle teacher-supplied problems and topics. Teachers/students may use established groups, new teacher-assigned groups, or student-formed groups. Each group should contain 4-5 students. Teachers read a text passage they or students choose; describe a scenario; or pose a question to discuss. They give students several minutes to review homework/notes, briefly read new related material, and/or review essay/paper drafts. Teachers then give each student in each group a specified number of uninterrupted minutes to speak in turn. After every group/circle student has taken a turn, the teacher opens general discussion, setting the following ground rules: (1) Students can only speak about others' ideas. However, (2) teachers and classmates can ask students to clarify their ideas, give examples, connect them more closely to what they read, or elaborate. (3) Small groups can summarize overall points they established for other groups, including shared points, differences, and potential topics they missed.

Incorporating active student listening into lessons

Teachers should make clear to students the subject underpinning a day's activities and identify the learning objectives incorporated in those activities to give students a view of the "big picture." They should also give students a single word/phrase to summarize the prior day's subject and a single word/phrase to preview the current day's subject. Teachers should not only establish this recall, retrieval, prediction, and planning process as a daily habit; by doing so, they should also prompt students to develop the same daily habit in their note-taking. Teachers should review main concepts addressed earlier, and/or have students summarize the last lecture's main ideas, to make connections with preceding lessons. In both cueing and queuing student listening, teachers supply spoken presentation/lecture transitions analogously to those in written research papers/articles. By cueing students to write marginal notes/Word comments with questions or summaries at the ends of sections, teachers also help students demonstrate their comprehension.

Teachers can allow students to take photos, videos, and audio recordings of lessons/lectures to review as many times as they need. To encourage students to reword and recall instructional input, teachers can let students download class outlines from GoogleDocs, including hard-to-spell terminology/vocabulary words, jargon of specific disciplines, and links reminding students to follow up by accessing resources and readings to inform notes they take. Teachers should give outlines a two-column format: on the right, a wider column with teacher notes, to which students can add, and on the left, a narrower column for students to place notes and questions about previous lectures and reading. They should advise students to take their own notes in similar formats. Students and teachers alike can learn through speaking, writing, listening, and reading when they contribute narratives to supplement visual graphics they both provide, e.g., photos, concept maps, charts, advance organizers, illustrations, diagrams, etc. to support challenging concepts they analyze and explain.

Educator techniques to improve and augment classroom discussions

Students who feel comfortable with the teacher and the class are more likely to engage openly in discussion. Teachers who learn students' names encourage this. Lively discussions with all students participating are evidence teachers have made students comfortable. Teachers should pose questions rather than make comments: teacher comments discourage student creativity; questions invite various responses. A variety of student answers is evidence the questioning technique works. When student discussions stray off the subject, learning goals the teacher identified will not be met. Teachers redirect discussion by restating topics and questions they previously announced, and introducing new questions related to identified topics. When conversation refocuses on stated topics, teachers can identify specified learning goals/objectives students are meeting in their discussion on a checklist. In most classes, some students dominate conversations. Teachers can pose less challenging questions, which anyone can answer even without being prepared, to engage more reticent students, and then graduate to higher-level questions. They can evaluate all students' participation using attendance roll-based checklists.

Teaching strategies to encourage discussion

During class discussions, students often contribute erroneous information. Teachers must be tactful in correcting them. If students they correct then withdraw from the conversation or cease further contributions, the teacher has not corrected them appropriately. If corrected students continue to contribute, the teacher has succeeded in providing positive reinforcement rather than punishment with the correction. Some ways to do this include acknowledging how the student came to a conclusion but explaining it does not apply to the current context or explaining how the student's response might be correct in another situation. Teachers can also provide incentives for students to contribute to class discussions. Teachers may incorporate a component of participation in their course syllabi, keep records to tally whenever each student contributes to a discussion, or assign different students to lead class discussions in turn. These are some ways teachers can evaluate individual student participation in classroom discussions, and hence the effectiveness of their teaching strategies to encourage such participation.

Students often feel intimidated if "put on the spot" to answer/discuss questions without warning. Teachers can put them at ease by allowing time to prepare: Announce topics and questions for class discussion. Give students five minutes to jot notes for responses. Give five more minutes for exchanging and reflecting on notes with classmates before beginning whole-class conversation. Teachers may distribute discussion topics/questions at the end of one class for the next day's conversation or post questions/topics online the night before class. One technique for evaluating discussion is asking students early in the term to write papers about the characteristics of good and bad class discussions, and then talk about these. Teachers then compose a list of classroom discussion goals and give all students copies. Another technique is an informal survey: ask students around midterm to evaluate the overall quality of class discussions. Share responses with the class, and inform them of teacher plans incorporating student feedback for enhancing discussions during the rest of the term.

Teachers can encourage in-class discussion by promoting group meetings and discussions outside the classroom. Interacting with students outside class also promotes a sense of community. Teachers demonstrate to students that they care about them as individual persons and about their educational development by asking them about their holiday/summer plans, about how they are feeling during midterm and final exam periods, and about their other classes. Teachers can find online articles related to class material and e-mail or text-message their students links to these for review. They can allow time at the beginnings of classes for announcements. They can also arrange classroom chairs in a semicircle to encourage conversation. These methods are all found effective in promoting a sense of community, which in turn encourages class discussions. To address different student learning styles and abilities, teachers can vary the levels and types of questions they ask them: asking them to give simple information, describe, compare, analyze, justify, compare, generalize, predict, or apply information.

Instructional practices for ELLs to acquire English as a second language

When instructing English Language Learners (ELLs), teachers should not simply state directions verbally; they should model specifically the things they expect students to do. This includes showing them how to perform each task, and giving them an example of the precise expected appearance of the finished results. Teachers should also give ELLs enough time to respond. They need more time than native English speakers to process the English the teacher speaks, translating it mentally into their native language; formulating a response mentally in their native language; translating that response into English; and then evaluating whether the translated English response they constructed makes sense, before they can finally answer. ELL students frequently require years of English exposure before they can "think in English" without going through these intermediate steps of translating. Teachers should also remember—when using idioms, figures of speech, and synonyms—to pantomime and/or explain these consistently as they are not logical, often do not have comparable equivalents in students' native languages, and must be taught explicitly.

Based on research findings, teachers are advised to observe ELL (English Language Learner) students closely. If teachers do not see obvious evidence that students understand what they are saying, they can elaborate by paraphrasing, supplying synonyms for many of the key vocabulary words they used; and summarize what they just said. Another strategy is to have students retell and/or explain what the teacher just said to their classmates. They can have students write their understanding of what the teacher said in a journal. Teachers may also arrange for ELL students to give them an agreed-upon signal to indicate whether they understand or not. Teachers should use varied visual aids, e.g., photographs, drawings, and/or concrete objects to illustrate/demonstrate concepts in subject areas. Abstract concepts present great difficulty to students learning a foreign language, who must gradually transition from concrete to abstract ideas in a language unfamiliar to them.

Rather than avoiding them, teachers can and should take advantage of ELL students' cultural and linguistic backgrounds. This accomplishes several important things: it celebrates diversity, draws

- 84 -

on students' experience and knowledge to give teachers and classmates information about students' native countries and languages; and integrating students' cultural and linguistic backgrounds into the learning environment makes them more comfortable in a foreign setting and gives them a basis for making transitions and connections to the new culture and language. Teachers can assign small group work; making some groups homogeneous for familiarity and comfort, and others heterogeneous to provide native English-speaker peer models. Additionally and importantly, teachers should permit and encourage both kinds of groups to interact and discuss things. Teachers should select the vocabulary words they use judiciously; instruct students explicitly in them; and provide opportunities for students to practice using them. They can also pair students with language/reading/writing "buddies" for modeling and support; and let ELL students be "buddies" for younger ELLs.

Assessment of ELL students

When conducting assessments of ELL students, teachers must gain sufficient information to determine student strengths and needs; and which students need areas to target in designing instruction. With ELLs, traditional written assessments may not be ideal. Instead, teachers may want to use more authentic assessment measures, e.g., oral assessments and performance assessments, to demonstrate actual student learning. It is important to remember that observable student behaviors they can see and hear are not necessarily accurate indices of what students really know internally. Teachers should not deprive ELL students of motivation by expecting too little of them; at the same time, the high expectations they communicate should be realistic. They must consider dual factors: according to research, ELLs may require several years to reach English-language acquisition levels comparable to those of native English-speaking peers; yet they also often demonstrate very rapid growth spurts in English literacy acquisition, so they should not be considered "slow" learners.

SIOP model for teaching ELLs

One approach found effective in research and classroom practice for ESL instruction is the Sheltered Instruction Observation Protocol (SIOP) model. It features a lesson-planning checklist with 30 components, which when applied systematically are effective for all students; and moreover support ELL student success in mainstream classrooms. A major reading obstacle for ELLs is inadequate vocabulary. Research finds that at least five elements are required for effective instructional programs in vocabulary development: (1) Intentional selection of words that are important beyond the specific task, are used across subject areas, and express new concepts; (2) direct instruction in new word acquisition strategies and word meanings; (3) the modeling of processes and techniques for acquiring new words; (4) exposing students through multiple, various experiences to new vocabulary and occasions for using new words they acquire—e.g., ongoing review, intentional word-based activities, and reading widely; and (5) a system whereby students can track the new vocabulary words they learn.

The research-based, field-tested Sheltered Instruction Observation Protocol (SIOP) model enables teachers to improve connecting content with language for ELL students, making content more understandable and accessible to them; and addressing varying student proficiency levels in classrooms. SIOP component #2, "Write clearly defined language objectives", induces classroom teachers to focus intentionally on language. This helps teachers and identify, model, and teach ELLs specific language forms, functions, and structures, and set realistic expectations for them; it also aids native English-speaking students having difficulty with academic English requirements. Experts advise teachers to study and understand language proficiency standards and design instruction—including student language objectives—connected to standards. SIOP component #8, "Explicitly link past learning and new concepts", reminds teachers to plan lessons incorporating student experiences and backgrounds. Basing instruction on a commonly shared classroom experience can prevent teachers from making unjustified assumptions about existing student knowledge/experience/background. Strategies include helping students consciously connect literature to their experience by constructing pre-reading and post-reading questions/prompts about literary characters' events and feelings similar to their own.

Research, including studies of actual classroom application, has found the Sheltered Instruction Observation Protocol (SIOP) model effective, for both teaching English as a second language (ESL) and overcoming native English-speaking student difficulties with academic English. Of 30 components, SIOP component #9 is "Emphasize key vocabulary." Vocabulary is critical to ELL students for English reading comprehension. A five-step vocabulary-building activity recommended by experts (cf. Marzano, Pickering, and Pollock; Wallace, Johns Hopkins School of Education, 2004) follows: (1.) The teacher defines a new word by reading, explaining, and/or demonstrating its meaning. (2.) The teacher represents the word nonverbally and visually, conducting a "think-aloud" to help students recognize central elements of the visual representation and how these relate to the new word. (3.) Students say and/or write their own definitions of the new word. (4.) Students make their own nonverbal, visual representations of the new word, working in small groups or pairs. (5.) Students develop more in-depth comprehension of the concept the word represents, revisiting the visual graphic to modify and/or expand it.

Major themes found in best language teaching practices

Research reviewing the literature on effective language instruction (Harris and Ó Duibhir, 2011) on behalf of Ireland's National Council for Curriculum and Assessment (NCCA) identifies these themes among others: (1) Corrective feedback: In multiple studies, students receiving recasts of morphological/syntactic errors performed better than those receiving no feedback; and those receiving prompts performed better than those receiving recasts. Prompts as corrective feedback appeared particularly beneficial for elementary (9~10-12 years) students more than older learners. (2) Content and language integrated learning (CLIL): Using a second language (L2) to teach both language and content is found more effective for both language proficiency and curriculum learning than teaching a language as a subject. (3) Intensive language programs: These have been investigated in Quebec, Canada with French and English, among other studies. Intensive instruction is based on the premise that developing basic spontaneous communication levels ASAP is requisite for L2 proficiency. It differs from CLIL and the immersion instruction that informs CLIL by focusing on language itself, not learning content via a language.

Researchers (Harris and Ó Duibhir, 2011) reviewed the literature on language instruction methods and identified themes emerging commonly among many studies. Of these, two influences they identified were teacher factors and orientation of language programs. In a number of studies, language instruction programs that adopted communicative orientations were found to have either equivocal, negative, or mixed results in class performance. In two studies, language proficiency was found to have an impact on the communicative orientations of language classes and programs. One of those two studies found evidence strongly supporting communicative orientations in language classes and programs as beneficial. Some researchers have maintained, however, that the element critical to learning success is achieving the ideal balance between analytical and communicative activities. Other studies have compared communicative courses to those emphasizing grammar, finding no connection between communicative orientation and student proficiency, but identifying

[handwritten margin notes: "Corrective Feedback", "Intensive lang program", "CLIL"]

[handwritten at bottom: "the element critical to learning success is achieving ideal balance between analytical -86- + communication activities."]

teacher expertise as significant. The reviewers suggested such teacher skill might also accomplish the balance between analytical and experiential activity mentioned by others.

Open educational resources

Open educational resources are freely available, public-domain learning, teaching, and research resources that anyone can access on the worldwide web, including textbooks, digital libraries, games, and podcasts. CK-12 FlexBooks are digital K-12 customizable textbooks, aligned with educational standards. Their high-quality content offers both core text material and adaptive learning opportunities. CK-12 has also partnered with the four Leadership Public Schools (LPS), where teachers collaborate to apply open-source materials for specific student learning needs, in developing College Access Readers—a series of online books embedding literacy supports to address individual student needs, encompassing underperforming to advanced learners. Nonprofit Khan Academy offers digital resources including a comprehensive video library, practice exercises, and assessments for K-12 math, science, humanities, history, and finance. North Carolina's **NC!** Mooresville Graded School District created a Digital Conversion Initiative promoting educational technology use, including state standard-aligned digital textbooks; laptops, and other tools. Arizona's Vail Unified School District also has established digital textbooks replacing traditional **Cool!** books, with an online tool enabling access by all district schools.

Adolescent reading instruction

According to findings of the What Works Clearinghouse (WWC, Kamil, 2008), five classroom teaching practices are recommended to improve teen literacy: (1) Research finds strong support for giving adolescent students explicit instruction in vocabulary. (2) Research also finds strong evidence for giving explicit and direct instruction in strategies for reading comprehension. (3) Research has found moderate evidence to support giving teenage students opportunities to engage in extended discussions about the meaning and interpretation of text they read. (4) Moderate support has also been found through research for enhancing adolescent student engagement and motivation for literacy learning. (5) Strong evidence has been discovered through research studies for trained specialists to provide specialized and intensive interventions to help adolescent students who are struggling with reading.

The conclusions of research conducted by the Center on Instruction (COI) into effective instructional methods in academic literacy for adolescent students have yielded the following recommendations: (1) Throughout the school day, educators should give students explicit instruction and supportive practice in using strategies for reading comprehension that have been proven effective. (2) Educators should use a higher quantity and quality of continued, open discussion about the content that adolescent students are reading. (3) Educators should establish and sustain high standards for adolescent students in the text that they read; the vocabulary that they learn and use; the questions that they are asked; and the conversations that they have. (4) Educators should work to enhance the degree to which adolescent students are motivated to read and are engaged with reading. (5) Educators should teach adolescent students content knowledge that is essential in order that they master the concepts critical to their understanding and success.

Reading comprehension skills

Reading comprehension requires interactions among skills including student background knowledge, knowledge of vocabulary, decoding skills, and verbal reasoning skills. Depending on individual task requirements, these skills interact at different intensity levels. Reading comprehension is not an end product but an ongoing process. Therefore, required skills do not interact equally through any exact formula. Previous student knowledge about certain subjects, e.g., about another country, helps inform reading comprehension. Student comprehension levels are reduced if text is at their grade level, but their vocabulary development is not. Students having difficulty with decoding, even at lower levels than their grade levels, experience significant detriments to speed and accuracy in both reading and comprehending text. In general education, instructional practices for adolescent literacy are focused on Language Knowledge strands; in intensive literacy interventions, instructional practices for adolescents are focused on both Language Knowledge and Word Knowledge strands. Research into reading-specific literacy instruction emphasizes strategies before, during, and after reading, to organize and augment reading experiences and enable text comprehension and application.

Adolescent literacy instruction strategies to use before, during, and after reading

Instructional activities initiated before adolescent students read have a number of purposes: To activate the previous knowledge of the students; to generate questions they may want to ask about the subject and reading before they read; to discuss the vocabulary words they will encounter in the text when they read it; to encourage students to make predictions about what they will be reading; and to help students to identify a purpose for their reading. Activities initiated during reading include the following purposes: To engage students with the text; to help students to self-monitor their own reading comprehension; to teach students how to summarize the text; to help them integrate new information from the text with their existing knowledge; to help them make and verify predictions about the text; to enable them to create graphic organizers to aid comprehension; and to facilitate their use of mental imagery related to the text.

After students read some text, teachers will initiate various instructional activities to support and evaluate their reading comprehension. Some of the purposes of instructional activities conducted after reading text include the following: To have students reflect on the content of the lesson; to identify where they found this content in the text they read; to have students consider and study questions the teacher provided to guide their reading, and have them give answers to those questions based on what they read and their own prior knowledge; to have students evaluate the accuracy of predictions they previously made about the text during instructional activities conducted before and during reading; to have students engage in discussion of the text to express, share, and compare their responses to the text; and to have students summarize or retell the narrative, events, or information they read in the text using their own words, demonstrating comprehension and application.

Seven Strategies of Highly Effective Readers

"Seven Strategies of Highly Effective Readers" (McEwan, AdLit.org, WETA 2014) are Activating, Inferring, Monitoring-Clarifying, Questioning, Searching-Selecting, Summarizing, and Visualizing-Organizing. Activating refers to activating the reader's previously existing background knowledge. Activation is "priming the cognitive pump"; in other words, the reader recalls from his or her long-term memory his or her past experiences and existing knowledge that are relevant to the current reading; and applies this established information and understanding to facilitate deriving and constructing meaning from the new information in the text that s/he reads. Inferring refers to combining what the text states explicitly with what the text does not say, but which is implicit within it; and combining both of these with what the reader already knows. Putting together what is said and unsaid in the text with the reader's own knowledge enables the reader to find and create meaning from reading the text.

③The Monitoring-Clarifying strategy involves the reader's thinking about what s/he is reading, and how s/he is reading it. This is done both during reading and after reading. The reader monitors the action of reading in order to assess whether s/he understands the text. In addition, the reader uses the clarifying component of this cognitive strategy to make clearer anything that s/he does or did not understand well enough; and to clear up any confusion s/he may have experienced in not correctly comprehending the text. ④The Questioning strategy is the reader's process of engaging in "learning dialogues" with the author or text; classmates/peers; and teachers. The reader generates questions about the text; asks himself or herself questions; and answers those questions.

⑤The Searching-Selecting strategy involves searching among various sources to find information, and then selecting from it the specific information that is appropriate for answering questions about the text, define terms and words used in the text, solve problems the text presents, clarify any misunderstood information, and/or collect information from the text. ⑥The Summarizing strategy involves using one's own words, which differ from the words that the original text used, to restate the meaning that the reader perceives was conveyed by the text. ⑦The Visualizing-Organizing strategy involves creating a graphic organizer, and/or a mental image, that the reader can use to the end of finding and constructing meaning from the text

Steps to teach cognitive strategies to facilitate comprehension

According to some experts (cf. McEwan, 2014), teachers can follow several steps to teach students how to apply the same cognitive strategies when they read that excellent readers routinely employ to comprehend the text that they read. First, the teacher should give the student(s) direct instruction in each cognitive strategy—e.g., inferring, questioning, summarizing, etc. This direct instruction should include the following: the teacher should give the student(s) a definition of the strategy, and explain it. The teacher should explain what purpose is served by the strategy during the act of reading. The teacher should also identify the most important characteristics of the strategy. Then the teacher should give the student(s) concrete (not abstract) examples of the strategy, and non-examples, i.e. examples of actions that do *not* equal the strategy. Following direct instruction, the teacher should use think-alouds to model the use of the cognitive strategy for students. Then the teacher should give the student(s) guided practice in applying the strategy.

Mindless reading vs. highly effective reading

Some researchers (Schooler, Reichle, and Halpern, 2004) describe many students who struggle with reading as mistakenly thinking staring at a page of print while "zoning out" is reading; they dub this "mindless reading". In contrast, highly effective readers apply cognitive strategies to process the text they read. Other researchers (Afflerbach, 1990b) have asked research questions like how excellent readers' previous knowledge influences their reading strategies in identifying a text's main concept. A related qualitative research study (Pressley and Afflerbach, 1995) asked such excellent readers to engage in think-alouds about what was going on in their minds as they read text. The investigators recorded these think-alouds in verbal protocols, which they then classified and analyzed to answer their research questions. These protocols provide representations of expert readers' constantly evolving mental processes while reading. The researchers identified reading as "constructively responsive"—i.e. excellent readers continuously change their cognitive processes in response to the particular text they read.

Summarizing

Part of the process of giving students direct instruction in cognitive strategies to facilitate reading comprehension is providing examples and non-examples of the strategy. One cognitive strategy excellent readers use for comprehension is summarizing. Summarizing facilitates and demonstrates reading comprehension, and better enables retention, by restating the text's main idea(s) and essential meaning in one's own words, omitting unimportant details. Some examples of good text summaries a teacher could give students include a brief report by a sports journalist (written or spoken) of a game—football/baseball/basketball/hockey/boxing, etc.—focusing on only the highlights; a short obituary of a famous person from a TV news program/magazine/newspaper; or some of the New York Times Bestsellers List's one-sentence book descriptions. Some non-examples teachers could present include paragraphs that include many minute details; are very long; or that completely retell the entire text instead of identifying the main point. Teachers might use unsuccessful student work—anonymously!—as non-examples.

Summarizing is using one's own words to restate the meaning one perceives of the text one has read. Readers may summarize text either verbally, using different words than the original; or visually, using a graphic organizer. The purpose of summarizing text is to enable the reader to distinguish what elements of the text are most important for them to remember after they have finished reading it. Many texts, especially those including many details, may contain only one or two main concepts. Identifying those major concepts ("big ideas") and rephrasing them helps readers remember them. Crucial attributes of the summarizing strategy include: Summaries are short. They include the text's major concept/"big idea(s)". They are to the point. Summaries leave out less important information. They reduce lists to a short phrase or word. A summary does not reproduce original text word for word or retell it literally. Rather, it demonstrates reader comprehension by expressing the text's main meaning using different wording/phrasing.

Self-monitoring

Functionally, knowing when reading makes sense and when it does not is self-monitoring. Some students can correctly read all words in a text; but when asked what it was about, they cannot say because they were not self-monitoring—i.e. actively thinking about the reading. To self-monitor, readers must (1) know what they do and (2) do not understand; and (3) apply suitable strategies to clear up comprehension issues. Some self-monitoring strategies include: (1) Identify the problem's location: What part of the text one did not comprehend; what word(s) were unfamiliar/confusing; and what did not make sense. (2) Paraphrase problematic passages/sentences: Consider what the author was trying to say, restating in one's own words. (3) Review the text: Look for what one finds unclear mentioned previously in text; and if found, what the author wrote about it. (4) Preview the text: Look forward in text for information that may resolve the problem, like illustrations, graphs, or charts; or if the next section/chapter explains/elaborates on something one did not understand.

When reading, students should cross-check, asking themselves whether an unfamiliar word looks and sounds correct and makes sense to them. When encountering a problem during reading, they should go back to the beginning of the paragraph/sentence and reread it. To predict, students should consider what they think will happen next in the text; what they expect a word to be; and whether what the reading makes sense to them. When encountering an unfamiliar word, students should skip it and continue reading to the end of the sentence, using the context to consider what word would fit there. Once they have read the rest of the sentence, they should go back and reread it and try to figure out what the unfamiliar word is. Students should use their background knowledge while reading by considering what they already know about the text topic: they may make useful connections. While reading longer texts, students should <u>stop,</u> review the events so far in the text; and <u>visualize</u> (mentally picture) them.

Problems with today's CCSS assessments

Most students today are unaccustomed to writing essay or even short-answer responses to state and commercial norm-referenced tests. But the new Common Core State Standards (CCSS) assessments in English Language Arts (ELA) require both close reading and extended writing. Classroom practices most often involve only constructing oral answers for the familiar audience of the teacher and classmates, and receiving immediate correction and clarification. Yet the CCSS/ELA tests require extended writing for remote audiences, with no immediate feedback or chances to correct or clarify writing. Moreover, many students do not carefully read questions, causing response errors. For example, they give one piece of textual supporting evidence when the question requires two. They write their own ideas, omitting textual evidence. They give enough evidence, but do not clearly state any conclusion. They disregard specific question verbs; e.g., they describe when the question requires explaining. They do not clearly connect the evidence with their conclusion. And they write incompletely as if for familiar audiences, which remote audiences find unclear.

Effective writing instruction

Researchers find that teachers need to give students in grades 4-12 explicit instruction in writing strategies, including pre-writing planning; revising their drafts, and editing their writing. Teaching writing strategies includes modeling, guiding, and allowing practice in both general processes, like brainstorming or editing; and in more specific procedures, like the steps to follow in composing narrative, persuasive/argumentative, and informational essays. Research also has found that teachers need to give students explicit instruction in how to summarize the text that they read. By learning how to summarize reading matter, students engage in practice with writing clearly and concisely to communicate accurately what the text's central ideas are. Teachers should start by showing students explicit strategies; then help them apply these themselves; give them enough opportunities to practice using them; and eventually fade their modeling and assistance gradually as students gain proficiency with summarizing.

Collaborative writing exercises
Cooperative learning exercises and projects are found by research studies to enhance student progress, both in school generally and with writing specifically. Students benefit from taking turns practicing both performance and evaluative roles and from giving and receiving peer feedback. They learn both to improve their own writing skills, and also how to judge others' writing. Evaluating others' work not only develops the critical thinking skills associated with Evaluation (cf. Bloom's Taxonomy); it also teaches students how to be more objective in self-assessing their own writing products. In addition, cooperative learning activities develop students' social skills for interacting with their peers, communicating with others, accepting (constructive) criticism gracefully and productively; and giving constructive feedback to others diplomatically. Students can meet individual performance goals as well as group ones as long as teachers provide them with appropriate expectations and structure for both. Teachers can assign students, for example, to take turns reviewing each other's writing for their use of descriptive adjectives, or supporting evidence, etc.

Roles, use, and benefits of goals
Research into effective writing instruction of upper elementary and secondary students has found that among other things, teachers need to establish specific goals for students to attain in each

writing assignment. Teachers may identify and communicate goals to students; or teachers can assign students to develop goals for themselves as a class. For the latter, teachers will need to review student-developed goals for appropriateness to student abilities and needs; applicability to learning unit content; consistency with teacher-established learning goals and objectives for the class/unit/lesson; and realism/reasonableness that students can achieve them. Some examples of goals for individual writing assignments include using specific components of a particular genre of writing, e.g., stating at least three justifying/supporting reasons for a position in an opinion paper; adding more specific adjectives and adverbs to a descriptive essay; or adding more ideas to an essay's content. Specific goals motivate students; and teachers' positive reinforcement for achieving goals furthers student motivation.

Computer use for word processing
Studies have found that students achieve better writing performance when teachers permit them to use computers with word-processing software to support the activities involved in completing their writing assignments. Teachers need to instruct students in using computer hardware and software correctly. Although many students are already quite proficient using computers on their own, others still need instruction. Also, some students have developed great facility with certain computer applications, e.g. gaming, messaging, surfing, and searching online; however, they may not have as much experience or practice with others, e.g. using word-processing programs appropriately for writing. Students need to learn both how spell-checkers and grammar-checkers can help beginning, intermediate, and advanced writers alike; and also how these tools will not catch every writing and typing error (e.g. legitimate but wrong words may not be identified, like "fir" vs. "for"), and will often even "correct" things incorrectly. Teachers should demonstrate for students how they can readily format, delete, insert, move, and otherwise manipulate text with word-processing technology.

Process writing
The process approach to writing includes such elements as these: Authentic audiences – teachers can identify, or ask and help students to identify, a specific type or group of readers/listeners for whom they will be writing. This helps them focus their writing to accomplish certain purposes; to use identified types of logic or reasoning, and select certain writing tones and specific word use, to appeal to their specific audiences. Personal responsibility for writing – through process writing approaches, students learn to take ownership of what they write. This contributes to more independent choices about what and how they write; greater care in editing, revising, and otherwise crafting their work; more independent practice of writing skills; and greater motivation to achieve excellence in final written products. Student interactions – the process approach involves more frequent, consistent peer interactions throughout the composition process. This develops critical thinking, evaluative skills, and social skills. Self-evaluation – students learn through the process approach to assess their own writing more objectively and constructively.

Inquiry
Students will need interest and skills in inquiry to succeed in school throughout all subject areas and activities. The role of inquiry may be more obvious in scientific learning activities, when students are instructed to ask research questions and conduct investigations and experiments to discover answers to those questions through systematic procedures. However, inquiry is equally important to writing instruction and learning. In addition to what—i.e. what they will write, and about what, students need to know why—reasons for writing and purposes of writing; and how—specific procedures for writing to achieve purposes by communicating ideas and points. Teachers can assign writing that requires using inquiry skills. One inquiry skill is identifying a definite goal for writing; for example, teachers assign students to describe a playground conflict. Another inquiry

skill is using specific strategies for investigating concrete data; for example, teachers assign students to observe the altercation, and record behaviors and their responses. Teachers can then guide students in writing to convey what they learned.

Modeling

Studies have shown that students learn better from being given demonstrations of what they are expected to do, rather than simply being told without any accompanying examples. When instructing students in writing, teachers should present models of each writing genre and technique they expect them to produce. These models should be not only clear illustrations, but also high in quality. Teachers can model in two ways: (1) They can write their own sentences, explaining why they chose specific vocabulary words and sentence structures to communicate certain ideas/feelings/moods/tones, etc. This is useful anytime literary quotations do not immediately come to mind and/or they have not researched any; and to tailor personally an example to emphasize a particular element. (2) They can use literary quotations reflecting specific genres and techniques. These are useful because many great authors have produced better examples of these; they have greater credibility; they lend themselves to teacher and class analysis; and they provide superior models for students to emulate in their own writing.

Prewriting

Teachers can help students generate and organize ideas before writing through prewriting activities. These can include identifying and retrieving knowledge that students already have; for example, brainstorming and making notes of what things they know about a particular topic. Students can also research unfamiliar subjects. Teachers can guide them in trying different search terms and keywords for useful online searches. They can also provide print materials, and direct students to find and look in books, including reference materials and informational texts; journal, magazine, and newspaper articles, etc. for prewriting research. Whether student compositions will be based on their existing knowledge and experiences; on information they have found through research; or on both, teachers can show them how to create graphic organizers or use existing templates to represent ideas visually before writing about them. Graphic organizers help students who think more visually than verbally; and they help all students with prewriting organization.

Sentence combining

Research studies have found that explicit instruction in how to combine sentences is an effective method for teaching writing skills. Students at intermediate writing levels may have developed fluency with connecting their sentences into paragraphs, but they may still be writing mainly in simple sentences. Teachers need to instruct them in advancing their sentences to become more sophisticated. They can do this by taking samples from the students' own compositions. Teachers show two or more simple sentences students have written that are related to one another in content, category, logic, reasoning, sequence, train of thought, etc. They show how to combine these into one longer sentence and give students practice. Teachers should also differentially define compound, complex, and compound-complex sentences for students, explaining that compound sentences are independent clauses (=simple sentences) connected by coordinators; complex sentences have an independent clause plus a dependent clause, connected by a subordinator; and compound-complex sentences contain multiple independent clauses plus one or more dependent clauses; and give examples of each.

Elements necessary beyond teaching specific strategies

Researchers have concluded that whichever instructional strategies a teacher selects to use in combination, they must always afford students plenty of time for practicing and actually writing. Studies find that writing practice and learning cannot be limited because of time constraints and still be successful. Even more time is required for students who struggle with writing. Teachers may need to give these students explicit instruction, not just in composition procedures; also in the transcription skills of spelling, handwriting, and typing. Students who have difficulty with both reading and writing typically not only have trouble with decoding for reading, but also have corresponding problems with encoding for writing. Regardless of writing abilities and levels, with all students, teachers need to help students develop self-regulation skills. These include establishing learning and writing goals for themselves; self-monitoring their progress toward these goals; self-assessing their attainment of the goals; and self-reinforcing the efforts they make and the learning outcomes they achieve. These enhance student competence and independence.

Individual student needs

Based on study results, researchers conclude that even the strongest evidence-based practices in writing instruction should not be used exclusively or in isolation. Rather, they recommend teachers use combinations of the research-based practices they find most suited to their particular students' needs as supplements to their existing writing curricula and teaching practices. Experts also advise no one instructional strategy to teach writing will work for every student. Moreover, a writing curriculum cannot consist of only the instructional strategies found most effective by research studies, even all of them taken together. Researchers advise that teachers should identify the specific needs of each individual student in learning writing, and of the class as a whole. They should select from and combine identified best practices, tailoring the mixture to their student and class needs; and incorporate it into their current writing curriculum and practices. Experts also emphasize the importance of monitoring how successful each strategy they implement is, and modifying each as indicated.

Strategies to teach self-monitoring

To help students lacking experience with tasks requiring close reading and extended written responses, teachers should give them open-ended questions and opportunities to respond using connected discourse. They can read student responses aloud in class and ask if they are off-task; or whether they explain, summarize, list, describe, support, or whichever verb(s) the question specified. This prepares students to self-monitor their own written answers. They should teach students the habit of checking their written answers the same as they check math solutions. Students should check if the answer type fits the question specifications; whether it makes sense, and all necessary components are included. Teachers can give students self-monitoring guidance via checklists with questions like these: If someone were not sitting near me, could they understand what I wrote without needing clarification? Would I be convinced by the textual evidence I supplied? Is my answer complete and thorough? Could I add textual details to reinforce it? And does what I wrote answer the question?

Hypothetical class writing assignment

A middle school teacher assigned the class essay writing to prepare for the Common Core State Standards (CCSS) assessment in English Language Arts (ELA). Teacher instructions included describing in detail how a short story author created and built tension, giving three textual examples and explaining how they illustrated author technique. Student Chris chose an appropriate Poe story, but summarized author techniques instead of describing in detail; quoted one textual example, not three; and did not clearly link it to the conclusion by explaining. <u>Instructional activities:</u> The teacher helps Chris correct insufficient example use with a "bull's-eye" chart: Outer rings represent increasing degrees of completeness, e.g., "some related ideas but not an answer"; "ideas barely answer the question"; "ideas answer the question, including supporting evidence"; the bull's-eye is "a thorough answer with ample support". A self-monitoring rubric asks whether student response followed instruction verb(s), helping Chris note that describing in detail, not summarizing is required, etc. A self-monitoring checklist item asking if the response addressed the assignment/question reinforces Chris's strength of choosing an appropriate author and story.

Hypothetical middle school class essay-writing assignment

Imaginary student Pat's teacher assigned the class essays to prepare for the English Language Arts (ELA) Common Core State Standards (CCSS) assessment. Directions included providing textual evidence; explaining how author devices worked; including an introduction, body, and conclusion; and writing thoroughly for comprehension by an unfamiliar audience. Pat provided ample textual evidence, but described without explaining. Pat found the ample evidence sufficient and omitted a conclusion. Also, Pat wrote in an abbreviated/'shorthand" style which the teacher; small group classmates; and close friends could understand, but would be unclear to unfamiliar audiences. <u>Instructional activities:</u> A guiding checklist asking things like "Would somebody who is not sitting near me/doesn't know me understand my writing without clarification?" The teacher supplies a self-monitoring rubric whereby students highlight verbs in test question/assignment directions; and then ask themselves whether they followed these—e.g. after highlighting "explain", Pat reexamines the composition, seeing description but no explanation. A rubric item asking whether work is complete/missing anything necessary helps Pat supply the omitted conclusion. Peer feedback sharing reinforces Pat's strength of providing ample textual evidence.

Tomlinson's principles of differentiated instruction

Tomlinson (*The Differentiated Classroom: Responding to the Needs of All Learners,* 1999, in Walch, 2009) represents differentiated instruction with the expression "One size doesn't fit all." Principles in her philosophy of education include: (1) Educators must view students as individuals. Despite assignment by age to grade levels, individual student learning styles, interests, and learning readiness differ. (2) Individual differences are sufficiently significant to require teacher accommodation, differentiating by content, process, and students' products. She states, "Curriculum tells us what to teach; differentiation gives us strategies to make teaching more successful." (3) When connections are established among students' prior learning experiences, interests, and the curriculum, students learn best. (4) Teachers should give students flexible grouping opportunities. Grouping by whole-group, interests, homogenous, heterogeneous, individually, etc. are determined by various lessons. (5) To inform effective instructional planning, continuing assessment is needed. (6) Howard Gardner's Multiple Intelligences theory informs self-examination of teacher attitudes about learning, and teachers' addressing students' diverse learning manners and styles, affording more relaxed learning environments for every student.

Howard Gardner's Multiple Intelligences

In Gardner's Multiple Intelligences theory, the Musical/Rhythmic intelligence is the ability to appreciate and/or produce music and rhythms. Students high in it may like moving to musical rhythms; composing songs, melodies, harmonies, and/or lyrics; singing; playing a musical instrument(s); and/or listening to music. Teachers can support them by providing them with activities wherein they can illustrate concepts and skills by using songs or music. The Bodily/Kinesthetic intelligence involves the ability to use one's own body with control and skill in activities like crafts, sports, and dance. Students high in it frequently learn best via hands-on activity. Teachers can support them by providing them with activities wherein they can relate concepts to physical movements; that involve movement; that use manipulatives; and which allow and/or require their direct physical and hands-on participation. The Interpersonal intelligence type is the capacity to sense and understand others' emotions. Students high in it like socializing and communicating, and they empathize with others. Long-range group projects, brainstorming, cooperative learning groups/projects, and creative groupings, like self-directed, homogeneous, heterogeneous, etc., will support them.

Whereas the Interpersonal intelligence type involves the ability for sensing and understanding other people's emotions, the Intrapersonal intelligence type involves the ability for being in touch with and understanding one's own emotions. Teachers should encourage students high in this intelligence to self-reflect, and explain their thinking; give them quiet time for independent work; and offer them questions to guide journal entries they write that support metacognition ("thinking about thinking"). What Gardner termed the Naturalist intelligence type involves the ability to form connections and relationships with aspects of the natural world, and to detect patterns in nature. Students high in it frequently enjoy collecting natural objects, such as shells, feathers, rocks, fossils, etc.; classifying such natural objects; collecting butterflies and other insects; and/or reading and/or writing about nature. They may also like adopting and caring for animals. Activities to support them include having them look for natural patterns; organize data using Venn diagrams; and classify objects according to their similarities and differences.

The Visual/Spatial intelligence accurately perceives the visual world and can visualize and transform three-dimensional realities in two-dimensional media. ELA teachers can support this intelligence by letting students make drawings; providing them with graphs and illustrations; giving them mapping activities; and having them explore problems in spatial visualization. The Verbal/Linguistic intelligence understands and appreciates the functions, structures, and meaning of language. Students high in this intelligence can effectively communicate in both spoken and written forms. ELA teachers can support them by assigning oral presentations, written compositions, research projects, and inviting them to discuss their ideas verbally in classes. The Logical/Mathematical intelligence can identify symbolic form and patterns therein, and numerical and logical patterns. Students high in this intelligence can follow lines of reasoning and like solving problems that require inductive or deductive logic. ELA teachers can encourage them by giving them problems in estimation, critical thinking, designing and using spreadsheets; tasks involving data organization and analysis; and helping them use numerical data analysis to make predictions.

Differentiated ELA instructional activity for students with two different learning styles

A "Today's Frankenstein" (Walch, 2009) activity has students discussing Frankenstein and his monster in Mary Wollstonecraft Shelley's *Frankenstein* (1818, 1823) and create a contemporary monster diagram incorporating subsequent scientific progress to date. It addresses ELA Standards 1 and 2 for reading; 3 for applying text comprehension strategies; and 12 for using spoken, written, and visual language to accomplish students' own purposes. It utilizes skills for research; using graphic organizers; summarizing and updating the novel to create the contemporary version; and using personal knowledge for creating the diagram and call-outs. Differentiation strategies include: Letting students strong in bodily/kinesthetic intelligence to act out monster movements for the diagram; encouraging students NOT high in visual/spatial intelligence to draw diagrams for communication without spending excessive time trying to perfect them; and supplying diagrams with call-outs while identifying and explaining the features' purposes for students with reading difficulties.

In Walch's (2009) "Today's Frankenstein" activity, teachers can differentiate their instruction for students with varying strengths and needs. <u>Procedures:</u> Teachers assign students to read a synopsis of Mary Shelley's *Frankenstein.* The class discusses the reading; teachers have students take notes. Teachers have students use their own knowledge to develop diagrams of an updated monster incorporating scientific progress since the 1800s. Teachers inform students the author was 19 years old when she wrote the novel, having them imagine they are contemporary counterparts of Victor Frankenstein. Teachers have students create flowcharts listing features of the monster; purposes of each feature; each feature's appearance, and its placement. They have students use completed flowcharts for developing diagrams. <u>Informal assessment measures:</u> Teachers listen to class discussion, noting how students describe traits of main characters; and how they identify figurative language the author used to describe the monster. To assess and encourage creativity, teachers write students individual notes, praising specific uses of clarity and creativity in communicating information; and suggesting ways to improve these.

Differentiated instruction as indices in evaluating its effectiveness

To support the content taught, differentiated classrooms should apply multiple materials and components, including principles, generalizations, attitudes, concepts, skills, and actions. The most common differentiation in this kind of instruction is the way in which individual students obtain access to the content that they learn. Access to content is essential. Also essential is aligning learning objectives and tasks to learning goals. Learning goals are commonly evaluated through high-stakes, state- and/or national-level standardized tests. Breaking goals down into successive increments via task analysis creates tasks that build skills along a continuum. With learners beginning at different skill levels, this makes it easier to identify the next steps in their instruction. Instructional concepts should not be overly detail-oriented, factual, or exhaustive; but rather general and broad, involving principles and skills to be learned. All students should be taught using the same concepts, with only complexity levels differentiated individually.

Grouping in differentiated instruction

In differentiated instruction, teachers must use flexibility in grouping students. Teacher strategies to keep grouping procedures flexible are considered essential by experts. As students develop their knowledge of new content, they are expected to interact and collaborate with their classmates. Teachers can introduce major concepts ("big ideas") in the content through whole-class discussions; then they can divide classes into pairs or small groups to work on learning activities. Teachers may coach the student groups or pairs in completing the tasks they assign; or students may have peer coaching from within the groups. Student grouping should not be fixed but dynamic, with regular regrouping as the content, assignments, and ongoing assessments dictate. Flexible grouping is a foundation of differentiated instruction. Teachers must conduct initial and ongoing assessments of student preparation and development. Relevant pre-assessment enables successful, functional differentiation. Integrating ongoing assessment informs teacher provision of supports, options, and approaches for diverse student needs, abilities, and interests.

Assessment of differentiated instruction

Teachers can more easily differentiate instruction meaningfully for diverse students through meaningful assessment. Pre-assessment identifies current student functioning levels and areas of need; ongoing assessment informs student progress/lack thereof, progress rates, increasing performance levels, diminishing needs for scaffolding/instruction, changing student interests, and new needs to address. Assessment may use formal testing instruments and/or various informal measures including performance assessments, portfolio assessments, surveys, checklists, and interviews. Teachers should never rely on only one assessment instrument; multiple measures are required for accurate, realistic, comprehensive information. Assignments and assessment should be differentiated, as instruction is: students should be actively engaged and usually feel challenged. Teachers should vary test/performance items so individual students can respond in different ways best expressing/demonstrating their knowledge and understanding. In addition to varying means of expression, alternative procedures, processes; varying assessment types, difficulty levels, and scoring should be provided. Assessment should not simply measure instruction, but extend instruction as a teaching tool, asking questions about optimum learning and student needs—before, during, and after teaching sessions.

Lexiles

A Lexile is a number that identifies a reading level. Reading tests use Lexiles to indicate the levels of student reading abilities. Their original source is The Lexile Framework® for Reading. This formula matches up books and articles with readers according to their reading abilities, not grade levels. A number, from less than 200 to above 1700, followed by L (for Lexile, e.g., 500L) is a Lexile measure indicating whether a reader or a text is beginning, intermediate, advanced and precisely where in that range. Lexile measures have the most widespread use today among reading level indices. Over 20 million students nationwide receive Lexile measures in schools annually; and over 80 million articles and over 100,000 books have been assigned Lexile numbers. One analogy (EBSCO Support, 2013) is to think of a Lexile as a shoe size: given the correct number, one can select reading which, like a pair of shoes, is the "right fit" for one's reading interests and abilities.

While a student might look for books and articles with the exact same Lexile number as s/he has received from a reading test or on his/her own*, they are advised rather to look for reading materials in a range, between 50L above and 100L below their reading level. If students or their teachers have not received a Lexile number through school testing, they can access the EBSCO*host* website online to obtain an estimate of their reading levels, and search among magazines they enjoy reading. They can use school library computers to log into the site and select one of the available databases that contains Lexile numbers; e.g., *Primary Search, Middle Search Plus,* or *MAS Ultra.* Students should check **Full Text** on the **Basic Search** screen and then type in the name of a magazine they want to read in the **Publication** field; and click **Search.** The EBSCO*host* site will retrieve all articles in the specified magazine, each with a different Lexile number. This indicates the range of reading levels in the magazine.

If students have not been given Lexile measures via standardized reading tests in school, and their teachers do not know their Lexile measure, students can estimate their approximate Lexiles by searching the *EBSCOhost* website's databases of magazine articles with Lexile numbers by typing in the name of a magazine they are interested in reading. Students can select articles of interest to them and try reading them. If they find an article too hard to follow, its Lexile is probably above theirs. If an article is too easy to read, its Lexile is likely below their reading ability. Estimating approximate Lexiles informs selecting reading material appropriate to reading ability and interest.

lexiles = book
shoe sizes

The Lexile website has a free Lexile Book Database at http://lexile.com/fab/. (FAB stands for Find a Book.) Students can look for books they like reading to estimate their own Lexile levels. Students and teachers who know student Lexiles can use these databases to find articles and books to read with matching levels.

Differential definitions of formative and summative assessment

It should be simple enough to define formative assessment as monitoring student progress during the instructional process, or as ongoing practice; and summative assessment as periodically evaluating achievement at the end of a learning segment, to assess success in meeting learning goals and objectives; assign grades, and provide accountability. However, in recent years, experts find these definitions have become confused. Regardless, they conclude that a balance of both is necessary to collecting information. If a teacher relies more on one or the other, it becomes more difficult to visualize student classroom achievement accurately. Summative assessments are less frequent than formative assessments and occur after instruction, hence not useful for information about classroom-level learning, or adjusting instruction and implementing interventions during learning. They are useful for evaluating curriculum alignment, student program placement, school improvement goal, and program effectiveness. Formative assessments are useful for informing teachers and students and modifying instruction and learning as they occur, helping students attain learning standards-based goals in specified times.

Summative assessment

At the levels of the classroom and the school district, summative assessment is most often used for the purpose of contributing to the process of determining grades that teachers will give to student. It is also used for the purpose of providing accountability to government education departments, school district officials, school administrators, etc. to comply with laws mandating that schools be accountable for students' learning by proving, through measures of student achievement, that students have learned what educators have been charged with teaching them to meet government and school district learning standards. Some examples of the many types of summative assessments that exist include: national norm-referenced standardized tests; state standardized assessments; school district interim assessments; school district benchmark assessments; tests on textbook chapters; unit tests given at the ends of teaching/learning units; tests given at the ends of school semesters or terms; report card letter or number grades given to students; and Adequate Yearly Progress (AYP) scores reported for school accountability.

Formative assessment

Formative assessment gauges ongoing student progress, helping teachers decide their next steps in the instructional process before summative assessments are due. Students are not held accountable, as with summative assessments like scores/grades, for concepts/skills they are still learning. This is analogous to practicing how to drive before taking the road test. If beginning learners were graded every time they practiced, their final scores would reflect their driving skills inaccurately by incorporating low practicing/learning grades into the average. Grading the learner's interim progress also would not help guide the student or instructor about each new thing s/he needed to do to improve his/her driving skills; only continuing practice would. Thus the road test is a summative assessment, in that it occurs after learning, and (usually) only once the student has had sufficient practice to pass it. The summative assessment is an accountability measure: the driving test demonstrates whether or not the individual has learned the skills needed for a driver's license. Driving practice is comparable to classroom instruction/learning and formative assessment.

Whenever teachers apply best instructional practices to the end of collecting student learning data, they are using the practices formatively. Experts point out that teaching and formative assessment cannot really be separated from one another, as good teachers do both together. The only way these are differentiated is by how teachers use the information they acquire. What teachers do with the data they collect about student learning includes how they apply it to inform their ongoing instruction; and how they share it with students and use it to engage them in their own learning. One instructional strategy that teachers can use in formative assessment is observation. This is not simply walking through the classroom to check that students are working assigned tasks or see if they need help. Teachers need to observe specific learning behaviors of individual students and record them. They can use this information to give students feedback about their learning, and/or share it with them during 1:1 conferencing.

Student self-assessment and teacher descriptive feedback
In addition to evaluating learning in progress as opposed to evaluating learning after it is complete as summative assessment does, another distinguishing feature of formative assessment is that students are more involved in the assessment process. Experts note that students should be involved in assessment, both as resources for their classmates and as evaluators of their own learning. Their involvement is essential to implementing and practicing formative assessment to its full potential. Research indicates that students' engagement in their work contributes to their ownership of it, which in turn increases their motivation for learning. Student ownership and self-assessment do not imply lack of teacher participation. Teachers are necessary to identify learning goals, establish clear success criteria, and design assessment tools and tasks that return proof of what students have learned. Studies show that teachers' descriptive feedback is the most significant teaching strategy for advancing student learning. It gives students insight into their areas of good performance; connects with classroom learning; and provides specific information about how to attain the next step in the learning process.

Instructional strategies
One classroom instructional strategy that teachers can use both to teach students and to aid in gathering formative information about student learning progress is student record-keeping. Teachers can assign students to keep running records of their own work. This stimulates motivation, engagement, and ownership. It gives students better insight into their own learning as it is reflected through their work in the classroom. It also helps students realize where they began and how far they have progressed toward learning goals, beyond just receiving grades. Two more related classroom instructional strategies that teachers can apply are self-assessment and peer assessment. In self-assessment, students use skills of metacognition ("thinking about thinking") to reflect about what and how they are learning. This engages them in their own learning. Especially when teachers have already involved students in establishing goals and criteria, the next logical step in the learning process is self-assessment. In peer assessment, students come to view one another as mutual resources to compare the quality of their work to preset criteria, and to understand their own and each other's work and learning.

Students have to understand what learning goals and objectives their teacher has identified, and what criteria the teacher has established to measure achievement of those goals and objectives, if they are to succeed. When teachers share these with students, they are communicating clear expectations; and also engaging students in the learning process. For example, teachers ask students to participate in deciding behavioral norms for the classroom culture; and to collaborate with them in defining what quality work is, and producing it. They ask students to help them decide what to include in classroom success criteria. Teachers give students examples of the type and quality of work they expect. These can include products from outside sources, e.g. literary, journalistic, and other works; successful classroom tests; and successful samples of students' classroom work. This helps students comprehend where they are in the learning process; where they need to go from there; and effective procedures to get them there.

Questioning

Teachers can stimulate students to think in more depth about learning topics, and can access better insights about the extent of students' comprehension and the depth of their understanding, by asking them better questions. Teachers should embed questioning practices into their lesson plans and teaching/learning units. When teachers ask students the kinds of questions that prompt them to think more deeply about learning content, they engage the students in classroom dialogues which not only reveal their learning, but moreover extend it further. Teachers can use time-saving questioning and formative assessment strategies during their classroom instruction; for example, red "stop" and green "go" cards or "thumbs up" and "thumbs down" cards, or "exit slips" they use at the end of class, are ways to check student understanding and learning during a lesson. Another way to employ questioning as a formative assessment strategy is to guide students in asking better questions themselves.

Impacts of classroom formative assessment on student achievement

Experts agree that elements essential to formative assessment include collecting student learning data, giving feedback to students, involving students, and adjusting instruction based on the information gathered. However, some researchers (e.g. McMillan, Venable & Varier, 2013), through both evaluating multiple studies and examining meta-analyses conducted by others, are of the opinion that much research into how formative assessment affects student performance has tended to emphasize the components of collecting data and giving feedback, but has given comparatively little attention to the adjustment/correction of instruction. They have also found that while researchers agree on the importance to formative assessment of student engagement—which can take the form(s) of self-assessment and/or peer assessment—most studies used formative assessment interventions of reflective student self-assessment more often than cooperative peer assessment; for example, only one of five studies reviewed used collaborative peer assessments, while the other four used self-assessment measures.

Performance in K-12 schools

Among researchers, there is consensus that feedback plays a crucial role in classroom formative assessment. However, in some literature reviews, it has been found among studies including feedback as an element that some did not describe the type of feedback specifically enough. Others varied in feedback timing: some teachers studied gave students immediate feedback, others delayed feedback. Some teachers gave feedback to individual students, others to groups of students. Some teachers gave students both individual and group feedback. Some studies paid more attention to feedback given following instruction than during instruction, which is inconsistent with formative assessment. Another finding among multiple studies was that most research devoted more attention to the collection of student data and the provision of feedback to students, while not attending sufficiently to the component of adjusting instruction based on the information gathered. Multiple researchers point out that effective formative assessment requires such adjustments. Investigators also find insufficient attention paid in studies to student reflection and self-assessment.

Authentic assessment

Some educational researchers and authors use the term "authentic assessment" to mean realistic, i.e. tasks similar to those in the real world. However, others (e.g. Frey, Schmitt, & Allen, 2012) say the concept of authenticity as used in the discipline is more complex and includes more than just realism. They comment some educators also label assessments as "authentic" if their tasks are cognitively complex, or performance-based. Others think student involvement in establishing scoring criteria; or requiring student collaboration; or methods for ensuring reliability, e.g. portfolio systems and multiple instruments/indices; and frequently, for ensuring validity, e.g. needing a public defense or having a formative assessment purpose, define authentic assessment. The above-referenced researchers find many of these unnecessary to defining assessment authenticity. Eliminating those, they find essential elements defining authentic classroom assessment are that tasks deeply engage students by being both intrinsically interesting and cognitively complex; and that they evaluate and/or develop abilities and skills having value beyond the assessment per se.

Incredible Interactive Notebook

The Incredible Interactive Notebook is identified by Pole (2013) as a concept from the Teachers Curriculum Institute (TCI), originally introduced by Addison-Wesley in *History Alive!* and defined as consisting of notes students take on their reading, viewing, listening, discussions, and corresponding, which may be written or graphic; and/or a daily journal that students record of their class notes from lectures, discussions, and reading plus their metacognitive and reflective responses about their own note-taking. It enables students to preview their assignments; graphically organize their reading notes; and process their assignments. It is recommended as a way to enhance the quality of instruction for ELL students. Interactive notebooks are identified as personal student tools; tools for scaffolding (support); collections of students' learning; and tools for authentic assessment. They provide places where students can make personal notes and illustrations that make sense to them. They encourage student engagement, organization, critical thinking, and combining visuals with words.

For the Incredible Interactive Notebook (cf. Pole, 2013), students can decorate their notebook covers by gluing pictures, attaching stickers, and/or drawing on them. They should then create an Author's Page; a Table of Contents; and a page with Teacher Expectations and/or a rubric. Teachers instruct students to number the notebook pages 10-20 at a time; and not to take the notebooks home. Suggestions for the Author's page include the student's name, nickname, birthday; favorite food(s), music, sport(s), color(s), movie(s), books(s), place(s); three words the student would use to describe herself/himself; where s/he would like to take a vacation; and what s/he would like to be/do in the future. A rubric example has criteria for student work of completeness, thoughtfulness, clarity, creativity, and making connections, with assessment categories of Excellent = all work meets these; Satisfactory = majority of work meets these; and Needs Improvement = some work meets these criteria.

On the left side of each notebook page, students place their input or application of concepts they learned; record their ideas/feelings/opinions; connect to learning standards; and apply skills they have developed. Some examples include: Brainstorming notes; drawings; photos; Venn diagrams; concept maps; thought maps; poems; word clusters; charts; graphs; graphic organizers; any other creative products; and K.I.M. Vocabulary charts. K.I.M. stands for Key idea, Information, and Memory clue. Students have a box or table with the top three cells containing these three headings horizontally. For example, under Key idea, they write/type vocabulary words. Under Information, next to each vocabulary word they write/type dictionary definitions. Under Memory clue, they might make a drawing, often with words, to help remember the definitions/meanings. On page right sides, they place learning standards; teacher-driven material; handouts; title and unit pages; notes; foldable media; word clusters; and personal responses. *Like those foldables*

Example entries

One student has cut out construction paper in the shape of Texas and written facts about Texas on it, e.g. cities, nickname; state bird and flower and drawings of these, etc. On a page entitled "Point of View", a student has cut out a printed chart with cells saying First Person, Second Person, Third Person Objective, Third Person Limited, and Third Person Omniscient; with a handwritten note under the latter, "(all-knowing)" and attached this to the left side of the page. Underneath, the student has written notes about each POV, including respectively associated pronouns. On a page entitled Multiplying Decimals and Whole Numbers, a student has drawn tables with some cells filled in with different colors and labeled with the relevant decimal numbers; with the multiplication written next to them. On another page, a student has written the title, in a drawing of an open book, and the main idea of a story, with definitions of "problem" and "solution" between the former and latter. Another has paper strips attached with printed names of the planets accompanied by drawings of each. Or a student has made labeled drawings of different graph types, etc.

Hypothetical middle school essay-writing assignment

Consider a hypothetical middle school student named Chris. The ELA class that Chris is in is preparing for a test on the ELA CCSS. The teacher has assigned all of the students to write essays with certain instructions, including the following: "Describe in detail how an author creates and builds tension during a short story, providing at least three examples from the text. Quote these examples; analyze each one, and explain how it supports your claim that it creates or builds tension in the story." Chris has written an essay about a short story by Edgar Allen Poe. In the essay, Chris summarizes Poe's tension-building techniques using brief phrases. Chris also includes one story quotation as an example of a technique. The conclusion states, "Therefore, Poe creates and builds tension throughout this story." Strengths: Chris correctly chose an author/story that create/build tension; and included an example of an author technique. Weaknesses: Instead of *describing* author technique *in detail*, Chris *summarized*; provided *one* example, not *three*; and did not explain/connect the conclusion clearly to supporting evidence.

Imaginary middle school essay assignment

An imaginary student, Pat, is in a middle school class whose teacher assigned an essay as practice for the CCSS/ELA assessment. Teacher instructions included, "Explain how an author establishes mood and uses description appealing to the senses in a short story, giving textual evidence. Include an essay introduction, body, and conclusion." Pat's essay describes the author's creation of mood, providing quotations of several textual examples. The essay ends with the last of these examples. Having provided plenty of textual evidence, Pat feels nothing further is needed in the essay. Pat wrote in a minimalist style that Pat's teacher, small reading group classmates, and closest friends would readily understand. Strengths: Pat provided ample textual evidence of author devices establishing mood and sensory imagery appealing to reader imagination. Weaknesses: Pat *described* instead of *explaining,* as instructions specified. Pat omitted the required essay conclusion. And Pat wrote in an incomplete style suitable for familiar audiences but unclear to the assessment's remote audience, for which the essay was practice.

Practice Test

Practice Questions

(D) 1. *Who's Afraid of Virginia Woolf?* was written by…
  a. Mother Goose.
  b. Virginia Woolf.
  c. Harold Pinter.
  (d.) Edward Albee.

(B) 2. Which of the following was written by Mary Ann Evans under the *nom de plume* George Eliot?
  a. *Emma* Jane Austen
  (b.) *Agatha*
  c. *Pride and Prejudice* Jane Austen
  d. *Sense and Sensibility* Jane Austen

(D) 3. Which of the following works was written closest in time to the literary English Renaissance?
  (a.) *Beowulf*
  b. *Everyman*
  c. *The Canterbury Tales*
  d. *The Pilgrim's Progress*

(C) 4. The historical and social context of Arthur Miller's play *The Crucible* is informed by…
  (a.) The 17th-century Salem witch trials.
  b. The 1950s communism "Red Scare."
  c. *The Crucible* is informed by A and B
  d. None of these informs *The Crucible*

A× B 5. Which of the following works are considered part of the same genre? Choose ALL answers that apply.
  a. *King Lear* and *Oedipus Rex* Tragedies
  b. *Animal Farm* and *Brave New World* Dystopian
  c. *The Faerie Queene* and *The Gift of the Magi*
  d. *The Open Window* and *For the Union Dead*
  e. *The Waste Land* (Eliot) and *The Waste Lands* (King)

B 6. Within the genre of poetry, which subgenre is typically a tripartite poem written to mourn a death?
  a. Epic
  (b.) Elegy
  c. Epigram
  d. Epistolary

7. Which of the following terms would NOT be used correctly regarding a sonnet?
  a. Sestet
  b. Couplet
  c. Quatrain
  d. Paragraph

8. Of the following, which is/are true of the haiku but not the limerick as a poetic form? Choose ALL answers that apply.
  a. This form typically is written with a total of 17 syllables.
  b. This form typically is written with a total of five verses.
  c. This form typically is written in AABBA rhyme scheme.
  d. This form typically captures a nature scene or moment.
  e. This form typically describes a funny and/or silly topic.

9. As an example of figurative language, who first used the "ship of state" metaphor?
  a. Longfellow
  b. Aeschylus
  c. Alcaeus
  d. Plato

10. A teacher has students read literary nonfiction by Martin Luther King, Jr. To help them make inferences from text, she does a Think-Aloud. Text clues are: seeing a "White Only" sign made King feel sad until he recalled his mother's words, and hearing his father's words when preaching made him feel better. Student knowledge is: parents make us feel better when we are unhappy. Which of the following would be the most appropriate student inference?
  a. Seeing segregation signs in his youth made King feel bad.
  b. King's feelings and beliefs were influenced by his parents.
  c. When unhappy, his parents' words made King feel better.
  d. When we are unhappy, our parents can make us feel better.

The following question is based on the first sentence of Ernest Hemingway's short story "The Short Happy Life of Francis Macomber" (1936)

> It was now lunch time and they were all sitting under the double green
> fly of the dining tent pretending that nothing had happened.

11. The way Hemingway begins this story gives textual evidence of which literary device?
  a. First-person narrative
  b. *Deus ex machina*
  c. *In medias res*
  d. *Duodecimo*

12. Which of the following is the most accurate definition of the theme in a work of literature?
  a. A central insight or idea underlying and controlling the work.
  b. An author's world view or revelation expressed in one word.
  c. The moral of a story that the author wants to teach readers.
  d. The main conflict that was involved in the work of literature.

13. In the novel *Great Expectations* (1860-1861), Charles Dickens develops the theme of revenge through...
    a. The relationship of Miss Havisham and Estella.
    b. The relationships of all of the characters.
    c. The relationship of Magwitch and Pip.
    d. The relationship of Orlick and Pip.

14. In the Gilgamesh Epic, the Islamic Quran, and the Old Testament book of Genesis, which of the following most represents a universal theme they commonly share?
    a. A flood occurring all over the world and destroying everybody.
    b. A flood as God's way to eliminate humans behaving wickedly.
    c. A flood before which a man is told to build a ship to escape it.
    d. A flood after which a survivor sends birds out to test its end.

15. Which author writes exclusively from one point of view in the book(s) named?
    a. George R. R. Martin in the series *A Song of Ice and Fire*
    b. J. K. Rowling in her *Harry Potter* series of novels
    c. Barbara Kingsolver in *The Poisonwood Bible*
    d. None of these uses a single point of view

16. In analyzing the plot structure of a short story, during which part of the plot does the main character experience a turning point?
    a. Exposition
    b. Climax
    c. Rising action
    d. Falling action

17. One element of literature establishes the emotional climate in a work through the author's choice of setting, details, imagery, objects, and words. One example of this element is mystery. Which of the following is this element?
    a. Tone
    b. Mood
    c. Conflict
    d. Point of view

18. Ernest Hemingway's short story "Hills Like White Elephants" (1927) describes a conversation between "the girl" (Jig) and "the man"(the American). The dialogue includes this from the girl: "Would you please please please please please please please Stop talking." How does this inform the girl's character, the relationship, and the situation? Choose ALL correct answers.
    a. It shows she repeats herself a great deal.
    b. It shows the man talks too much for her.
    c. It shows they have discussed this before.
    d. It shows she is frustrated over the topic.
    e. It shows she is not ready for a discussion.

19. In Kate Chopin's short story "The Story of an Hour" (1894), Chopin's description of Louise Mallard as "young, with a fair, calm face, whose lines bespoke repression and even a certain strength" contributes to her character development to help explain which plot event most?
  a. Her reaction to seeing her husband alive.
  b. The controlling behavior of her husband.
  c. Why her immediate grief ended so soon.
  d. Her joy when her husband was not dead.

20. In "Old Times on the Mississippi" (1876), Mark Twain writes, "I... could have hung my hat on my eyes, they stuck out so far." This is an example of which literary device?
  a. Third-person narrative
  b. Personification
  c. Hyperbole
  d. Irony

Answer the following question based on the excerpt below. Choose ALL correct answers.

Parker surveyed the infield. Ninety feet away at first base, his teammate Jones crouched like a tiger, taking a big lead. Beyond the pitcher at second base, Hernandez slouched a few feet from the bag. Out of the corner of his eye, Parker made out Curtis hopping around at third base. The other team's infielders stood around the infield, staring at Parker, knees bent, waiting to make a play.

Beyond the dirt of the infield paced the outfielders, small, blurry figures in the tall grass. The stands that surrounded the field held a sea of faces. The scoreboard high above the orange fence at straight-away center field, four hundred twenty feet from home plate, told the tale: bottom of the ninth inning, two outs, and the home team was down by three runs. Parker held up a sweaty hand to the blue-suited umpire behind the catcher and croaked, "Time."

"Rookie!" someone yelled from the stands.

(--McGraw-Hill Education Group)

21. In this passage, which is true of similes, metaphors, and context clues?
  a. "A sea of faces" is a metaphor.
  b. "Jones crouched like a tiger" is a simile.
  c. "Jones crouched like a tiger" is a metaphor.
  d. "Taking a big lead" is a context clue to "Jones crouched like a tiger."
  e. "The stands that surrounded the field" is a context clue to "a sea of faces."

Answer the following question based on this excerpt from the poem "O Captain! My Captain" (1865) by Walt Whitman.

O Captain! my Captain! our fearful trip is done,
The ship has weather'd every rack, the prize we sought is won,
The port is near, the bells I hear, the people all exulting,
While follow eyes the steady keel, the vessel grim and daring;
But O heart! heart! heart!
O the bleeding drops of red,
Where on the deck my Captain lies,
Fallen cold and dead.

22. Which of the following poetic devices does Whitman use in this excerpt? Choose ALL correct answers.
    a. Elegy
    b. Symbolism
    c. Allusion
    d. Metaphor
    e. Apostrophe

23. Through the structure of his poem, "Proem: To the Brooklyn Bridge" (1930), Hart Crane conveys and reinforces senses of...
    a. Stability, regularity, and connection.
    b. Impermanence, change, and insecurity.
    c. Irregularity, chaos, and confusion.
    d. Eternity free of progress and/or change.

24. As a reading strategy, ELA teachers can best give students practice in making predictions to support comprehension through which activity?
    a. Predicting what or whom a book is about
    b. Predicting what a novel's character will do
    c. Predicting a significant event in a narrative
    d. Predicting (B) and/or (C), rather than (A)

25. Which of the following teacher questions can help students develop the literacy skill of text-to-self connection? Choose ALL correct answers.
    a. How does this book remind you of any other books you have read?
    b. Does anything in the book remind you of anything in your own life?
    c. Are there events in this book similar to events in the real world?
    d. How are some events in this book different from real-life events?
    e. Are there any characters in this book you can relate to personally?

26. Which instructional activity is the best example of the research-based strategy of activating students' prior knowledge before reading?
    a. Before students read a text, the teacher instructs them in relevant background information.
    b. Before and after they read a text, the teacher has students make a KWL chart on its subject.
    c. After students have read a text, the teacher asks them what they know about the subject.
    d. The teacher asks students to express their opinions and reactions on a topic after reading.

27. What have studies found about how teachers interpret and apply research to reading instruction challenges?
    a. Teachers make data-based instructional decisions better individually than in small groups.
    b. Teachers are generally better at data comprehension than data location in graphs or tables.
    c. Teachers do far better at interpreting relationships among variables than question-posing.
    d. Teachers plan differentiated instruction better with real (not hypothetical) student scores.

28. Which of the following literary theories would most inform Conrad's *Heart of Darkness*?
    a. Aristotle's theory of unity
    b. Feminist and gender theories
    c. Post-colonial theories
    d. Marxist theories

29. Regarding literal versus figurative language in informational texts, the words "politician" and "statesman"...
   a. Have both the same denotation and connotation.
   b. Have both different denotations and connotations.
   c. Have the same denotation but different connotations.
   d. Have the same connotation but different denotations.

30. When reading an expository text, the reader would most appropriately draw which kinds of inferences?
   a. Cause-and-effect and/or problem-solution
   b. What events occurred and what people did
   c. What the author wants readers to believe
   d. Ideas that support the author's message

31. Among Common Core Standards (CCS) in "anchor" performance skills that all must students must demonstrate for reading informational texts, which is required of 11th- and 12th-graders that is not required of 6th- through 10th-graders?
   a. Citing textual evidence to support their inferences and analyses
   b. Identifying specific textual evidence to defend their conclusions
   c. Being able to differentiate strong from weaker textual evidence
   d. Being able to recognize which elements are left unclear in a text

32. Students are analyzing the text of Abraham Lincoln's *Gettysburg Address*. They are identifying Lincoln's main ideas and details supporting those ideas. Which of the following would be paraphrases of main ideas rather than supporting details? Select ALL correct answers.
   a. The Founding Fathers created the United States of America
   b. The US was conceived in liberty and dedicated to equality
   c. Now the US is engaged in the great struggle of a Civil War
   d. We are here today to dedicate the Gettysburg battlefield
   e. It is a fitting and proper thing to commemorate our troops

33. In a paired reading strategy for identifying the main idea in informational text, two students silently read a selection. Then, taking two-column notes of main ideas and supporting details, they take turns with the following steps. Which choice sequences these steps in the correct order?
   a. The pair develops main idea consensus, a student paraphrases the main idea, a student explains agreement or disagreement, they take turns finding supporting details
   b. A student paraphrases the main idea, a student explains agreement or disagreement, the pair develops main idea consensus, they take turns finding supporting details
   c. They take turns finding supporting details, a student explains agreement or disagreement, a student paraphrases the main idea, the pair develops main idea consensus
   d. A student explains agreement or disagreement, they take turns finding supporting details, the pair develops main idea consensus, a student paraphrases the main idea

- 109 -

34. An informational text states that a Yugoslavian nationalist assassinated Austria-Hungary's heir to the throne, Archduke Franz Ferdinand; this triggered a diplomatic crisis, wherein Austria-Hungary issued the Kingdom of Serbia an ultimatum; in reaction to this ultimatum, a number of previously formed international alliances were then reinforced; and therefore within several weeks, the major world powers had gone to war; consequently, the fighting soon spread worldwide. This is an example of which kind of structural or organizational pattern?
    a. Descriptive
    b. Cause and effect
    c. Sequence and order
    d. Comparison-contrast

35. A teacher helps students analyze informational text to see how authors connect and distinguish ideas by giving them sentence frames. For example, "_____ are _____, meaning they eat _____." Students fill these in, such as "Rabbits are herbivores, meaning they eat only plants" or "Frogs are carnivores, meaning they eat only meat." These are examples of...
    a. Making analogies among animals.
    b. Grouping animals into categories.
    c. Comparing animals by similarities.
    d. Contrasting animals' differences.

36. Of the following informational text features, which is/are NOT usually found in the back of a book? Choose ALL correct answers.
    a. Index
    b. Graphs
    c. Glossary
    d. Appendix
    e. Footnotes

37. Which of the following sentences uses the word "smart" with a negative connotation, rather than a positive connotation or simply the word's denotation?
    a. Eliot's teacher said he was not quite gifted, but too smart for a general class.
    b. Eliot was smart to have studied the day before the test; he got a good grade.
    c. Eliot was identified by his teacher as one of the smart students in her classes.
    d. Eliot got into trouble when he gave a smart answer to his teacher's question.

38. Of the following attributes of technical language used in informational texts, which represent(s) the character of the mood rather than the character of the tone?
    a. Concise
    b. Impersonal
    c. Professional
    d. Self-deprecating versus grandiose

Answer the following question based on the text provided below.

> Cells are our bodies' building blocks. Our body systems contain organs made of tissue, and body tissues are composed of cells. All living organisms, including humans, are made of cells.

39. Of the following questions related to the text above, which one is implicit rather than explicit?
    a. What is the main idea of the text?
    b. Which things are composed of cells?
    c. How do we know birds are made of cells?
    d. What is the role that cells play in our bodies?

40. In scientific informational texts, which of these are authors LEAST likely to do?
    a. Explicitly state their point of view about the research they did
    b. Explicitly state the purpose of the research they are reporting
    c. Explicitly state their interpretation of the study evidence or data
    d. Explicitly state which variables they investigated and in whom

41. When reading a research report or other scientific informational text whose author does not overtly state his or her point of view, how can the reader analyze the text to identify the author's purpose and/or point of view?
    a. The reader can consider with what main idea the author seems to want readers to agree.
    b. The reader can consider the author's main point, but examining word choice will not help.
    c. The reader can consider word choice instead of facts and examples affecting reader attitudes.
    d. The reader can consider facts used more than what an author wants to achieve by writing.

42. How would an author best use rhetoric to provide readers with supporting evidence of a main point in an informational text?
    a. By evocative descriptions
    b. By making good analogies
    c. By telling personal stories
    d. By reporting case studies

43. In the poem "To His Coy Mistress" (1650~1652), Andrew Marvell writes, "The grave's a fine and private place, / But none, I think, do there embrace." Which rhetorical strategy does he employ in these lines?
    a. Satire
    b. Hyperbole
    c. Verbal irony
    d. Understatement

44. A telecommunications salesman is writing informational text to persuade customers to agree to buy the products and services he is selling. One tactic includes advising the customer, "You are hemorrhaging money!" This is an example of which method of persuasion?
    a. A generalization
    b. Using a metaphor
    c. Rhetorical question
    d. Negative connotation

45. Of the following criteria for critically evaluating how effective an informational text author's methods of appealing to the reading audience, which is related to whether readers believed the author, and why they did or did not?
    a. Clarity
    b. Accuracy
    c. Cohesion
    d. Credibility

46. When should scientists use technical rather than non-technical language to write about technical subjects?
    a. When reporting research results to colleagues in their field
    b. When writing science fiction for a popular reading audience
    c. When writing material to support school science instruction
    d. When writing material to support scientific lobbying efforts

47. In the steps that a reader can follow to evaluate an informational text writer's arguments, which should come first?
    a. Identifying the conclusion the argument makes
    b. Judging the validity or supportiveness of premises
    c. Clarifying premises or reasons with paraphrases
    d. Identifying the supporting premises or reasons

48. Among the following reasons that readers must deduce informational author purposes and motivations for writing, which is most important for identifying purposes an author may have had but did not state in the text?
    a. Determining an author's purpose enables readers to know what to expect from the text.
    b. Discovering the author's motivation for writing allows readers to read for relevant details.
    c. Knowing author motivation and purpose enables critical reader evaluation of author and text.
    d. When authors define purposes contradicting some text, they may have hidden agendas.

49. In three pieces of informational writing, Sample 1's author provides evidence tangential to his argument. Sample 2's author cites anecdotal evidence which is inaccurate. Sample 3's author cites accurate, directly related evidence, but it is an isolated example uncorroborated by any other sources. Which choice correctly matches these samples with incompletely met criteria?
    a. Sample 1's evidence is not sufficient, Sample 2's is not relevant, and Sample 3's is not factual.
    b. Sample 1's evidence is not factual, Sample 2's is not sufficient, and Sample 3's is not relevant.
    c. Sample 1's evidence is not relevant, Sample 2's is not factual, and Sample 3's is not sufficient.
    d. Samples 1 and 3 evidence are insufficient, and Sample 2's evidence is factual but irrelevant.

50. Someone argues, "But if you legalize this drug, all drugs will be legalized." In rhetoric, this is an example of which type of logical fallacy?
    a. Straw man
    b. Red herring
    c. Slippery slope
    d. *Post hoc ergo propter hoc*

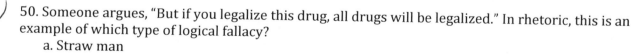

Answer the next two questions based on the sentence below.

> "Although we liked Bill and Hillary, we did not go to their party because there were too many people there for us."

51. In the sentence above, what is "Although we liked Bill and Hillary"?
    a. A prepositional phrase
    b. An independent clause
    c. A dependent clause
    d. A complete sentence

52. In the sentence above, which parts are prepositional phrases?
    a. "to their party"; "for us"
    b. "Although we liked"; "because there were"
    c. "we did not go"; "because there were"
    d. "because there were"; "too many people"

Answer the next two questions based on the following sentence.

> "Nancy also felt that the party was too crowded, but the hosts, who relied so much on her, would have been hurt if she had not attended."

53. What type of sentence is the sentence above?
    a. Simple
    b. Complex
    c. Compound
    d. Compound-complex

54. In the sentence above, which parts are the independent clauses?
    a. "Nancy also felt..."; "who relied so much on her"
    b. "Nancy also felt..."; "the hosts would have been hurt..."
    c. "who relied so much on her"; "if she had not attended"
    d. "that the party was too crowded"; "who relied so much on her"

55. In the words *proactive, progress,* and *projecting, pro-* is a(n) _____ and means _____.
    a. suffix; good/on top of/over
    b. prefix; before/forward/front
    c. affix; after/behind/in back of
    d. prefix; against/under/below

56. The syllable *–tion* is a(n) _____ and turns a _____ into a _____.
    a. Suffix; verb; noun
    b. Affix; noun; pronoun
    c. Prefix; noun; verb
    d. Infix; noun; adjective

Answer the next question based on the following sentences.

> "She has made remarkable progress as a student."
> "After a good beginning, her work did not progress."

A+C

57. Which can we determine about the word *progress* from context clues in each sentence? Choose ALL correct answers.
    a. It is a noun in the first sentence, with its first syllable stressed.
    b. It is a verb in the first sentence, with the first syllable stressed.
    c. It is a verb in the second sentence, with its second syllable stressed.
    d. It is a noun in the second sentence, with the second syllable stressed.
    e. It is a verb in the first sentence and a noun in the second, both are pronounced the same.

Answer the next question based on the two sentences below.

> "Don't mind the dog; his bark is worse than his bite."
> "I can tell this tree is an aspen because of its bark."

B

58. Based on the sentence contexts, which is true about the word *bark*?
    a. It is impossible to tell its meaning because its spelling and pronunciation are the same in both.
    b. The reference to the dog in the first sentence, and the tree in the second, define its meaning.
    c. "Bark" refers to a sound in the second sentence, and to a plant covering in the first sentence.
    d. The meaning of this word is different in each sentence, but in one of them it is spelled wrong.

59. In *Romeo and Juliet,* Shakespeare writes Romeo's line, "What light from yonder window breaks?" What is the syntax of this sentence?
    a. Subject-object-verb
    b. Subject-verb-object
    c. Object-subject-verb
    d. Verb-object-subject

60. Edna St. Vincent Millay has written, "Search the fading letters finding / Steadfast in the broken binding / All that once was I!" If the last line were rearranged into more common everyday syntax, how would it read?
    a. All that I was once
    b. Once I was all that
    c. That I once all was
    d. That all I was once

61. A student is introducing a quotation in a paper. Among verbs the student can select to describe what the quoted author wrote, which is most similar in nuance to "insists"?
    a. Maintains
    b. Suggests
    c. Explains
    d. Points out

62. In "Do not go gentle into that good night," Dylan Thomas writes, "Old age should burn and rave at close of day; / Rage, rage, against the dying of the light... Grave men, near death, who see with blinding sight / Blind eyes could blaze like meteors and be gay, / Rage, rage against the dying of the light." The literary figure of speech Thomas uses here is...
   a. Anaphora.
   b. Alliteration.
   c. Assonance.
   d. Apostrophe.

63. A student writing a paper on a topic within a specialized discipline, which she has researched using textbooks published in that field, wants to make sure she has correctly spelled certain words that are part of the terminology peculiar to that discipline. Which reference should she best consult?
   a. Spell checker
   b. Style manual
   c. Dictionary
   d. Glossary

Answer the next question based on the following quotation of dialogue from a novel.

> "Running after t'lads, as usuald!... If I war yah, maister, I'd just slam t'boards i' their faces all on 'em, gentle and simple! Never a day ut yah're off, but yon cat o'Linton comes sneaking hither; and Miss Nelly, shoo's a fine lass!"

64. What kind of dialect is represented in the character's speech?
   a. Early 20th-century American Southern English
   b. English spoken in 18th-century colonial India
   c. English spoken in 17th-century rural Scotland
   d. 19th-century Yorkshire working-class dialect

65. Mark Twain's *The Adventures of Huckleberry Finn* (1885) contains the following quotation of dialogue: "...we's safe! Jump up and crack yo' heels. Dat's de good ole Cairo at las', I jis knows it." Twain was representing the typical dialect of which character?
   a. The uneducated, poor white protagonist, Huck
   b. Huck's best friend, educated white Tom Sawyer
   c. Huck's companion, African-American slave Jim
   d. Jim's (former) owner, wealthy old Miss Watson

66. Which of these correctly represents findings about research-based vocabulary instruction?
   a. Children need word repetition consisting of drills for vocabulary development.
   b. Children need only be exposed to new words once or twice to remember them.
   c. Children learn the vocabulary in texts best indirectly through simply reading them.
   d. Children require direct instruction and multiple word exposure in various contexts.

67. In the seven steps readers can follow for evaluating the argument by an author of persuasive or argumentative writing, what is accurate about the fifth, sixth, and seventh steps?
   a. Authors strengthen their arguments by omitting detracting information.
   b. Authors persuade readers better appealing to emotion than using logic.
   c. Author arguments are valid if reasoning is logical, with sequential points.
   d. Authors can produce credible arguments which are not necessarily valid.

68. In explanatory writing, which of the following does the writer typically NOT do?
    a. Differentiate among the members of a given category
    b. Assume some information is factual, accurate, or true
    c. Prove certain information is factual, accurate and true
    d. Define terms, analyze processes, or develop concepts

69. If a writer's purpose is to create portraits of people for a reading audience whose interest is in different personalities, motivations, and their expression in various behaviors and relationships, which mode of writing is most appropriate?
    a. A fictional novel
    b. A how-to manual
    c. A persuasive essay
    d. An explanatory paper

70. Two mothers of young children write their observations about parenting. Writer A publishes her writing daily for a wide reading audience. Writer B also writes daily, but privately. Which two forms of writing best identify their activities?
    a. Blog; journal
    b. Journal; letters
    c. Letters; essays
    d. Essays; speeches

71. What do the books *Pamela* and *Clarissa* by Samuel Richardson; *Dangerous Liaisons* by Pierre Choderlos de Laclos; *The Sorrows of Young Werther* by Johann Wolfgang von Goethe; *The History of Emily Montague* by Frances Brooke; and *Frankenstein* by Mary Shelley all have in common?
    a. They are all picaresque novels.
    b. They are all first novels in their countries.
    c. They are all novels written in epistolary form.
    d. They are all novels written in the 18th century.

72. Which of the following is critically effective for the purposes and audiences of blog writing?
    a. Writing with correct punctuation
    b. Writing with longer paragraphs
    c. Writing with longer sentences
    d. Writing with smaller font size

73. To suit their purposes and audiences, which makes blog writing more readable? Choose ALL correct answers.
    a. Avoiding blank spaces within text
    b. Not interrupting text with images
    c. Using all capitals, italics, and boldface
    d. Consistently sequencing in posts
    e. Putting text in narrower columns

74. Which two kinds of writing commonly share the characteristic of using subjective, expressive language--among other techniques—to accomplish their purposes with reading audiences?
    a. Speculative and persuasive
    b. Descriptive and speculative
    c. Persuasive and descriptive
    d. Narrative and explanatory

75. Among the following transitional words or phrases, which one indicates contrast?
    a. Regardless
    b. Furthermore
    c. Subsequently
    d. It may appear

76. When writing an essay, which of the following attributes belongs in the introduction?
    a. Getting the reader's attention
    b. Developing the thesis statement
    c. Giving examples of the thesis idea
    d. Giving the reader a sense of closure

77. When students are writing the conclusions of their essays, which of the following should they do?
    a. Paraphrase their main thesis statement
    b. Repeat their main thesis statement verbatim
    c. Apologize for their opinions and/or their writing
    d. Always summarize their essay in every conclusion

78. In research fields, what does "literature" mean?
    a. All the written works in a language
    b. The profession of a writer or author
    c. All existing material on a subject
    d. Any kinds of printed materials

79. What is true about the problem statement in a research paper?
    a. It follows the title of the paper and precedes the abstract.
    b. It tells why the writer cares about the issue s/he identifies.
    c. It cannot be attributed with establishing the paper context.
    d. It will not demonstrate the import of the variables of focus.

80. For evaluating the credibility of a source when doing research, which of these is true?
    a. The author's reputation is more important than whether s/he cites sources.
    b. The source should always be as recent as possible, regardless of the subject.
    c. The author's point of view and/or purpose is not relevant to the credibility.
    d. The kinds of sources various audiences value influences credibility for them.

81. Which of the following is a primary source?
    a. A report of an original research experiment
    b. An academic textbook's citation of research
    c. A quotation of a researcher in a news article
    d. A website description of another's research

82. Among effective research practices, which of the following is most accurate?
    a. If one finds unlimited material, one should broaden one's research question.
    b. If one finds too little related material, one's research question is too narrow.
    c. If one knows the research question first, one can get lost among all the data.
    d. If one finds no existing literature on a new topic, no type of searching helps.

83. When asking a research question, which of the following should a researcher do first?
    a. Search the literature for knowledge gaps related to the topic
    b. Search the literature for definitive answers to that question
    c. Search the literature for additional research needs or openings
    d. Search the literature for consensus or controversy on the topic

84. Which statement is accurate about using digital text markup tools in school?
    a. Teachers need much training to learn to italicize or boldface certain words in text.
    b. There is no difference for students between using physical and digital highlighters.
    c. Neither teachers nor students need much training to use digital tools to mark text.
    d. That teacher/student digital markups can be deleted or changed is a disadvantage.

85. Among digital networking's educational advantages, which most transforms social interactions?
    a. Linking digitally saved resources to one another
    b. Embedded links to references and learning supports
    c. Virtually instant access to global communications
    d. Diverse formats more similar to diverse learners

86. When using research-based writing instruction strategies, which should be gradually faded?
    a. Brainstorming
    b. Explicit instruction
    c. Teacher modeling
    d. Collaborative work

87. When teachers assign students to small groups for collaborative writing, which of these applies?
    a. Teachers should only set individual performance expectations for individual, not group work.
    b. Teachers should expect student groups to self-manage, and not interfere by giving structure.
    c. Classmates in collaborative groups should give each other positive feedback, not corrections.
    d. Classmates in collaborative groups should give each other constructive and positive feedback.

88. Regarding research-based instructional strategies for collaborative student writing groups, what is correct about developing and setting goals?
    a. Setting specific goals for writing undermines student motivation.
    b. Only the teachers should develop writing goals for the students.
    c. Teachers should expect students to develop their writing goals.
    d. Both the teachers and the students may develop writing goals.

89. What advice to teachers does research indicate about writing instruction strategies?
    a. Explicitly instruct sentence combining to develop sophisticated sentences.
    b. Computer word-processing is a crutch that defeats student independence.
    c. A process writing approach is incompatible with research-based strategies.
    d. Help students analyze writing models, but do not let them imitate models.

90. Which of these accurately reflects research findings about effective writing instruction methods?

    a. Procedural strategies like mnemonics, graphic organizers, outlines, and checklists are wastes of time.

    b. Studies show teaching cognitive strategies is helpful only to students of certain ages and ability levels.

    c. Students need explicit instruction, modeling, think-alouds, and scaffolding to learn how to write well.

    d. Teaching self-regulation improves only student awareness of their writing strengths and weaknesses.

91. What is correct about how teachers can use rubrics as a research-based assessment method?

    a. Teachers should use rubrics to conduct formative (not summative) student work assessments.

    b. Teachers should use rubrics for lesson objectives, both to guide and to assess students' work.

    c. Teachers should use rubrics to conduct summative (not formative) student work assessments.

    d. Teachers should use rubrics in place of stating learning objectives and modeling performance.

92. Which of the following is true about how teachers should use formal and informal instruments for formative assessment in the classroom?

    a. Teachers should use multiple formal and informal assessments as bases for student grouping.

    b. Teachers should use only formal test instruments for conducting their formative assessments.

    c. Teachers should select one specific formal or informal assessment instrument to use exclusively.

    d. Teachers should use formative assessments only for evaluating students, not for teaching them.

93. For supporting language acquisition in ESL/ELL students, what is most accurate about research-based instructional practices?

    a. Teachers should only state directions verbally to give ELLs English decoding practice.

    b. Teachers should encourage ESL students to respond rapidly to get them up to speed.

    c. Teachers should use idioms without explanations to familiarize ELL students to these.

    d. Teachers should give ELL students models and examples of what they expect in tasks.

94. What is correct about evidence-based instructional strategies to use with ELL students?

    a. Asking ELL students to explain and/or retell what teachers said to classmates is useful.

    b. To get ELLs to concentrate on language, teachers should avoid incorporating visual aids.

    c. Teachers should not "talk down" to ELLs by presenting abstract ideas in concrete forms.

    d. Teachers may have ELLs signal when they don't understand, but not elaborate verbally.

95. Research finds that the challenge of assessing learning in ESL student is best met by…

    a. Written tests.

    b. Oral assessments.

    c. Performance assessments.

    d. (B) and (C) more likely than (A)

96. Which of the following is most accurate about the relationship between the physics of thinking and speaking as these inform classroom instruction in listening actively?

a. Because thinking outpaces speech, students' minds wander, so listening is less effective than reading.

b. The disparity between speaking and thinking speeds is conducive to active listening via summarizing.

c. The process of listening is an inherently social interaction; the process of learning is not equally social.

d. The process of learning is essentially a reciprocal one, but the process of listening is not as reciprocal.

97. What statement is correct regarding effective teacher techniques for classroom discussions?

a. Teachers' making comments instead of asking questions encourages creativity in student responses.

b. When some students dominate discussion, teachers engage others with more challenging questions.

c. To meet learning goals, teachers can redirect off-subject discussion by restating topics and questions.

d. A checklist based on the class attendance roll is not the best way to assess all students' participation.

98. If a student has an assignment to speak before the whole class on a given topic and include a visual aid, which of the following technological tools would be most appropriate?

a. PowerPoint

b. A poster

c. A blog

d. A wiki

99. What have research studies found about the effectiveness of technology-based instructional techniques compared to traditional face-to-face classroom instruction? Choose ALL correct answers.

a. The majority of studies found better results from blended online and face-to-face instruction.

b. The majority of studies found better results from traditional face-to-face than online teaching.

c. The majority of studies found better results from online-only teaching than blended teaching.

d. One study had better writing from face-to-face, but no comprehension disparities in methods.

e. One study of two blended courses got better results with an online teacher than in classrooms.

100. Which of the following activities would support a student who is high in Gardner's Logical-Mathematical intelligence type?

a. Writing and giving an oral presentation

b. Designing and utilizing spreadsheets

c. Composing and performing a song

d. A cooperative learning project

101. Providing a learning assignment wherein a student is engaged in hands-on activities like manipulating objects, participating in sports, or dancing would appeal most to which of Gardner's Multiple Intelligences?
    a. The Intrapersonal
    b. Bodily-Kinesthetic
    c. The Naturalist
    d. The Visual-Spatial

102. In differentiated instruction classrooms, which is the most common type of differentiation?
    a. The way individual students access content
    b. The way that learning goals are assessed
    c. The concepts individual students are taught
    d. The amount of detail in teaching concepts

103. How can Lexile measures best help teachers and students choose texts to fit student abilities and interests?
    a. By identifying the grade levels of many books and articles
    b. By finding only texts exactly matching a student's number
    c. By identifying text and student reading levels via numbers
    d. By assigning a number to every book and article published

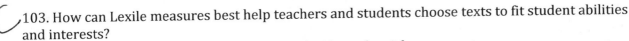

104. According to research findings, which of the following is/are most strongly recommended for teaching adolescent reading? Choose ALL correct answers.
    a. Explicit instruction in vocabulary
    b. Explicit comprehension instruction
    c. Extended open discussions of texts
    d. Enhancing student literacy motivation
    e. Enhancing student literacy engagement

105. Among effective reading strategies, which one involves recalling relevant past experience and existing knowledge to construct meaning from the new information in text that one reads?
    a. Inferring
    b. Activating
    c. Questioning
    d. Summarizing

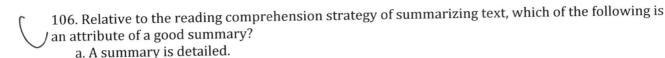

106. Relative to the reading comprehension strategy of summarizing text, which of the following is an attribute of a good summary?
    a. A summary is detailed.
    b. A summary is thorough.
    c. A summary has main ideas.
    d. A summary literally repeats.

107. Which element of the process approach to writing is most related to metacognition?
    a. Self-evaluation
    b. Student interactions
    c. Authentic audiences
    d. Personal responsibility

108. Of the following statements, which is correct about formative and summative assessments?
    a. Summative assessments help students meet learning standards-based goals on time.
    b. Formative assessments allow teachers to adjust instruction to make it more effective.
    c. Summative assessments typically involve students more in the assessment processes.
    d. Formative assessments are more often used for accountability and calculating grades.

109. As one approach to gathering student input, what is correct about a K.I.M. chart for learning vocabulary?
    a. The K in K.I.M. stands for Know, the I for Identify, and the M for Meaning.
    b. Under the K in a K.I.M. chart, the student enters the definitions of the word.
    c. Under the K in a K.I.M. chart, the student enters the new vocabulary words.
    d. When students make K.I.M. charts, they never include drawings or pictures.

110. Concerning student self-monitoring strategies in reading, which statement is true?
    a. If students did not comprehend something, they should identify what and locate it in the text.
    b. If students did not comprehend something, trying to restate it in their own words will not help.
    c. If students did not comprehend something, reviewing for previous text instances wastes time.
    d. If students did not comprehend something, previewing text by looking ahead makes it worse.

Constructed-Response Questions

Reading Question (Interpret literature)

In the following poem, identify the following: What is the extended metaphor used by the poet? Give several specific examples. What poetic form or type of poem is this work? What was the historical occasion for which Whitman wrote this poem? Identify examples of visual and auditory imagery the poet uses. Identify multiple instances of the use of apostrophe in the poem. Explain how the poet uses repetition, and to what effect(s). Identify the rhyme scheme and meter of the poem. Refer to section and line numbers as needed.

O Captain! My Captain!
By Walt Whitman
From *Leaves of Grass* (1891 edition)

1

O CAPTAIN! my Captain! our fearful trip is done;
The ship has weather'd every rack, the prize we sought is won,
The port is near, the bells I hear, the people all exulting,
While follow eyes the steady keel, the vessel grim and daring;
    But O heart! heart! heart!   *5*
     O the bleeding drops of red,
       Where on the deck my Captain lies,
         Fallen cold and dead.

2

O Captain! my Captain! rise up and hear the bells;
Rise up—for you the flag is flung—for you the bugle trills,   *10*
For you bouquets and ribbon'd wreaths—for you the shores a-crowding,
For you they call, the swaying mass, their eager faces turning;
    Here Captain! dear father!
     This arm beneath your head!
       It is some dream that on the deck,   *15*
         You've fallen cold and dead.

3

My Captain does not answer, his lips are pale and still,
My father does not feel my arm, he has no pulse nor will,
The ship is anchor'd safe and sound, its voyage closed and done,
From fearful trip the victor ship comes in with object won;   *20*
    Exult O shores, and ring O bells!
     But I with mournful tread,
       Walk the deck my Captain lies,
         Fallen cold and dead.

Textual Interpretation

In the poem below, identify what predominant literary device Longfellow uses, what thing he compares to what other thing. State the occasion for which he wrote this poem. Quote specific words that he uses throughout as parts of the predominant literary device. Explain why he capitalized the words "Master" and "Workmen" in lines 6 and 7. What other literary device does he use in the last line? Identify the meter and rhyme scheme of the poem. Is the main conceit in this poem original, or had other authors used it before Longfellow? If so, name some who did.

O Ship of State
(1850)

Henry Wadsworth Longfellow (1807-1882)

Thou, too, sail on, O Ship of State!
Sail on, O UNION, strong and great!
Humanity with all its fears,
With all the hopes of future years,
Is hanging breathless on thy fate!
We know what Master laid thy keel,
What Workmen wrought thy ribs of steel,
Who made each mast, and sail, and rope,
What anvils rang, what hammers beat,
In what a forge and what a heat
Were shaped the anchors of thy hope!
Fear not each sudden sound and shock,
'T is of the wave and not the rock;
'T is but the flapping of the sail,
And not a rent made by the gale!
In spite of rock and tempest's roar,
In spite of false lights on the shore,
Sail on, nor fear to breast the sea!
Our hearts, our hopes, are all with thee,
Our hearts, our hopes, our prayers, our tears,
Our faith triumphant o'er our fears,
Are all with thee,—are all with thee!

Answers and Explanations

1. D: Edward Albee (b. 1925), an American playwright, wrote this drama about how the relationship of a middle-aged couple, George and Martha, falls apart. He is also known for plays including *The Zoo Story, The Sandbox, The American Dream,* and *Tiny Alice.* Harold Pinter (C), a contemporary (1930-2008) of Albee, was also a playwright but was British. He is most known for plays *The Birthday Party, The Homecoming,* and *Betrayal.* Mother Goose (A) is a fictional author of many nursery rhymes and fairy tales. However, not from Perrault's *Tales of My Mother Goose* (1695), but Halliwell-Phillips' *The Nursery Rhymes of England* (c. 1886) was the traditional tale of the Three Little Pigs. The Disney version contained the familiar quotation, "Who's afraid of the big bad wolf?" Albee's play title is a take-off on this phrase, substituting the name of 19th-20th century British author Virginia Woolf (B). Woolf's writing frequently unveiled and condemned social pretense by members of the upper class—Woolf's and Albee's backgrounds. In an interview, Albee said, "Who's afraid of Virginia Woolf means who's afraid of the big *bad* wolf...who's afraid of living without false illusions." (The Paris Review, No. 39, Fall 1966)

2. B: *Agatha* is the title of a poem written by Mary Ann (or Marian) Evans (1819-1880), who used the pen name George Eliot. She said this was to have her work taken seriously, as female authors during her time were stereotyped as writing only fluffy romances. She may also have used the pseudonym for privacy. Eliot is best known for her novels *Adam Bede, The Mill on the Floss, Silas Marner, Romola, Middlemarch,* and *Daniel Deronda. Emma* (A), *Pride and Prejudice* (C), and *Sense and Sensibility* (D) were novels written by Jane Austen (1775-1817), who also wrote *Mansfield Park, Northanger Abbey,* and *Persuasion.* Eliot was strongly influenced by reading Austen's novels. While Austen's treatment was lighter and more ironic and Eliot's more serious and political, both women were famous for their realism, social commentary, character portraiture and analysis, and psychological insights.

3. D: *Beowulf* (A), of unknown authorship, is the oldest known epic poem written in Old English, the earliest surviving English literature written in the vernacular, and a major work of Anglo-Saxon literature. It is believed to have been written in the Middle Ages (c. 500-1500) between c. 975 and 1025. *Everyman* (B), whose full title is *The Summoning of Everyman* and whose author is also unknown, is a Christian morality play written in the Middle English dialect sometime in the late 1400s, hence also during the Medieval period. *The Canterbury Tales* (C) were also written in Middle English, by Geoffrey Chaucer c. 1390—again, during the Middle Ages. *The Pilgrim's Progress,* written by John Bunyan, was published in 1678 during the Tudor period—just after the end of the literary English Renaissance (c. 1500-1670) and before the Enlightenment (c. 1700-1800). Therefore, option (D) was written closest in time to literature's English Renaissance. Options (B) and (D) are both religious allegories.

4. C: Both American historical and social contexts of the Salem witch trials in the late 1600s (A) and the fear of communists in the 1950s (B) informed Miller's writing of *The Crucible* (1953). Miller used an overt depiction of the Salem witch trials as an allegory for the panic over Communism he witnessed—and was himself victimized by—during the time he wrote the play. This "Red Scare" was epitomized by McCarthyism, when Senator Joseph McCarthy spearheaded prejudicial investigation and blacklisting of many Americans, including many creative artists, for suspected or accused Communist affiliation or activities. Salem and McCarthyism shared parallel properties of government coercing private citizens to investigate and punish an unproven and ultimately nonexistent "threat." Therefore, option (D) is incorrect.

5. A and B: Shakespeare's *King Lear* (c. 1603-1606) and Sophocles' *Oedipus Rex* (c. 495 BCE) are both plays and tragedies (A). (Moreover, both are about kings and their downfalls.) *Animal Farm* and *Brave New World* are both dystopian novels (B). *Animal Farm* (1945) is George Orwell's political allegory on Stalinism using animal symbols. In *Brave New World* (1931), Aldous Huxley depicts a futuristic society, also with a totalitarian government that has exploited genetic engineering to control IQ levels for various job functions and uses pharmaceutical technology to control citizen dissatisfaction. *The Faerie Queene* is Edmund Spenser's allegorical epic poem (1590, 1596); *The Gift of the Magi* (C) is O. Henry's short story (1905)—the two works are not even in the same genre. Likewise, *The Open Window* is Saki's (1914) short story, while *For the Union Dead* is Robert Lowell's (1964) book of poems (D). Despite similar titles, *The Waste Land* and *The Waste Lands* (E) are not the same genre: The former is T. S. Eliot's seminal Modernist long poem (1922), while the latter is a novel (1991) by contemporary author Stephen King, a part of his Dark Tower series in the horror/fantasy/science fiction genre.

6. B: An elegy is a poem of mourning, traditionally divided into three parts: (1) a lament for the departed, (2) praise of the departed, and (3) solace for the loss of the departed. An epic (A) is a long poem written in stylized language, telling tales of heroic exploits and adventures, and combining both dramatic and lyrical conventions. An epigram (C) is a brief poem consisting of one or two lines and using memorable wording to express some wise, perceptive, or witty observation, sentiment, or adage. Epistolary (D) poems are written in the form of letters from one person to another and are read as such.

7. D: A paragraph (D) is a term used to describe prose, not poetry. While there are several different types of sonnets (Petrarchan, Shakespearean, and many more), they generally follow a tradition of being 14 lines long. Italian and Petrarchan sonnets begin with eight verses (or lines), i.e., an octave, with a set rhyme scheme; and end with six lines, i.e., a sestet (A) with a flexible rhyme scheme. Spenserian sonnets have three stanzas of four lines each, i.e., quatrains (C), unified by overlapping ABAB/BCBC/CDCD rhymes into a 12-line unit; followed by a final rhyming EE couplet (B), i.e., two-line section, which often sums up the main theme or idea. English and Shakespearean sonnets also use three quatrains, but with simpler, more flexible, alternating ABAB/CDCD/EFEF/ rhymes; and a final rhymed GG couplet.

8. A and D: The haiku is typically written with five syllables in the first line, seven in the second, and five in the third. Haiku typically have a total of three lines or verses; limericks typically have five (B). Limericks typically use a regular AABBA rhyme scheme (C); traditional haiku typically do not rhyme. Haiku often capture a scene and/or moment in nature (D). Haiku are typically not humorous or silly, whereas limericks typically are (E)—and also frequently feature bawdy humor.

9. C: Alcaeus, a lyrical poet of ancient (7th-6th century BCE) Greece, was the first person known to use the metaphor of sailing a ship to represent the government of a city-state or republic. The playwright Aeschylus (6th-5th century BCE), known for his tragedies (*The Oresteia, Prometheus Bound*), subsequently used this metaphor in his work *Seven Against Thebes*, also in ancient Greece. Thereafter another, very famous ancient Greek, philosopher and author Plato (5th-4th century BCE) employed the same metaphor in his *Republic*. In the 19th century, English poet Henry Wadsworth Longfellow used the same figurative meaning as an extended metaphor throughout his 1850 poem, "O Ship of State." In 1865, Walt Whitman again used this extended metaphor in his poem "O Captain! My Captain!" an elegy on Lincoln's death.

10. B: This is the only choice representing an inference because the students have to draw this conclusion based on clues in the text combined with their own existing knowledge. Option (A) is not

- 126 -

an inference but a clue stated in the text. Option (C) is also a clue stated in the text. Option (D) is what the students already know. These choices are the material the students have from the text and their own background knowledge. Only option (B) is an inference they draw based on that material.

11. C: Hemingway begins the story in the middle of the action. This literary device is called *in medias res,* Latin for "in the middle of things." Its tradition dates to ancient Roman poet Horace's advice to aspiring epic poets not to start with the beginning, but begin with the heart of their story. Textual evidence includes Hemingway's use of "It was now lunch time," implying things had happened before; and "...pretending that nothing had happened," implying something had happened previously. This story does not use first-person narrative (A) which would narrate with "I/me/my/we/us," but third-person narrative ("they," "he," and so on) The quotation does not contain *deus ex machina* (B), Latin for "God from a machine," a magical or unbelievable mechanism introduced to resolve a plot conflict. (Its origin is ancient Greek dramas wherein gods intervened onstage, often via elaborate machinery.) *Duodecimo* (D) is a bibliographic book format or size, similar to contemporary paperback size (*octavo* is similar to contemporary hardcover book size).

12. A: The theme as an element of a literary work is a central insight or idea, which underlies and controls the work. The author wants to communicate this idea, which may represent a revelation concerning human nature and/or the author's world view, to the readers and audiences. The theme of a literary work is NOT expressed in only one word (B); it pervades the entire work, controlling author choices about characters, conflict, plot action, and tone; and the work contains evidence to support the theme. The theme is NOT the moral of a story to be taught (C); morals are explicitly stated in fables, as lessons are stated in parables. However, in fiction, drama, poetry, and other forms of literature, themes are discovered by readers and audiences through the setting, characters, and plot. The theme is NOT the main conflict (D) in the work; it may, however, be related to what the main character learns through resolving that conflict.

13. B: All of these relationships involve conflicts that Dickens uses to develop the theme of revenge throughout the novel. Miss Havisham uses Estella (A) by raising her to break men's hearts, to gain revenge against men for her fiancé having left her at the altar. Estella in turn marries Drummle to get revenge on Miss Havisham for using her thusly. Magwitch uses Pip (C) by raising Pip's social status to get revenge against society for discriminating against Magwitch in court on the basis of social class. Orlick wants revenge against Pip (D) for a series of wrongs he feels Pip committed; and for enjoying a privileged life, which Orlick never experienced and envies.

14. B: Of the choices given, the only one all three texts share in common is that a great flood was how each religion's god eliminated humans whose behavior had become wicked beyond any other remedy. In Genesis, the flood is described as occurring all over the world (A). However, the Quran describes the flood as regional (which is closer to fact according to historians and archeologists, who identify a tidal wave in the Middle East as the actual source of these narratives). Also, none of these texts describes everybody being destroyed by the flood: the Quran says Allah only destroys those who disregard his messengers' communications, and the Gilgamesh Epic and Genesis both include survivors. While the Gilgamesh Epic and Genesis tell of a man being instructed to build a ship to escape the flood (C), and the shipbuilder in both stories sends birds out after the flood to test its end (D), the Quran does not include the ship or birds.

15. D: None of these authors writes exclusively from a single point of view in the books named. In the *A Song of Ice and Fire* series, George R. R. Martin (A) alternates writing from different characters' points of view in different chapters. In the *Harry Potter* novels, J. K. Rowling (B) frequently writes third-person limited narrative from Harry Potter's point of view, but also

switches to other characters' points of view at times. In her novel *The Poisonwood Bible,* Barbara Kingsolver (C) narrates in first person, but sometimes changes to third person for narrating major action scenes in which the first-person narrator is missing or not involved.

16. B: The parts of plot structure are exposition, rising action, climax, falling action, and dénouement or resolution. In the exposition (A), the setting is established, characters introduced, and plot background presented. During the rising action (C), the story builds up to the chief conflict or problem. During the climax (B) or crisis (the high point of the story), the main character's challenge reaches a peak, then a turning point occurs that determines the outcome. During the falling action (D), the story slows down as outcomes of the character's decisions or actions are revealed. During the dénouement or resolution, the author ties up loose ends, and the story is concluded with an unhappy or happy ending.

17. B: The mood of a literary work establishes the emotional atmosphere through the author's use of setting, details, imagery, objects, and words. One example is a mood of mystery. Tone (A) is the author's implied or stated attitude toward the subject matter of the work. For example, the author might create a humorous, joyous, bitter, ironic, earnest, serious, optimistic, or pessimistic tone through the use of details and word choice. For instance, a work's setting or a character might have a mysterious mood, but be treated with a humorous or ironic tone. Conflict (C) is a literary element that provides the basis for a plot. Examples of generalized conflicts include man versus nature, man versus society, man versus man, or man versus self. Point of view (D) is the literary element of who tells the story, such as a first person, third-person objective, third-person limited, or omniscient narrator.

18. C and D: The girl's repetition of "please" seven times, in the context of the dialogue, shows the couple has had this conversation many times (C), and that she is frustrated over repeated discussions of the topic (D). Though Hemingway does not directly state it, the topic, which the characters call "it," is whether she should have an abortion. Hemingway does not use repetition to show the character repeats herself a lot (A), or the man talks too much (B). He uses it to show that after numerous inconclusive discussions, she explodes. Earlier in the same dialogue, she has said, "Can't we maybe stop talking?" The dialogue does not show that she is unready to talk (E), but that she is fed up with talking without resolution. Hemingway sets the story at a railway station crossroads, symbolizing the girl's decisions about the pregnancy and the relationship also at a crossroads.

19. C: Chopin's character development of Mrs. Mallard in the quotation includes repression and strength. These explain her not showing shock or denial but weeping immediately on hearing of her husband's apparent death, but also its short duration: "When the storm of grief had spent itself she went away to her room alone." The quotation does not explain her reaction to seeing her husband alive (A): identification of Louise's "heart trouble" in the first sentence helps explain her heart attack, along with character development indicating her relief at freedom from her husband's domination (despite his always loving her and her "sometimes" loving him). It does not explain his behavior (B): the paragraph describing his "powerful will bending hers" explains his controlling nature. The "joy" Chopin describes is NOT at seeing her husband alive (D), which kills her; Louise felt this joy previously upon believing he was dead ("free, free, free!").

20. C: This is an example of hyperbole: extreme exaggeration to create an effect. In this case, Twain's purpose is to achieve the effect of humor. He describes his reaction, "I was helpless. I did not know what in the world to do. I was quaking from head to foot..." and then elaborates on this description by saying his eyes protruded so far he could have hung his hat on them, which is

obviously not literally possible. This is an 18th-century verbal precursor of 20th-century cartoon graphics in which a character's eyes "bug out" unnaturally far to indicate an extreme reaction. This is not an example of third-person narrative (A); it is first-person narrative. It is not personification (B), which is attributing human qualities or actions to inanimate objects or animals. It is not irony (D), which creates humor, sarcasm, satire, or sadness through stating something in terms opposite to its meaning.

21. A, B, D, and E: "a sea of faces" is a metaphor (A). Metaphors compare two different things without using the comparative words "like" or "as," but imply comparison by referring to the faces as a sea. "Jones crouched like a tiger" is a simile (B): it directly states comparison using "like." "Taking a big lead" is a context clue to "Jones crouched like a tiger" (D), indicating that Jones was preparing to run toward and pounce on second base immediately when the batter hit the ball, like a tiger would crouch when preparing to run after and pounce on prey. "The stands that surrounded the field" is a context clue to "a sea of faces" (E): The sentence "The stands that surrounded the field held a sea of faces" indicates the stands held many spectators. This informs the metaphor "a sea of faces" because a sea connotes a large volume. Option (C) is incorrect: "like a tiger" is a simile, not a metaphor.

22. A, B, C, D, and E: Whitman managed to use all of these poetic devices in his poem, and even in this single excerpted stanza. The poem is an elegy (A) on the death of Abraham Lincoln. Whitman uses the heart as a symbol (B) of his grief over the loss of President Lincoln. Whitman makes allusions (C) to the Union's victory in the Civil War, and to Lincoln's death. The entire poem uses an extended metaphor (D) wherein the United States is the ship, the "fearful trip" is the Civil War, and Lincoln was the ship's captain. When he addresses Lincoln directly, "O Captain! My Captain!" even though Lincoln is not there, Whitman uses apostrophe (E), i.e., naming and speaking directly to a real or imagined listener or thing.

23. A: Crane's ode to the bridge expresses great stability and regularity in a construction that took longer than most people's lifetimes. He conveys how building the bridge persevered regardless of weather, human activity, day or night—even the suicidal jump from it of a "bedlamite." He does this through the poem's structure, such as maintaining its regular pentameter throughout. Moreover, whenever addressing and/or describing the bridge itself, Crane renders this pentameter even more regular by making it consistently iambic. He even places caesuras (pauses within lines and words) symmetrically (indicated here by spaces between syllables): "And Thee, across the har bor, sil ver-paced /"; "O harp and al tar, of the fur y fused, /"; or "O Sleep less as the riv er un der thee, /". Crane also reinforces stability and endurance with frequent alliteration and assonance. Therefore, options (B) and (C) are incorrect. While Crane does portray the bridge as connecting humankind with God ("And of the curveship lend a myth to God") and eternity, option (D) is incorrect because he does NOT equate eternity with lack of progress: "All afternoon the cloud-flown derricks turn.../ Thy cables breathe the North Atlantic still."

24. D: Predicting what (like a quest or a war) or whom (such as a prince or three animals) a book is about is a common practice of students who fall back on the easiest answer to a teacher's request to make predictions. It is more useful for teachers to challenge students to try and predict what a character in a novel will do (B) or a significant event that may occur in a story (C). Teachers can explain to students that they can make predictions by looking for clues in book titles, front-cover illustrations, and illustrations inside a book before even reading it. They can also have students read just one passage from a book, and then have them predict what will occur next.

25. B and E: Asking students how a book reminds them of anything in their own lives (B) and whether there are any characters in the book they can relate to personally (E) help them make text-to-self connections. Asking students if anything in a book reminds them of any other book they have read (A) is a way of helping them make text-to-text connections. Asking students if events in a book are similar to events in the real world (C) or different from real-life events (D) are ways of helping them make text-to-world connections.

26. B: A KWL chart allows students to list, before they read, what they **K**now about a subject; what they **W**ant to know or learn about it; and, after reading, what they have **L**earned about it. This is a good example of a research-based instructional strategy for activating students' prior knowledge. Option (A) is not a good example because the teacher gives the students background information, rather than finding out what they already know. Option (C) is not a good example because the teacher asks students what they know about the subject after they have read a text, not before. Activating prior knowledge before reading enables students to build upon what they already know when they begin reading, as successful readers do, versus beginning to read without thinking, as less successful readers do. Similarly, the teacher should ask students their opinions and reactions about a topic before they read, not after (D), to activate their existing knowledge.

27. D: Research finds that most teachers can plan differentiated instruction based on the findings of studies, and that they do this better when using individual scores of real students than with invented scores of hypothetical students. Research has found that teachers make data-based instructional decisions better in small groups than individually, not vice versa (A). Studies show that most teachers can locate data in graphs or tables, but have more trouble with data comprehension than vice versa (B). Research also finds that the majority of teachers have difficulty with both interpreting relationships among variables and posing questions (C).

28. C: Conrad's novel deals with characters in colonial Africa, so post-colonial theories would most inform considering how the author treats those characters. Aristotle's theory of unity (A) would be more likely to inform *Oedipus Rex* by Sophocles, Homer's *Iliad* and *Odyssey*, and many other similar—especially classical—works meeting Aristotle's criteria for unity of plot. Feminist and gender theories (B) are more likely to inform a work like *The Awakening* (1899) by Kate Chopin and have popularly been applied to Shakespeare's *The Taming of the Shrew*; Hardy's *Tess of the D'Urbervilles*; D.H. Lawrence's *Women in Love*; and the works of Jane Austen, George Eliot, Charlotte Brontë, and Virginia Woolf, among many others. Marxist theories (D) are more likely to inform the interactions of characters according to their historical and cultural background, social class, and economic circumstances. For example, some have applied Marxist criticism to Ferrol Sams' novel *Run with the Horsemen* (1982) or Langston Hughes' poem "Union" (Collected Poems, 1921-1940).

29. C: Denotation is the literal meaning or dictionary definition of a word. Connotation is the figurative meaning of a word, including emotional or perceptual associations associated with the word but not included in its literal definition. The words "politician" and "statesman" have the same literal meaning or denotation. However, when used in context, "politician" may have either a neutral or negative connotation, whereas "statesman" usually has a positive connotation.

30. A: Expository texts are nonfiction works that give information, like how-to instructions or facts about a given subject. Therefore the most appropriate inferences for the reader to draw would be about cause-and-effect relationships, such as in history books, and/or about problems and their solutions. Reader inferences about what events occurred and things people did (B) are more appropriate when reading a nonfictional biography or autobiography. Reader inferences about what the author wants the audience to believe (C) and about ideas that support the author's

message (D) are more appropriate when reading persuasive or argumentative text, wherein the author works to convince readers of a position, opinion, or argument.

31. D: Common Core Standards for the English Language Arts require "anchor" performance skills for citing textual evidence to support their inferences and analyses (A) of 6th-graders. They require 7th-graders to do this, and additionally to identify several specific pieces of textual evidence to defend their conclusions (B). They require 8th-graders to do both of these, plus to be able to differentiate stronger from weaker textual evidence (C). They require all these, plus citing strong and thorough textual evidence, of 9th- and 10th-graders. They require 11th- and 12th-graders to do all of the aforementioned, as well as to be able to identify which elements in a text are left unclear (D).

32. A, C, and D: Lincoln's statement that our Founding Fathers created the US is a main idea. That it was "conceived in liberty, and dedicated to the proposition that all men are created equal" (B) represents details supporting the main idea of option (A). His statement, "now we are engaged in a great civil war," (C) is another main idea. A supporting detail is that this war is "testing whether that nation, or any nation so conceived and so dedicated, can long endure." His statement that "We have come to dedicate a portion of that field" is another main idea (D). Details supporting the latter main idea include that this field is "a final resting place for those who here gave their lives that that nation might live," and "It is altogether fitting and proper that we should do this" (E).

33. B: In this paired reading strategy, which improves reading comprehension and helps students identify the main idea in informational text, after silently reading a text selection, the pair of students takes turns following these steps: One student paraphrases what s/he thinks the text's main idea is. The other student agrees or disagrees, explaining why. The pair then develops a consensus as to the text's main idea. Then they take turns finding details in the text that support its main idea.

34. B: This is an example of the cause and effect structural pattern of informational text because it recounts the events leading up to World War I in a way that suggests how each event led to the next one by using words like "triggered," "in reaction to," "therefore," and "consequently." The descriptive (A) pattern uses sensory imagery enabling readers to see, hear, feel, smell, and taste things; and/or tells readers the what, who, when, where, and why of the topic. The sequence and order (C) pattern arranges events in chronological sequence, or gives instructions in the order to follow steps. Although this example also relates events in chronological sequence, it is a better example of cause and effect because each successive event is also attributed to the preceding one. The comparison-contrast (D) pattern identifies the similarities and differences among things or ideas. (A fifth pattern is problem-solution.)

35. B: These are examples of grouping animals into categories. Authors connect and distinguish ideas and things in informational texts by making analogies (A), like "a frog is to an insect as a lion is to an antelope"—in other words, predator to prey. Another example includes comparing their similarities (C) and/or contrasting their differences (D). For instance, some animals have simple life cycles; others, like frogs, undergo metamorphosis; and some insects undergo complete metamorphosis including egg, larval, pupal, and adult stages; while other insects, like grasshoppers, dragonflies, and cockroaches undergo incomplete metamorphosis with egg, nymph, and adult stages but no pupal stage.

36. B and E: The index (A), typically in the back of a book, alphabetically lists important topics in the book with their page numbers to aid easy location. Graphs (B), which visually display multiple information sets and their relationships plotted along vertical and horizontal axes, are typically

found throughout a text. Some may be in the back if they are included as part of an appendix. The glossary (C), also usually in the back of the book, is an alphabetized list of vocabulary words or technical terms with definitions to help readers understand unfamiliar or specialized language used in the book. An appendix (D) is an addition in the back of a book with important supplementary information not found in the main text. Footnotes (E) are found at the bottoms of individual pages, referenced in the text body with superscript numbers. Endnotes are like footnotes, but found at the back of the book.

37. D: This use of "smart" has a negative connotation: "a smart answer" here means a disrespectful or impertinent one. This is evident from the sentence context ("Eliot got into trouble"). Options (A) and (C) use the word "smart" with its literal denotation, meaning intelligent or competent. Option (B) uses "smart" with a positive connotation, meaning wise or judicious. The context "he got a good grade" informs this use: Eliot was smart to have studied, meaning he used good judgment when he prepared, evidenced by the positive outcome.

38. D: Writers of technical language, as in scientific informational texts, need to find a balance between seeming too self-deprecating or too grandiose. For example, "our findings will change the world" is grandiose, whereas "our findings are insignificant" is self-deprecating. "Our results are promising and indicate the need for further research" is more balanced. These are examples of the mood of the language. Technical language should be concise (A) by not using superfluous words, impersonal (B) and detached by using passive voice and avoiding overuse of the first person and the vernacular, and professional (C) by using more technical terminology rather than more familiar everyday vocabulary. These are examples of the tone of the language.

39. C: This question is implicit because the text does not explicitly state anything about birds. However, the reader can infer that birds are made of cells because the text does explicitly state that all living things are made of cells, and birds are living things. The other choices are all explicit questions because their answers are stated directly in the text (A: Cells are integral to the bodies of all living things; B: organs and tissues; D: the building blocks of our bodies).

40. A: Authors of scientific informational text, such as research study reports, are likely to state the purpose of their research (B). They are likely to state their interpretations of the evidence or data their study produced (C). And in any acceptable research report, they will always identify which variables they studied, the population in whom they studied them (D), the number of the sample size, the conditions of the experiment, and the research methodology used. However, they are least likely to state explicitly their point of view about their research (A), unlike authors of other types of informational text who directly state their viewpoint about the topic and/or their reason(s) for writing about it.

41. A: To determine an author's unstated point of view in scientific informational text like research reports, the reader can analyze the text to discover what main idea the author is communicating, with which the author likely wants readers to agree. The reader can also examine the author's choice of words (B) and how these affect the readers' perceptions of the text subject. The reader should also consider how the author uses facts and/or examples in the text, and how these choices affect the readers' attitudes (C) toward the topic. Additionally, the reader should consider what s/he thinks the author wanted to accomplish by writing the text (D).

42. D: Reporting case studies is the best example of using rhetoric to provide supporting evidence of an author's main point in an informational text. Writing evocative descriptions (A) is an example of using rhetoric to appeal to the reader's emotions in an informational text, not to provide

supporting evidence. Making good analogies (B) is an example of using rhetoric to illustrate and/or illuminate the author's point(s) rather than actually supporting them with evidence. Telling personal anecdotes (C) is an example of using rhetoric to give readers examples that are more accessible and realistic to illustrate their points, rather than to provide evidence supporting them.

43. D: This is an example of understatement. Using the *carpe diem* tradition as a seduction tactic, Marvell argues that life is short, so he and his mistress should "seize the day" and make love while they can. In the lines quoted, he understates the condition of death by saying people do not embrace in the grave—when they do not live at all, let alone embrace there. Satire (A) is ridiculing people and/or groups to expose and criticize their shortcomings. Jonathan Swift wrote biting satires, including *A Tale of a Tub, A Modest Proposal,* and *Gulliver's Travels.* Hyperbole (B) is extreme exaggeration, like saying "I've told you a million times" or "I have a ton of homework." Verbal irony (A) is using words opposite to their literal meaning: in *Directions to Servants* (1745), Swift wrote, "In Winter Time light the Dining-Room Fire but two Minutes before Dinner is served up, that your Master may see, how saving you are of his Coals"—satirizing servants' habits and lame excuses by presenting them as instructions.

44. B: This is an example of a metaphor. The literal meaning of hemorrhaging is copious bleeding. In this example it is used figuratively in a metaphor for losing money at a volume and rate comparable to severe blood loss denoted by hemorrhage. It is not a generalization (A). An example of using a generalization persuasively is "We all want peace, not war." It is not a rhetorical question (C) or a question at all. An example of using a rhetorical question (needing no answer) persuasively is "Wouldn't you rather get paid more than less?" The example is not of negative connotation (D), because the word "hemorrhage" already has a negative denotation—in other words, the literal meaning of hemorrhaging is never a good thing. An example of using negative word connotation persuasively is, "You could stay with this *expensive* plan..." followed by contrasting positive connotation: "...or choose the *money-saving* plan I'm offering."

45. D: Credibility is related to how believable readers felt the author's writing was, which is a major element of whether the author's appeals changed the readers' minds. Clarity (A), another criterion for evaluating methods of appeal, is related to how clearly the author presented the content. Accuracy (B), an additional criterion, is related to whether the content that the author included was factually correct. Cohesion (C), also an evaluative criterion, has to do with how well the author's arguments and appeals are connected and related to one another, which helps readers understand them and holds their interest.

46. A: Scientists should use technical language to write about technical subjects when they are reporting their research results to colleagues in their own field because they will understand it. However, scientists who also write science fiction (B) will need to write in non-technical language for the popular reading audience to understand it. When scientists write material to support school instruction in the sciences (C), they must also use non-technical language for students and teachers to understand it. And when they write material to support scientific lobbying efforts (D), they must use non-technical language for the politicians who hear or read it to understand the messages they are communicating and the appeals they are making for legislation and/or funding.

47. A: The first step a reader should take in evaluating the arguments in an informational text is to identify the conclusion the author draws with the argument. The second step is to identify what premises or reasons support this conclusion (D). The third step is to clarify these premises or reasons by paraphrasing them (C) in the reader's own words, which can also show whether the premises fit with the conclusion they should support. The reader can then list all premises in order,

followed by the conclusion, and note any assumptions or premises necessary to support the conclusion that the author may have omitted. The next step is judging whether a deductive reasoning argument is valid, or whether an inductive reasoning argument uses true premises that support the conclusion (B).

48. D: One way that a reader can determine that an informational text author may have had a hidden agenda is if the author's stated purposes for writing contradict other parts of the text. When the reader can identify motivations the author has not stated, the reader is better able to evaluate how effective the text is, whether they agree or disagree with it, and why. It is equally true that knowing author purpose enables readers to know what to expect from text (A), that knowing author motivation helps with reading for relevant details (B), and that knowing authors' purposes and motivations facilitates critical reader evaluation of author and text (C). However, option (D) is most related to the importance of discovering unstated author purposes for evaluating text.

49. C: Sample 1's author cites evidence that is tangential to his argument, hence it is not relevant. Sample 2's author cites anecdotal evidence which is inaccurate, hence it is not factual. Sample 3's author cites evidence which is factual (accurate) and relevant (directly related), but not sufficient (an isolated example uncorroborated by any other sources). Criteria for evaluating evidence used in informational text include that the evidence be relevant, factual, and sufficient to accomplish the author's purpose (for example, proving the author's point or points and/or persuading the reader).

50. C: This is an example of a slippery slope argument that is a logical fallacy. The fallacious form of the slippery slope is essentially a non sequitur—it argues that one thing will cause other things without showing any cause-and-effect relationship between them. A straw man (A) argument is a logical fallacy which, instead of refuting someone else's actual argument, refutes an exaggeration or caricature of it. A red herring (B) is a piece of irrelevant information introduced to distract attention from the real issue. *Post hoc ergo propter hoc* (D) is Latin for "After this, therefore because of this." It means arguing that one thing was caused by another that happened before it. This is a logical fallacy because, like correlation, chronological order does not equal causation.

51. C: "Although we liked Bill and Hillary" is a dependent clause. It is a clause because it has a subject, "we," and a verb, "liked." It is dependent or subordinate because it begins with a subordinating conjunction, "although." So it cannot stand alone as an independent clause (B), but depends on and modifies the independent clause "we did not go (to their party)." It is not a prepositional phrase (A) as it does not begin with a preposition. It is not a complete sentence (D) because it is not an independent clause.

52. A: "To their party" and "for us" are prepositional phrases because they begin with the prepositions "to" and "for," respectively. The first phrase modifies the predicate (verb) "go"; the second modifies the dependent clause "because there were (too many people there)": "for" is the preposition; the pronoun "us" is the object of the preposition. "Although we liked..." and "because there were..." (B) are both dependent clauses. "We did not go" (C) is an independent clause. "Too many people" is an adverbial phrase modifying the verb "were": "too" is an adverb modifying the adjective "many," which modifies the noun "people" (D).

53. D: This is a compound-complex sentence because it contains two independent clauses plus dependent clauses. A simple (A) sentence is a single independent clause. A complex (B) sentence consists of one independent clause and one dependent clause, such as "After she went to the party, she went home." A compound (C) sentence consists of two independent clauses connected by a conjunction, like "She went to the party, and then she went home."

54. B: "Nancy also felt that the party was too crowded" is an independent clause because it has a subject ("Nancy"), verb ("felt"), and could stand alone as a complete sentence. "The hosts would have been hurt" is also an independent clause. These two independent clauses are joined by the coordinating conjunction "but." "Who relied so much on her" (A) is a dependent clause modifying the subject of the second independent clause, "the hosts." "If she had not attended" (C) is an adjectival dependent clause, introduced by the subordinating conjunction "if" and modifying the predicate "would have been hurt" in the second independent clause. "That the party was too crowded" (D) is an adverbial dependent clause, introduced by the subordinating conjunction "that" and modifying the verb "felt."

55. B: The prefix *pro-* from Latin means before, earlier, prior to; for or forward; or front. Prefixes come at the beginnings of words. Suffixes come at the ends of words; and *pro-* does not mean good, on top of, or over (A). The Greek prefix *eu-* means good, the Latin prefix *supra-* means above, and the Latin prefix *super-* can mean over and above, among other meanings. Prefixes and suffixes are both affixes (C); however, *pro-* does not mean after, behind, or in back of. The Latin prefix *post-* means after or behind, and *retro-* means back or backward. *Pro-* does not mean against, under, or below (D). *Sub-* means under or below; *anti-* means against.

56. A: *–Tion* is a suffix because it comes at the end of a word. It turns a verb into a noun: *attend* becomes *attention, convert* becomes *conversion, present-presentation, converse-conversation, ambulate-ambulation,* and more. Prefixes, suffixes, and infixes are all affixes. However, *-tion* does not turn nouns into pronouns (B). Pronouns are *I, me, we, us, you, he, she, they, them, it* (personal pronouns); *this, that, these, those, such* (demonstrative pronouns); *who, whom, which, that* (relative pronouns); *somebody, anybody, everybody, each, every, all, some, none, one* (indefinite pronouns); *myself, ourselves, yourself, himself, herself, themselves* (intensive or reflexive pronouns); and many more. The *–tion* suffix does not come at beginnings of words and hence is not a prefix, and does not make nouns into verbs (C)—such as *fright* into *frighten*—but vice versa. Infixes come in the middles of words, like *s* in *mothers-in-law* or *passers-by*; or in expressions like "abso-blooming-lutely" in *My Fair Lady.* *–Tion* is not an infix and does not make a noun into an adjective (D), such as *danger* into *dangerous.*

57. A and C: We can tell from the context that in the first sentence, *progress* is a noun because it is the object of the verb "has made" and is modified by the adjective "remarkable." The object of the verb cannot be another verb, and adjectives modify nouns, not verbs. The noun "progress" is pronounced with the first syllable stressed. From the context, we can tell that in the second sentence *progress* is a verb because it modifies the noun subject "work." Nouns do not modify other nouns, and the subject needs a verb. The verb *progress* is pronounced with the second syllable stressed.

58. B: Because "his bark" refers to the dog in the first sentence, the context informs us that here "bark" means the vocal sound that a dog makes. Because "its bark" refers to the aspen tree in the second sentence, the context informs us that here "bark" means the covering of a tree trunk. Hence it is not true that it is impossible to tell the meaning in each sentence despite identical spelling and pronunciation (A). Option (C) reverses the meanings in the two sentences. The word "bark" is not misspelled in either sentence (D). "Bark" in the first sentence and "bark" in the second sentence are both homonyms—meaning they sound the same, and also homographs—meaning they are spelled the same, but they have different meanings.

59. A: "Light" is the subject of the sentence. "From yonder window" is a prepositional phrase beginning with the preposition "from," then the adjective "yonder," modifying the object "window," an indirect object modifying the verb "breaks." Subject-verb-object (B) is the typical syntax of most English sentences; Shakespeare changes this by placing the verb at the end of the sentence instead of after the subject and before the object as is most common. Option (C) would be "From yonder window what light breaks?" And option (D) would be "Breaks from yonder window what light?

60. A: Millay's meaning, in more ordinary syntax, is "all that I was once" (or "all that I once was"). She did not mean "Once I was all that" (B), "that I once all was" (C), or "that all I was once" (D). These either mean something different and/or do not make sense. She makes her syntax more unusual and poetic, first by placing the adverb "once" ahead of the subject and verb; and second by reversing the usual order of subject + verb, "I was" to verb + subject, "was I."

61. A: Nuances are subtle distinctions of word meaning in writing (or of color in art, among others). Of the choices offered, "maintains" is most similar in nuance of meaning to "insists," as both imply that the quoted author is adamant about the statement. "Suggests" (B) has a much less forceful, more diffident, or even hesitant nuance. "Explains" (C) implies that the quoted author clarifies something we might not understand otherwise. "Points out" (D) implies that the quoted author is calling our attention to something we might otherwise overlook. "Remarks," "comments," and "observes" have similar nuances to one another.

62. C: Assonance is using the same or similar vowel sounds internally in nearby words, as Thomas has done with the /e/ (or /ɛi/) sound in "age," "rave," "day," "rage" (repeated), "grave," "gay," and "rage"(repeated again); and with also with the /ai/ sound in "dying," "light," "blinding," "sight," "blind," "eyes," and "light" again. Anaphora (A) is repeating the same word or phrase at the beginnings of consecutive verses/clauses, as Winston Churchill did in his 1940 speech: "...We shall fight in France, we shall fight on the seas and oceans, we shall fight... in the air... we shall fight on the beaches, we shall fight on the landing grounds, we shall fight in the fields... we shall fight in the hills..." Alliteration (B) is repeating the same initial consonant sound in consecutive words, as Emily Dickinson did in "The soul selects her own society" or Wallace Stevens in "...in kitchen cups concupiscent curds" ("The Emperor of Ice Cream"). (In the song *Werewolves of London,* Warren Zevon combined alliteration and assonance in the verse, "Little old lady got mutilated late last night.") Apostrophe (D) is interrupting discourse to address an absent or nonexistent person, thing, or quality.

63. D: She should use the glossaries in the textbooks that were her research sources. Glossaries are alphabetized lists of vocabulary or terminology specifically used in the text with their definitions. These will give the correct spellings, and she can also use the definitions to ensure the correct spelling among very similar words. She should not use the spell checker (A) of her computer's word processing software program because these programs typically do not recognize specialized terminology or vocabulary specific to peculiar disciplines. She should not use a style manual (B), which she would only consult to find the correct format for citing references and the paper format specified in a particular style (MLA, APA, Turabian, and so on). She should not necessarily use a dictionary (C) before the glossaries in her reference texts because, although many good dictionaries include specialized terminology and vocabulary words, they may not include them all. If she is using specialized terms in her paper that she found in the research texts, the glossaries of said texts will most likely include these.

64. D: This quotation is dialogue spoken by the servant Joseph in the 1847 novel *Wuthering Heights* by Emily Brontë. It is typical of the English spoken by the working class in Yorkshire, the largest

county in Northern England, during the 19th century. People in the American South during the early 20th century (A) did not speak this way. Examples of their speech can be found in Harper Lee's novel *To Kill a Mockingbird* (1960), which represents Southern American dialect during the 1930s. Colonial Indian English dialects (B) vary widely phonologically, to the extent that they are not mutually understandable, including Babu, Butler/Bearer, Bazaar, and Hindi English. None of these sounds like the dialect in the quotation. Despite the use of the word "lass," the quotation's dialect does not represent rural Scottish dialect (C).

65. C: This quotation is dialogue spoken by Jim, the African-American slave. Twain was representing the typical dialect of an uneducated slave in the American South of the 19th century. Twain used a distinctly different dialect for the dialogue spoken by Huck, who is also uneducated and poor but white (A). Huck's friend Tom Sawyer also speaks with the casualness of youth and in a Southern regional white dialect, but his dialogue, reflecting more education, is more grammatical and contains fewer folk expressions than Huck's (B). Miss Watson also speaks like a 19th-century Southerner, but in contrast her speech reflects the refined, formal qualities of more extensive education, wealth, and age (D).

66. D: Research-based vocabulary instruction findings show that children need ample word repetition, but not through drilling (A). Multiple exposures to the same words in different contexts are more effective. Multiple and repeated exposures are important because children do not learn vocabulary through only one or two exposures to a new word (B). Research finds that they do not simply learn vocabulary in texts indirectly from reading (C); instead, teachers must give them direct instruction in the new vocabulary words they find in their texts.

67. C: In the fifth of seven reader steps for evaluating argumentative writing, readers assess whether the author's argument is complete. Some authors may not present enough supporting evidence. Or they may omit information that detracts from their argument, making their argument incomplete (A) rather than including such detracting material and then refuting it, which makes the argument more complete. The reader's sixth step is to determine the validity of the author's argument. While argumentation may sway reader opinion by influencing reader feelings, valid arguments also use clear, logical reasoning rather than relying solely upon emotional appeals (B); the points they make follow a sequence, with one leading to the next (C). The seventh reader step is to decide if the argument is credible. For an argument to be believable it must first be valid, hence option (D) is incorrect.

68. C: Proving that something is factual, accurate, or true is typically what a writer of argumentative or persuasive writing does. Writers of explanatory writing, in contrast, will assume that something is factual, accurate, and true (B) and then analyze, explain, and clarify this information to help readers understand it. This explanation can include differentiating among members of a given category (A); defining certain terms; analyzing or breaking down processes into their stages, phases, steps, or components; and/or developing concepts (D) for the reading audience. Argumentative writing works to convince readers that something is so; explanatory writing works to explain why something is so.

69. A: A fictional novel is a form of narrative writing that tells a story. In addition to plot and setting, characters are key elements of narrative. In developing characters, authors depict their personality characteristics, mannerisms, behaviors, and interactions with other characters for audiences interested in personalities, motivations, and relationships in stories. A how-to manual (B) is informational writing. The author's purpose is informing how to do something by giving sequential steps, diagrams, and/or descriptions of the order and/or manner in which it should be done, for

readers seeking specific instructions in how to complete a process or task. The writer of a persuasive essay (C) has the purpose of convincing readers to agree with a point or argument. The audience is interested in the issue being argued. The writer of an explanatory paper (D) would seek to clarify facts, ideas, or processes for an audience seeking to understand these.

70. A: Blogs (short for "web logs") are published online, where anybody with Internet access may read them. Bloggers may post occasionally, monthly, weekly, daily, or whenever they want. It is not uncommon for bloggers to post weekly or daily. Journals are more typical for private entries, similar to diaries. People often make journal entries daily or less often, similarly to blog posts but less publicly. (Some people also publish journals—in print or online as collections in books or e-books, or as ongoing online publications similar to blogs. However, journal writing is more often private, whereas blogging never is.) Letters (B) are typically to others, not private (except for therapeutic letters written to vent emotions but never sent); and though sometimes published online (such as letters to the editor, open letters, or newsletters, among others), usually not daily (C). Essays (C) are typically not written daily and privately or published online. Speeches (D) are typically written for oral delivery, not daily online publication or as private activities.

71. C: The titles named are all epistolary novels, or novels told in the form of series of letters written by their characters. They are not picaresque novels (A), which tell the adventures of a roguish antihero (*pícaro* means "rogue" in Spanish) and are often humorous and/or satirical. Popular examples include Miguel de Cervantes' *Don Quixote*, Henry Fielding's *Joseph Andrews* and *Tom Jones*, and Charles Dickens' *Martin Chuzzlewit. The History of Emily Montague* by Frances Brooke (1769) was the first novel written in North America, as well as an epistolary novel, but the others were not first novels in their countries (B). Mary Shelley's *Frankenstein* (1818) was written in the 19th century; therefore, not all of these novels were written in the 18th century (D).

72. A: Bloggers need to use correct punctuation to encourage continued reading of their posts. If they are not already confident in their grasp of punctuation, they should write in shorter sentences (C) until they are. Because reading on computer screens is harder than on paper, paragraphs in blogs must be significantly shorter than in print, not longer (B). Shorter paragraphs enable readers to "chunk" the information. Font sizes should be larger rather than smaller (D) to be easier on readers' eyes and more legible onscreen.

73. D and E: Bloggers need to be consistent throughout by writing their story or argument sequentially (D) with a beginning, middle, and end because online readers often do not read in order as often as readers of print media with consecutive pages do. Blank spaces within the text should not be avoided (A) but provided regularly, because readers' eyes and brains are taxed by blogs that are too visually busy. For the same reason, text should be broken up by images (B), which are also attention-getting and more visually appealing than solid text. Capital letters, italics, and boldface should be used only for highlighting, not throughout text (C). Online paragraphs should be narrower (E) than in print, such as 80 characters or fewer (including spaces) to make online reading easier.

74. C: Persuasive or argumentative writing uses a combination of logic, proof, supporting evidence; and subjective, expressive language to influence reader feelings and beliefs. Descriptive writing also appeals to reader emotions, as well as reader imaginations and senses, by vividly portraying sensory details to recreate experiences, events, and scenes so that readers feel they are also experiencing what is described. Speculative writing does not aim to convince readers as persuasive writing does (A). It does not aim to recreate experiences for readers as descriptive writing does (B). Rather, speculative writing invites readers to explore diverse ideas and their potential outcomes. As

such, it uses looser structure and less definitive points than persuasive or expository writing. Narrative writing aims primarily to tell a story. This may include affecting reader feelings through subjective, expressive language. However, explanatory (D) writing does not share this characteristic; it aims to inform readers and explain information to them.

75. A: *Regardless* is a transitional word that indicates contrast between the previous idea(s) or point(s) and the following one(s). Others include *nonetheless, even so,* and *however. Furthermore* (B) is a transitional word that indicates sequence. Others include *moreover, besides, also,* and *finally. Subsequently* (C) is a transitional word indicating time. Others include *thereafter, immediately, previously, simultaneously, so far, presently, since, soon,* and *at last. It may appear* (D) is a transitional phrase indicating concession. Others include *granted that, of course,* and *although it is true that.* Transitions can also indicate place, examples, comparison, cause and effect, repetition, summary, and conclusion. These all enhance coherence by connecting ideas and sentences.

76. A: The introduction of an essay should get the reader's attention, engage the reader's interest, state and integrate the main thesis within it, and give an overview of the essay's organization or structure (for example, by summarizing the main point and supporting evidence). Developing the thesis statement (B) and giving examples of the idea in the thesis (C) both belong in the body of the essay. Giving the reader a sense of closure (D) belongs in the conclusion of the essay.

77. A: When students write the concluding paragraphs of their essays and they restate their main thesis, it is better to paraphrase it rather than to repeat the same thesis statement from the essay's introduction word for word (B). Teachers should advise students NOT to apologize for the opinions they expressed or their writing technique (C) in essay conclusions. They should also instruct students that it is NOT necessary for them to use their conclusions to summarize the essay every single time (D).

78. C: The word "literature" has multiple meanings. A general meaning is all the written works in a given language (A), such as English literature. It can also mean the profession of a writer or author (B). "Literature" is also used to mean any kinds of printed materials (D), like a company's promotional or informational literature, including pamphlets, brochures, and the like. However, in research fields, "literature" means all the research previously published on a given subject (C), such as research on self-correction in the psychology field of applied behavior analysis, or on instructional strategies in the English language arts field of writing instruction.

79. B: In a research paper, the problem statement follows both the title and the abstract; it does not come before the abstract (A). It identifies the issue under study, and explains why the issue is important to the writer (B). It also establishes the context for the body of the paper (C). In addition, the problem statement defines the scope of the research being reported by identifying the specific variables of focus in the research, and shows what is important about these variables (D).

80. D: To evaluate source credibility, researchers consider not only an author's reputation in the field, but equally whether s/he cites sources (A). These two commonly (but not always) go hand-in-hand: generally, authors respected in their fields are responsible and cite sources. (In popular fields, some individuals gain favorable reputations without responsible scholarship. This is less common in rigorous academic fields.) In some rapidly changing fields, for instance information technologies, sources must be current; in others, such as 19th-century American history (barring new historical discoveries), information published decades ago may still be accurate (B). Researchers must consider author point of view and purpose, which affect neutrality. Sources from certain points of view can be credible, but may restrict subject treatment to one side of a debate (C).

Audience values influence what they consider credible (D): younger readers accept Internet sources more, academics value refereed journals, and local community residents may value mainstream sources like *Newsweek* magazine.

81. A: When a researcher has conducted an original experiment and reports the results, findings, and associated conclusions in a research report, that report is considered a primary source. Academic textbooks, journal articles, articles in other periodicals, and authoritative databases may all be primary sources. When an academic textbook cites research (B) by others, that citation is considered a secondary source as it refers to information originally presented by others. When a news article quotes a researcher's writing (C), that is also a secondary source. So is a description given on a website of another person's research (D).

82. B: If a researcher finds too little material about a research question, s/he should broaden the question, which may be too narrow to yield enough literature. If there is an unmanageable, seemingly unlimited amount of literature, s/he likely needs to narrow, not broaden the research question (A) because it is too general. Many people voluntarily doing research enjoy information and can get overwhelmed by all the data they find. Knowing the research question in advance can keep the wealth of information from impeding progress (C). On new topics, sometimes no research literature exists yet. This does not mean that no type of searching helps (D): Doing systematic searches can help, for example, first through periodical abstracts to get an overview of literature related to the topic, then through references cited in specific sources like individual research papers, and/or references cited in general sources like books about specific related topics.

83: B: The first thing a researcher should look for in a review of the existing literature related to a specific research question is whether that question has already been definitively answered. If so, the researcher should ask a different research question. If the question has not already been answered conclusively, then the researcher can look for gaps in knowledge about the topic that searching the literature reveals (A); review the literature to find what needs and opportunities for further research other researchers have identified (C); examine the literature to discern whether there is consensus, controversy, or both; and if so, what those opinions are about the topic (D). These considerations help inform the direction for research.

84. C: A big advantage of digital text tools is that teachers and students alike need minimal training to use them. Teachers can italicize or boldface certain words in text (A), like those with Latin or Greek roots, or literary devices like similes and metaphors (and more) to call them to students' attention. A big difference between physical highlighter pens and digital highlighters (B) is that marks made by highlighter pens cannot be removed or changed, whereas digital highlights can easily be removed, or simply hidden and then displayed again. They can be changed according to changing student needs, a distinct advantage rather than a disadvantage (D).

85. C: The fact that digital networking enables educators and learners to communicate nearly instantly with a variety of experts, mentors, and peers all over the world has transformed the social interactions available in the educational community, as well as otherwise. Additional advantages of digital networking include that digital educational resources can be linked to one another (A); that embedded hyperlinks afford students easy access to learning supports like electronic notepads, graphic organizers, supplementary information, reading comprehension prompts, encyclopedias, dictionaries and thesauruses, and more (B); and that the diversity of digital formats available provide experiences more similar in their diversity to that of individual students (D). These advantages are all transformative of learning itself. Option (C) is an advantage transformative

specifically of social interactions (including remote and long-distance) within the learning process, as well as of learning.

86. C: Writing instruction strategies proven effective by multiple research studies include brainstorming (A) to plan before writing; explicit instruction (B) of students by teachers in techniques for planning, revising, and editing compositions; explicit instruction in steps to follow for writing argumentation; collaborative work (D) among students to plan, write, edit, and revise their writing in groups; and teacher modeling (C) of writing strategies. Of these, teacher modeling should be introduced initially, and then gradually faded as students gain experience and confidence with practice until they independently apply the strategies consistently.

87. D: According to research-based writing instruction strategies, when teachers assign students to small collaborative writing groups, they should set individual performance expectations for within-group as well as individual work (A). Teachers should also support student groups by providing them with structure (B). Classmates in collaborative writing groups should give each other both positive feedback (C) for reinforcement and constructive feedback for correction as well.

88. D: Research studies have shown that setting specific goals for writing promotes student motivation (A) and sense of accomplishment. Developing student writing goals should not be a responsibility confined either to teachers (B) or students (C): both teachers and students (D) may develop writing goals, such as including more ideas within one paper, or incorporating specific elements of certain genres in compositions. Teachers and students may develop goals individually, in collaboration, and/or both: students together, teachers together, and students with teachers—including individual students, student groups, individual teachers, and team/co-teachers.

89. A: One research-based writing instruction strategy teachers can use is to give students explicit instruction in combining simple sentences into compound, complex, and compound-complex sentences. This develops student ability to compose more sophisticated sentences. Computer word-processing programs are not crutches and do not interfere with independent student writing skills (B); on the contrary, teachers can use these as a strategy to help students engage in the processes of planning, writing, and editing more easily. A process writing approach is another research-based instructional strategy, not an incompatible one (C). It allows students extended practice with planning, composing, and reviewing; interacting with classmates while writing; owning writing responsibility; writing for real audiences; and self-evaluating writing. Research finds that teachers should not only provide good models of writing types and help them analyze these, but also encourage them to emulate these models (D) in their own writing efforts.

90. C: Research studies have found that explicit instruction, teacher modeling, teacher think-alouds, and scaffolding (graduated, faded support) are all effective methods of writing instruction for all students. Research also shows that procedural strategies including mnemonic devices, graphic organizers, outlining, and checklists are helpful to students for planning and revision of writing; these are not wastes of time (A). Studies find that teaching cognitive strategies helps students of all ages and ability levels, not just some (B). Teaching self-regulation not only improves student awareness of their writing strengths and weaknesses, it also makes their writing work more strategic, empowers them to adapt the strategies they learn as they need, and increases their generalization and maintenance of the writing strategies they have learned (D).

91. B: Teachers should base rubrics on their identified lesson objectives. They should explain a rubric to students in advance, and have students refer to the rubric as a guide while they work. Teachers should then use the rubric to assess whether students have met all included learning

objectives. Rubrics can be used as both formative (A) and summative (C) assessment tools, meaning they were assessed either during or after the work, respectively. Rubrics are not replacements for clearly stating learning goals, objectives, expectations, and teacher modeling of expected performance (D): teachers should do all of these to enable optimal student performance, as well as supply a rubric to guide and assess student work. Teachers should also make very clear to students the relationship between learning goals and their performance.

92. A: Teachers should generally use a variety of formal and informal assessment instruments to get a complete picture of student achievement. This is especially applicable for grouping students, which teachers should never do for the long term based on the results of only one assessment instrument. To conduct formative assessments of learning in progress, teachers should use both formal and informal test instruments (B); and use several different kinds, rather than choosing only one formal instrument to use exclusively (C). Formative assessment results are valuable not only for evaluating student progress, but moreover for use in the classroom as teaching tools (D).

93. D: Teachers should give students learning English as a second language (ESL) and English language learners (ELLs) clear models and examples of what they expect them to do, how to do it, and how the completed results should look. Stating directions verbally in English alone (A) is insufficient for students learning a foreign language. Teachers must also give ELLs more time to respond (B) because it takes them longer to process the English they hear, mentally translate it into their own language, mentally formulate a response in their own language, translate that mentally into English, and judge whether their translation makes sense before they answer. It typically takes ESLs years before they can "think in English." When using idioms and figures of speech, teachers should explain these to ELLs (C) and add pantomime demonstrations to help them understand. These expressions are not logical and often have no L1 equivalents for ESLs, so they require explicit instruction.

94. A: Research finds one helpful instructional strategy for ELL student language acquisition is to have them explain and/or retell what the teacher just said to their classmates. This not only ensures their comprehension, it also gives them practice analyzing the English they hear, restating/paraphrasing English, and communicating to others in spoken English. Teachers should incorporate visual aids (B): studies show supplementing verbal input visually helps ELLs understand concepts in subject content areas as they are learning a foreign language. Research finds that students cannot grasp abstract concepts as readily in a foreign language, so teachers should give them concrete objects, pictures, and the like to illustrate and demonstrate ideas as students gradually transition from concrete to abstract in a new language (C). Teachers can arrange for ELLs to signal when they don't understand; they also closely observe ELLs, and if they do not indicate or demonstrate understanding, should elaborate (D) by summarizing, paraphrasing, and giving synonyms.

95. D: Written tests (A) traditionally used to assess learning in native English-speaking students are typically not as effective with ESL students, as they do not reveal and may even interfere with ESL student demonstration of what they know and have learned. Oral assessments (B) and/or performance assessments (C) are generally more authentic measures with students learning English.

96. B: Typical speech is roughly 125 words per minute, while typical thinking is estimated at roughly 500 words per minute. This natural disparity does not make listening less effective than reading (A). While the slower rate of speech and the faster rate of thought does allow students' minds to wander, teachers can have students make use of this time by instructing them to

summarize mentally the speech they hear as an active listening technique. This enables students to process, consider, and manipulate heard information and make richer, more creative decisions about it. Listening and learning share the common characteristics of being both social (C) and reciprocal (D).

97. C: An effective teacher technique for meeting learning goals in classroom discussions if students get off the subject is to restate the topics and questions they previously stated. Another good redirection technique is to ask new questions about the same topics. To encourage creative and varied student responses, teachers should ask questions instead of making comments, not vice versa (A). Teachers' making comments discourages students from doing the same, whereas asking questions invites them to offer different feedback. When some students dominate the discussion, a technique whereby teachers can engage more reticent students is to ask less challenging questions, not more (B): less challenging questions can be answered by any student, even unprepared ones. A checklist based on the class attendance roll is a good way to assess whether all students are participating (D).

98. A: A PowerPoint presentation is designed as a visual aid to summarize and highlight the main points in a speaker's talk. PowerPoint slides commonly feature brief verbal phrases and sentences; are often numbered or bulleted; and also may include pictures, diagrams, graphs, and more. The slides not only visualize the speaker's main points for audiences, guide listeners through the presentation, and facilitate note-taking and outlining by listeners, they also help keep the speaker organized and on the subject. The slides provide an outline of the presentation; the speaker supplies the additional details. A poster (B) is a visual aid, but not a technological tool. It would also not add as much to the presentation as a PowerPoint. A blog (C) and a wiki (D) are both designed for audiences to read online, not to read while someone is speaking or to listen to someone reading them aloud.

99. A, D, and E: Most research studies have found that blended instruction, which combines online and traditional face-to-face classroom teaching, achieves the best student outcomes. Most studies have not found traditional face-to-face instruction superior to online (B) or online-only instruction superior to blended instruction (C). In one study, student writing performance was better from traditional face-to-face instruction, but student oral and written comprehension was not significantly different regardless of teaching method (D). In another study comparing two courses, both blending face-to-face teaching with web-based activities, students performed better with an online teacher than students with a teacher in classrooms did (E).

100. B: In his Multiple Intelligences theory, Howard Gardner defines the Logical-Mathematical intelligence type as the ability to identify symbolic, numerical, and logical forms and patterns. A teacher could support a student high in this intelligence by assigning activities like designing and utilizing spreadsheets, organizing and analyzing data, and making estimates and predictions. Writing and giving an oral presentation (A) is an activity that would support a student high in Gardner's Verbal-Linguistic intelligence type, who excels in spoken and written language and verbal communication. Composing and performing a song (C) is an activity that would support a student high in Gardner's Musical-Rhythmic intelligence, as that student can appreciate and/or produce music and rhythms. A cooperative learning project (D) is an activity that would support a student high in Gardner's Interpersonal intelligence type, who can detect and understand others' emotions and interacts well with others.

101. B: Students high in the Bodily-Kinesthetic intelligence learn best through hands-on activities like dancing, sports, and using manipulatives. Those high in Intrapersonal (A) intelligence excel at

being in tune with, understanding, and explaining their own feelings; they learn best through reflective, metacognitive, and independent activities. Those high in the Naturalist (C) intelligence type relate to the natural world and can identify and appreciate patterns in nature. They learn best by observing, studying, classifying, and collecting natural objects and/or studying or interacting with animals. Students high in the Visual-Spatial (D) intelligence excel at visual perception and converting three-dimensional reality into two-dimensional media forms. They learn best through drawing, mapping, reading and making graphs and illustrations, and spatial visualization problems.

102. A: In classrooms based on differentiated instruction, the most common differentiation is the way in which individual students access the content they learn, as individual student differences often dictate differential means of access. It is common for learning goals to be assessed by standardized testing, which is not differentiated as often (B) except when individual students require alternative assessment. All students in the differentiated classroom should be taught the same concepts (C). The only differentiation is the level of complexity at which concepts are taught, which is individualized. Instructional concepts should not be detailed, but broad and generalized (D) for all students to acquire the same principles and skills.

103. C: Lexile measures assign numbers to many books and articles that identify their reading levels, from below to 200L to above 1700L. These are reading levels not to be confused with grade levels (A). Students can also be assigned Lexile measure numbers through their scores on standardized reading tests they may be given in school. Teachers and students can select texts that correspond to a range around a student's Lexile measure; 50L above and 100L below the student's number is a recommended range. Lexile measures do not find these texts; teachers and/or students do. They are not advised to find only texts exactly matching a student's number (B), as this would overly restrict available reading material and is unnecessary. Students can generally read and enjoy texts in a range around their level. Lexile measures are not assigned to every book and article published (D); over 80 million articles and over 100,000 articles have Lexile measure numbers, providing identification of ample reading matter for those wishing to use this system.

104. A and B: Findings of research into adolescent literacy instruction indicate the strongest support for giving adolescent students explicit instruction in vocabulary (A) and reading comprehension (B). Research also finds support for extended and open student discussion of the texts they are reading, for enhancing teen students' motivation for literacy (D), and for enhancing teen students' engagement in literacy (E). All of these are found important by research, but options (A) and (B) have been proven the most important of all.

105. B: *Activating* is the term experts use to identify the reading strategy whereby the reader activates prior knowledge and applies it to the new information in reading to construct meaning from it. *Inferring* (A) is a strategy whereby the reader combines what the text states explicitly with what it does not state but implies, and combines these both with what s/he already knows to draw inferences. *Questioning* (C) is the reading strategy whereby the reader engages in "learning dialogues" with the text, author, classmates, and teachers to ask and answer questions about the text. *Summarizing* (D) is the reading strategy whereby the reader paraphrases or restates what s/he perceives as the text's meaning.

106. C: A good summary of text captures the main ideas, omitting the details (A) and other less important information (B). A summary does not literally retell (D) the text or repeat it word for word. It shows reader comprehension by paraphrasing the major meaning of the text in the reader's own words.

107. A: Metacognition is the ability to "think about thinking," or the ability to reflect on, analyze, and understand one's own thinking processes. Through the process approach to writing, students learn how to evaluate their own writing in more objective and constructive ways. In the process approach, students interact more often and consistently with their peers while writing. This element of student interactions (B) is more related to collaboration and social skills than metacognition. Another element of process writing is the identification of authentic audiences (C): knowing for whom they are writing helps students focus on achieving specific purposes and identifying which kinds of reasoning, logic, tone, and word choice to appeal to those audiences. This is more other-oriented than metacognitive or self-oriented. Process writing also includes the element of personal student responsibility for writing (D). Such ownership enables greater independence in student choices, craft, practice, and motivation more than self-analysis of cognitive processes.

108. B: Because they are done during learning in progress, formative assessments enable teachers to make changes to their instruction via the feedback the assessment gives them. If one strategy or technique is not working, they can modify it or substitute another one, increase or decrease the pace of procedures, increase or decrease repetitions, or change instructional modalities (among others) to tailor instruction to the individual student's learning rates, needs, styles, preferences, and interests to optimize learning. Hence formative assessments also help students meet standards-based goals on time. Summative assessments cannot do this (A) because they are given after instruction is completed and less often, so they do not allow time to change ongoing instruction to expedite progress. Formative assessments typically involve students more in the assessment processes, not summative assessments (C). Summative assessments are more often used to provide accountability and to calculate student grades, not formative assessments (D).

109. C: The acronym *K.I.M.* in a K.I.M. vocabulary chart stands for Key idea, Information, and Memory clue. Hence option (A) is incorrect. Under the "K" for Key idea, the student enters a vocabulary word (C); hence option (B) is incorrect. Under the "I" for Information, the student enters the definition of the word. Under the "M" for Memory clue, students often make a drawing or attach a picture, sometimes including written or printed captions, to remind them of the word's meaning; hence option (D) is incorrect.

110. A: One self-monitoring strategy to aid reading comprehension is for students to locate the problem by isolating what part of the text they did not understand, which words were difficult, and specifically what did not make sense to them. Another self-monitoring strategy for students is trying to paraphrase the text they had trouble understanding, which often helps (B). An additional strategy is to review the text for earlier instances of the same topic or information the student finds unclear to see if those shed light on the current instance. This can inform reading and is not a waste of time (C). Another self-monitoring strategy is to preview the text to see if explanations, elaboration, illustrations or other graphics later in the text might clarify what students are currently reading. Looking ahead does not make a comprehension problem worse (D), and sometimes solves it.

Secret Key #1 - Time is Your Greatest Enemy

Pace Yourself

Wear a watch. At the beginning of the test, check the time (or start a chronometer on your watch to count the minutes), and check the time after every few questions to make sure you are "on schedule."

If you are forced to speed up, do it efficiently. Usually one or more answer choices can be eliminated without too much difficulty. Above all, don't panic. Don't speed up and just begin guessing at random choices. By pacing yourself, and continually monitoring your progress against your watch, you will always know exactly how far ahead or behind you are with your available time. If you find that you are one minute behind on the test, don't skip one question without spending any time on it, just to catch back up. Take 15 fewer seconds on the next four questions, and after four questions you'll have caught back up. Once you catch back up, you can continue working each problem at your normal pace.

Furthermore, don't dwell on the problems that you were rushed on. If a problem was taking up too much time and you made a hurried guess, it must be difficult. The difficult questions are the ones you are most likely to miss anyway, so it isn't a big loss. It is better to end with more time than you need than to run out of time.

Lastly, sometimes it is beneficial to slow down if you are constantly getting ahead of time. You are always more likely to catch a careless mistake by working more slowly than quickly, and among very high-scoring test takers (those who are likely to have lots of time left over), careless errors affect the score more than mastery of material.

Secret Key #2 - Guessing is not Guesswork

You probably know that guessing is a good idea. Unlike other standardized tests, there is no penalty for getting a wrong answer. Even if you have no idea about a question, you still have a 20-25% chance of getting it right.

Most test takers do not understand the impact that proper guessing can have on their score. Unless you score extremely high, guessing will significantly contribute to your final score.

Monkeys Take the Test

What most test takers don't realize is that to insure that 20-25% chance, you have to guess randomly. If you put 20 monkeys in a room to take this test, assuming they answered once per question and behaved themselves, on average they would get 20-25% of the questions correct. Put 20 test takers in the room, and the average will be much lower among guessed questions. Why?

1. The test writers intentionally write deceptive answer choices that "look" right. A test taker has no idea about a question, so he picks the "best looking" answer, which is often wrong. The monkey has no idea what looks good and what doesn't, so it will consistently be right about 20-25% of the time.
2. Test takers will eliminate answer choices from the guessing pool based on a hunch or intuition. Simple but correct answers often get excluded, leaving a 0% chance of being correct. The monkey has no clue, and often gets lucky with the best choice.

This is why the process of elimination endorsed by most test courses is flawed and detrimental to your performance. Test takers don't guess; they make an ignorant stab in the dark that is usually worse than random.

$5 Challenge

Let me introduce one of the most valuable ideas of this course—the $5 challenge:

- *You only mark your "best guess" if you are willing to bet $5 on it.*
- *You only eliminate choices from guessing if you are willing to bet $5 on it.*

Why $5? Five dollars is an amount of money that is small yet not insignificant, and can really add up fast (20 questions could cost you $100). Likewise, each answer choice on one question of the test will have a small impact on your overall score, but it can really add up to a lot of points in the end.

The process of elimination IS valuable. The following shows your chance of guessing it right:

If you eliminate wrong answer choices until only this many remain:	Chance of getting it correct:
1	100%
2	50%
3	33%

However, if you accidentally eliminate the right answer or go on a hunch for an incorrect answer, your chances drop dramatically—to 0%. By guessing among all the answer choices, you are GUARANTEED to have a shot at the right answer.

That's why the $5 test is so valuable. If you give up the advantage and safety of a pure guess, it had better be worth the risk.

What we still haven't covered is how to be sure that whatever guess you make is truly random. Here's the easiest way:

- *Always pick the first answer choice among those remaining.*

Such a technique means that you have decided, **before you see a single test question**, exactly how you are going to guess, and since the order of choices tells you nothing about which one is correct, this guessing technique is perfectly random.

This section is not meant to scare you away from making educated guesses or eliminating choices; you just need to define when a choice is worth eliminating. The $5 test, along with a pre-defined random guessing strategy, is the best way to make sure you reap all of the benefits of guessing.

Secret Key #3 - Practice Smarter, Not Harder

Many test takers delay the test preparation process because they dread the awful amounts of practice time they think necessary to succeed on the test. We have refined an effective method that will take you only a fraction of the time.

There are a number of "obstacles" in the path to success. Among these are answering questions, finishing in time, and mastering test-taking strategies. All must be executed on the day of the test at peak performance, or your score will suffer. The test is a mental marathon that has a large impact on your future.

Just like a marathon runner, it is important to work your way up to the full challenge. So first you just worry about questions, and then time, and finally strategy:

Success Strategy

1. Find a good source for practice tests.
2. If you are willing to make a larger time investment, consider using more than one study guide. Often the different approaches of multiple authors will help you "get" difficult concepts.
3. Take a practice test with no time constraints, with all study helps, "open book." Take your time with questions and focus on applying strategies.
4. Take a practice test with time constraints, with all guides, "open book."
5. Take a final practice test without open material and with time limits.

If you have time to take more practice tests, just repeat step 5. By gradually exposing yourself to the full rigors of the test environment, you will condition your mind to the stress of test day and maximize your success.

Secret Key #4 - Prepare, Don't Procrastinate

Let me state an obvious fact: if you take the test three times, you will probably get three different scores. This is due to the way you feel on test day, the level of preparedness you have, and the version of the test you see. Despite the test writers' claims to the contrary, some versions of the test WILL be easier for you than others.

Since your future depends so much on your score, you should maximize your chances of success. In order to maximize the likelihood of success, you've got to prepare in advance. This means taking practice tests and spending time learning the information and test taking strategies you will need to succeed.

Never go take the actual test as a "practice" test, expecting that you can just take it again if you need to. Take all the practice tests you can on your own, but when you go to take the official test, be prepared, be focused, and do your best the first time!

Secret Key #5 - Test Yourself

Everyone knows that time is money. There is no need to spend too much of your time or too little of your time preparing for the test. You should only spend as much of your precious time preparing as is necessary for you to get the score you need.

Once you have taken a practice test under real conditions of time constraints, then you will know if you are ready for the test or not.

If you have scored extremely high the first time that you take the practice test, then there is not much point in spending countless hours studying. You are already there.

Benchmark your abilities by retaking practice tests and seeing how much you have improved. Once you consistently score high enough to guarantee success, then you are ready.

If you have scored well below where you need, then knuckle down and begin studying in earnest. Check your improvement regularly through the use of practice tests under real conditions. Above all, don't worry, panic, or give up. The key is perseverance!

Then, when you go to take the test, remain confident and remember how well you did on the practice tests. If you can score high enough on a practice test, then you can do the same on the real thing.

General Strategies

The most important thing you can do is to ignore your fears and jump into the test immediately. Do not be overwhelmed by any strange-sounding terms. You have to jump into the test like jumping into a pool—all at once is the easiest way.

Make Predictions

As you read and understand the question, try to guess what the answer will be. Remember that several of the answer choices are wrong, and once you begin reading them, your mind will immediately become cluttered with answer choices designed to throw you off. Your mind is typically the most focused immediately after you have read the question and digested its contents. If you can, try to predict what the correct answer will be. You may be surprised at what you can predict.

Quickly scan the choices and see if your prediction is in the listed answer choices. If it is, then you can be quite confident that you have the right answer. It still won't hurt to check the other answer choices, but most of the time, you've got it!

Answer the Question

It may seem obvious to only pick answer choices that answer the question, but the test writers can create some excellent answer choices that are wrong. Don't pick an answer just because it sounds right, or you believe it to be true. It MUST answer the question. Once you've made your selection, always go back and check it against the question and make sure that you didn't misread the question and that the answer choice does answer the question posed.

Benchmark

After you read the first answer choice, decide if you think it sounds correct or not. If it doesn't, move on to the next answer choice. If it does, mentally mark that answer choice. This doesn't mean that you've definitely selected it as your answer choice, it just means that it's the best you've seen thus far. Go ahead and read the next choice. If the next choice is worse than the one you've already selected, keep going to the next answer choice. If the next choice is better than the choice you've already selected, mentally mark the new answer choice as your best guess.

The first answer choice that you select becomes your standard. Every other answer choice must be benchmarked against that standard. That choice is correct until proven otherwise by another answer choice beating it out. Once you've decided that no other answer choice seems as good, do one final check to ensure that your answer choice answers the question posed.

Valid Information

Don't discount any of the information provided in the question. Every piece of information may be necessary to determine the correct answer. None of the information in the question is there to throw you off (while the answer choices will certainly have information to throw you off). If two seemingly unrelated topics are discussed, don't ignore either. You can be confident there is a relationship, or it wouldn't be included in the question, and you are probably going to have to determine what is that relationship to find the answer.

Avoid "Fact Traps"

Don't get distracted by a choice that is factually true. Your search is for the answer that answers the question. Stay focused and don't fall for an answer that is true but irrelevant. Always go back to the question and make sure you're choosing an answer that actually answers the question and is not just a true statement. An answer can be factually correct, but it MUST answer the question asked. Additionally, two answers can both be seemingly correct, so be sure to read all of the answer choices, and make sure that you get the one that BEST answers the question.

Milk the Question

Some of the questions may throw you completely off. They might deal with a subject you have not been exposed to, or one that you haven't reviewed in years. While your lack of knowledge about the subject will be a hindrance, the question itself can give you many clues that will help you find the correct answer. Read the question carefully and look for clues. Watch particularly for adjectives and nouns describing difficult terms or words that you don't recognize. Regardless of whether you completely understand a word or not, replacing it with a synonym, either provided or one you more familiar with, may help you to understand what the questions are asking. Rather than wracking your mind about specific detailed information concerning a difficult term or word, try to use mental substitutes that are easier to understand.

The Trap of Familiarity

Don't just choose a word because you recognize it. On difficult questions, you may not recognize a number of words in the answer choices. The test writers don't put "make-believe" words on the test, so don't think that just because you only recognize all the words in one answer choice that that answer choice must be correct. If you only recognize words in one answer choice, then focus on that one. Is it correct? Try your best to determine if it is correct. If it is, that's great. If not, eliminate it. Each word and answer choice you eliminate increases your chances of getting the question correct, even if you then have to guess among the unfamiliar choices.

Eliminate Answers

Eliminate choices as soon as you realize they are wrong. But be careful! Make sure you consider all of the possible answer choices. Just because one appears right, doesn't mean that the next one won't be even better! The test writers will usually put more than one good answer choice for every question, so read all of them. Don't worry if you are stuck between two that seem right. By getting down to just two remaining possible choices, your odds are now 50/50. Rather than wasting too much time, play the odds. You are guessing, but guessing wisely because you've been able to knock out some of the answer choices that you know are wrong. If you are eliminating choices and realize that the last answer choice you are left with is also obviously wrong, don't panic. Start over and consider each choice again. There may easily be something that you missed the first time and will realize on the second pass.

Tough Questions

If you are stumped on a problem or it appears too hard or too difficult, don't waste time. Move on! Remember though, if you can quickly check for obviously incorrect answer choices, your chances of guessing correctly are greatly improved. Before you completely give up, at least try to knock out a couple of possible answers. Eliminate what you can and then guess at the remaining answer choices before moving on.

Brainstorm

If you get stuck on a difficult question, spend a few seconds quickly brainstorming. Run through the complete list of possible answer choices. Look at each choice and ask yourself, "Could this answer the question satisfactorily?" Go through each answer choice and consider it independently of the others. By systematically going through all possibilities, you may find something that you would otherwise overlook. Remember though that when you get stuck, it's important to try to keep moving.

Read Carefully

Understand the problem. Read the question and answer choices carefully. Don't miss the question because you misread the terms. You have plenty of time to read each question thoroughly and make sure you understand what is being asked. Yet a happy medium must be attained, so don't waste too much time. You must read carefully, but efficiently.

Face Value

When in doubt, use common sense. Always accept the situation in the problem at face value. Don't read too much into it. These problems will not require you to make huge leaps of logic. The test writers aren't trying to throw you off with a cheap trick. If you have to go beyond creativity and make a leap of logic in order to have an answer choice answer the question, then you should look at the other answer choices. Don't overcomplicate the problem by creating theoretical relationships or explanations that will warp time or space. These are normal problems rooted in reality. It's just that the applicable relationship or explanation may not be readily apparent and you have to figure things out. Use your common sense to interpret anything that isn't clear.

Prefixes

If you're having trouble with a word in the question or answer choices, try dissecting it. Take advantage of every clue that the word might include. Prefixes and suffixes can be a huge help. Usually they allow you to determine a basic meaning. Pre- means before, post- means after, pro - is positive, de- is negative. From these prefixes and suffixes, you can get an idea of the general meaning of the word and try to put it into context. Beware though of any traps. Just because con- is the opposite of pro-, doesn't necessarily mean congress is the opposite of progress!

Hedge Phrases

Watch out for critical hedge phrases, led off with words such as "likely," "may," "can," "sometimes," "often," "almost," "mostly," "usually," "generally," "rarely," and "sometimes." Question writers insert these hedge phrases to cover every possibility. Often an answer choice will be wrong simply because it leaves no room for exception. Unless the situation calls for them, avoid answer choices that have definitive words like "exactly," and "always."

Switchback Words

Stay alert for "switchbacks." These are the words and phrases frequently used to alert you to shifts in thought. The most common switchback word is "but." Others include "although," "however," "nevertheless," "on the other hand," "even though," "while," "in spite of," "despite," and "regardless of."

New Information

Correct answer choices will rarely have completely new information included. Answer choices typically are straightforward reflections of the material asked about and will directly relate to the question. If a new piece of information is included in an answer choice that doesn't even seem to relate to the topic being asked about, then that answer choice is likely incorrect. All of the information needed to answer the question is usually provided for you in the question. You should not have to make guesses that are unsupported or choose answer choices that require unknown information that cannot be reasoned from what is given.

Time Management

On technical questions, don't get lost on the technical terms. Don't spend too much time on any one question. If you don't know what a term means, then odds are you aren't going to get much further since you don't have a dictionary. You should be able to immediately recognize whether or not you know a term. If you don't, work with the other clues that you have—the other answer choices and terms provided—but don't waste too much time trying to figure out a difficult term that you don't know.

Contextual Clues

Look for contextual clues. An answer can be right but not the correct answer. The contextual clues will help you find the answer that is most right and is correct. Understand the context in which a phrase or statement is made. This will help you make important distinctions.

Don't Panic

Panicking will not answer any questions for you; therefore, it isn't helpful. When you first see the question, if your mind goes blank, take a deep breath. Force yourself to mechanically go through the steps of solving the problem using the strategies you've learned.

Pace Yourself

Don't get clock fever. It's easy to be overwhelmed when you're looking at a page full of questions, your mind is full of random thoughts and feeling confused, and the clock is ticking down faster than you would like. Calm down and maintain the pace that you have set for yourself. As long as you are on track by monitoring your pace, you are guaranteed to have enough time for yourself. When you get to the last few minutes of the test, it may seem like you won't have enough time left, but if you only have as many questions as you should have left at that point, then you're right on track!

Answer Selection

The best way to pick an answer choice is to eliminate all of those that are wrong, until only one is left and confirm that is the correct answer. Sometimes though, an answer choice may immediately look right. Be careful! Take a second to make sure that the other choices are not equally obvious. Don't make a hasty mistake. There are only two times that you should stop before checking other answers. First is when you are positive that the answer choice you have selected is correct. Second is when time is almost out and you have to make a quick guess!

Check Your Work

Since you will probably not know every term listed and the answer to every question, it is important that you get credit for the ones that you do know. Don't miss any questions through careless mistakes. If at all possible, try to take a second to look back over your answer selection and make sure you've selected the correct answer choice and haven't made a costly careless mistake (such as marking an answer choice that you didn't mean to mark). The time it takes for this quick double check should more than pay for itself in caught mistakes.

Beware of Directly Quoted Answers

Sometimes an answer choice will repeat word for word a portion of the question or reference section. However, beware of such exact duplication. It may be a trap! More than likely, the correct choice will paraphrase or summarize a point, rather than being exactly the same wording.

Slang

Scientific sounding answers are better than slang ones. An answer choice that begins "To compare the outcomes…" is much more likely to be correct than one that begins "Because some people insisted…"

Extreme Statements

Avoid wild answers that throw out highly controversial ideas that are proclaimed as established fact. An answer choice that states the "process should used in certain situations, if…" is much more likely to be correct than one that states the "process should be discontinued completely." The first is a calm rational statement and doesn't even make a definitive, uncompromising stance, using a hedge word "if" to provide wiggle room, whereas the second choice is a radical idea and far more extreme.

Answer Choice Families

When you have two or more answer choices that are direct opposites or parallels, one of them is usually the correct answer. For instance, if one answer choice states "x increases" and another answer choice states "x decreases" or "y increases," then those two or three answer choices are very similar in construction and fall into the same family of answer choices. A family of answer choices consists of two or three answer choices, very similar in construction, but often with directly opposite meanings. Usually the correct answer choice will be in that family of answer choices. The "odd man out" or answer choice that doesn't seem to fit the parallel construction of the other answer choices is more likely to be incorrect.

Special Report: How to Overcome Test Anxiety

The very nature of tests caters to some level of anxiety, nervousness, or tension, just as we feel for any important event that occurs in our lives. A little bit of anxiety or nervousness can be a good thing. It helps us with motivation, and makes achievement just that much sweeter. However, too much anxiety can be a problem, especially if it hinders our ability to function and perform.

"Test anxiety," is the term that refers to the emotional reactions that some test-takers experience when faced with a test or exam. Having a fear of testing and exams is based upon a rational fear, since the test-taker's performance can shape the course of an academic career. Nevertheless, experiencing excessive fear of examinations will only interfere with the test-taker's ability to perform and chance to be successful.

There are a large variety of causes that can contribute to the development and sensation of test anxiety. These include, but are not limited to, lack of preparation and worrying about issues surrounding the test.

Lack of Preparation

Lack of preparation can be identified by the following behaviors or situations:
- Not scheduling enough time to study, and therefore cramming the night before the test or exam
- Managing time poorly, to create the sensation that there is not enough time to do everything
- Failing to organize the text information in advance, so that the study material consists of the entire text and not simply the pertinent information
- Poor overall studying habits

Worrying, on the other hand, can be related to both the test taker, or many other factors around him/her that will be affected by the results of the test. These include worrying about:
- Previous performances on similar exams, or exams in general
- How friends and other students are achieving
- The negative consequences that will result from a poor grade or failure

There are three primary elements to test anxiety. Physical components, which involve the same typical bodily reactions as those to acute anxiety (to be discussed below). Emotional factors have to do with fear or panic. Mental or cognitive issues concerning attention spans and memory abilities.

Physical Signals

There are many different symptoms of test anxiety, and these are not limited to mental and emotional strain. Frequently there are a range of physical signals that will let a test taker know that he/she is suffering from test anxiety. These bodily changes can include the following:

- Perspiring
- Sweaty palms
- Wet, trembling hands
- Nausea
- Dry mouth
- A knot in the stomach
- Headache
- Faintness
- Muscle tension
- Aching shoulders, back and neck
- Rapid heart beat
- Feeling too hot/cold

To recognize the sensation of test anxiety, a test-taker should monitor him/herself for the following sensations:

- The physical distress symptoms as listed above
- Emotional sensitivity, expressing emotional feelings such as the need to cry or laugh too much, or a sensation of anger or helplessness
- A decreased ability to think, causing the test-taker to blank out or have racing thoughts that are hard to organize or control.

Though most students will feel some level of anxiety when faced with a test or exam, the majority can cope with that anxiety and maintain it at a manageable level. However, those who cannot are faced with a very real and very serious condition, which can and should be controlled for the immeasurable benefit of this sufferer.

Naturally, these sensations lead to negative results for the testing experience. The most common effects of test anxiety have to do with nervousness and mental blocking.

Nervousness

Nervousness can appear in several different levels:

- The test-taker's difficulty, or even inability to read and understand the questions on the test
- The difficulty or inability to organize thoughts to a coherent form
- The difficulty or inability to recall key words and concepts relating to the testing questions (especially essays)
- The receipt of poor grades on a test, though the test material was well known by the test taker

Conversely, a person may also experience mental blocking, which involves:
- Blanking out on test questions
- Only remembering the correct answers to the questions when the test has already finished.

Fortunately for test anxiety sufferers, beating these feelings, to a large degree, has to do with proper preparation. When a test taker has a feeling of preparedness, then anxiety will be dramatically lessened.

The first step to resolving anxiety issues is to distinguish which of the two types of anxiety are being suffered. If the anxiety is a direct result of a lack of preparation, this should be considered a normal reaction, and the anxiety level (as opposed to the test results) shouldn't be anything to worry about. However, if, when adequately prepared, the test-taker still panics, blanks out, or seems to overreact, this is not a fully rational reaction. While this can be considered normal too, there are many ways to combat and overcome these effects.

Remember that anxiety cannot be entirely eliminated, however, there are ways to minimize it, to make the anxiety easier to manage. Preparation is one of the best ways to minimize test anxiety. Therefore the following techniques are wise in order to best fight off any anxiety that may want to build.

To begin with, try to avoid cramming before a test, whenever it is possible. By trying to memorize an entire term's worth of information in one day, you'll be shocking your system, and not giving yourself a very good chance to absorb the information. This is an easy path to anxiety, so for those who suffer from test anxiety, cramming should not even be considered an option.

Instead of cramming, work throughout the semester to combine all of the material which is presented throughout the semester, and work on it gradually as the course goes by, making sure to master the main concepts first, leaving minor details for a week or so before the test.

To study for the upcoming exam, be sure to pose questions that may be on the examination, to gauge the ability to answer them by integrating the ideas from your texts, notes and lectures, as well as any supplementary readings.

If it is truly impossible to cover all of the information that was covered in that particular term, concentrate on the most important portions, that can be covered very well. Learn these concepts as best as possible, so that when the test comes, a goal can be made to use these concepts as presentations of your knowledge.

In addition to study habits, changes in attitude are critical to beating a struggle with test anxiety. In fact, an improvement of the perspective over the entire test-taking experience can actually help a test taker to enjoy studying and therefore improve the overall experience. Be certain not to overemphasize the significance of the grade - know that the result of the test is neither a reflection of self worth, nor is it a measure of intelligence; one grade will not predict a person's future success.

To improve an overall testing outlook, the following steps should be tried:
- Keeping in mind that the most reasonable expectation for taking a test is to expect to try to demonstrate as much of what you know as you possibly can.
- Reminding ourselves that a test is only one test; this is not the only one, and there will be others.
- The thought of thinking of oneself in an irrational, all-or-nothing term should be avoided at all costs.
- A reward should be designated for after the test, so there's something to look forward to. Whether it be going to a movie, going out to eat, or simply visiting friends, schedule it in advance, and do it no matter what result is expected on the exam.

Test-takers should also keep in mind that the basics are some of the most important things, even beyond anti-anxiety techniques and studying. Never neglect the basic social, emotional and biological needs, in order to try to absorb information. In order to best achieve, these three factors must be held as just as important as the studying itself.

Study Steps

Remember the following important steps for studying:
- Maintain healthy nutrition and exercise habits. Continue both your recreational activities and social pass times. These both contribute to your physical and emotional well being.
- Be certain to get a good amount of sleep, especially the night before the test, because when you're overtired you are not able to perform to the best of your best ability.
- Keep the studying pace to a moderate level by taking breaks when they are needed, and varying the work whenever possible, to keep the mind fresh instead of getting bored.
- When enough studying has been done that all the material that can be learned has been learned, and the test taker is prepared for the test, stop studying and do something relaxing such as listening to music, watching a movie, or taking a warm bubble bath.

There are also many other techniques to minimize the uneasiness or apprehension that is experienced along with test anxiety before, during, or even after the examination. In fact, there are a great deal of things that can be done to stop anxiety from interfering with lifestyle and performance. Again, remember that anxiety will not be eliminated entirely, and it shouldn't be. Otherwise that "up" feeling for exams would not exist, and most of us depend on that sensation to perform better than usual. However, this anxiety has to be at a level that is manageable.

Of course, as we have just discussed, being prepared for the exam is half the battle right away. Attending all classes, finding out what knowledge will be expected on the exam, and knowing the exam schedules are easy steps to lowering anxiety. Keeping up with work will remove the need to cram, and efficient study habits will eliminate wasted time. Studying should be done in an ideal location for concentration, so that it is simple to become interested in the material and give it complete attention. A method such as SQ3R (Survey, Question, Read, Recite, Review) is a wonderful key to follow to make sure that the study habits are as effective as possible, especially in the case of learning from a textbook. Flashcards are great techniques for memorization. Learning to take good notes will mean that notes will be full of useful information, so that less sifting will need to be done to seek out what is pertinent for studying. Reviewing notes after class and then again on occasion will keep the information fresh in the mind. From notes that have been taken summary sheets and outlines can be made for simpler reviewing.

A study group can also be a very motivational and helpful place to study, as there will be a sharing of ideas, all of the minds can work together, to make sure that everyone understands, and the studying will be made more interesting because it will be a social occasion.

Basically, though, as long as the test-taker remains organized and self confident, with efficient study habits, less time will need to be spent studying, and higher grades will be achieved.

To become self confident, there are many useful steps. The first of these is "self talk." It has been shown through extensive research, that self-talk for students who suffer from test anxiety, should be well monitored, in order to make sure that it contributes to self confidence as opposed to sinking the student. Frequently the self talk of test-anxious students is negative or self-defeating, thinking that everyone else is smarter and faster, that they always mess up, and that if they don't do well, they'll fail the entire course. It is important to decreasing anxiety that awareness is made of self talk. Try writing any negative self thoughts and then disputing them with a positive statement instead. Begin self-encouragement as though it was a friend speaking. Repeat positive statements to help reprogram the mind to believing in successes instead of failures.

Helpful Techniques

Other extremely helpful techniques include:
- Self-visualization of doing well and reaching goals
- While aiming for an "A" level of understanding, don't try to "overprotect" by setting your expectations lower. This will only convince the mind to stop studying in order to meet the lower expectations.
- Don't make comparisons with the results or habits of other students. These are individual factors, and different things work for different people, causing different results.
- Strive to become an expert in learning what works well, and what can be done in order to improve. Consider collecting this data in a journal.
- Create rewards for after studying instead of doing things before studying that will only turn into avoidance behaviors.
- Make a practice of relaxing - by using methods such as progressive relaxation, self-hypnosis, guided imagery, etc - in order to make relaxation an automatic sensation.
- Work on creating a state of relaxed concentration so that concentrating will take on the focus of the mind, so that none will be wasted on worrying.
- Take good care of the physical self by eating well and getting enough sleep.
- Plan in time for exercise and stick to this plan.

Beyond these techniques, there are other methods to be used before, during and after the test that will help the test-taker perform well in addition to overcoming anxiety.

Before the exam comes the academic preparation. This involves establishing a study schedule and beginning at least one week before the actual date of the test. By doing this, the anxiety of not having enough time to study for the test will be automatically eliminated. Moreover, this will make the studying a much more effective experience, ensuring that the learning will be an easier process. This relieves much undue pressure on the test-taker.

Summary sheets, note cards, and flash cards with the main concepts and examples of these main concepts should be prepared in advance of the actual studying time. A topic should never be eliminated from this process. By omitting a topic because it isn't expected to be on the test is only setting up the test-taker for anxiety should it actually appear on the exam. Utilize the course syllabus for laying out the topics that should be studied. Carefully go over the notes that were made in class, paying special attention to any of the issues that the professor took special care to emphasize while lecturing in class. In the textbooks, use the chapter review, or if possible, the chapter tests, to begin your review.

It may even be possible to ask the instructor what information will be covered on the exam, or what the format of the exam will be (for example, multiple choice, essay, free form, true-false). Additionally, see if it is possible to find out how many questions will be on the test. If a review sheet or sample test has been offered by the professor, make good use of it, above anything else, for the preparation for the test. Another great resource for getting to know the examination is reviewing tests from previous semesters. Use these tests to review, and aim to achieve a 100% score on each of the possible topics. With a few exceptions, the goal that you set for yourself is the highest one that you will reach.

Take all of the questions that were assigned as homework, and rework them to any other possible course material. The more problems reworked, the more skill and confidence will form as a result. When forming the solution to a problem, write out each of the steps. Don't simply do head work. By doing as many steps on paper as possible, much clarification and therefore confidence will be formed. Do this with as many homework problems as possible, before checking the answers. By checking the answer after each problem, a reinforcement will exist, that will not be on the exam. Study situations should be as exam-like as possible, to prime the test-taker's system for the experience. By waiting to check the answers at the end, a psychological advantage will be formed, to decrease the stress factor.

Another fantastic reason for not cramming is the avoidance of confusion in concepts, especially when it comes to mathematics. 8-10 hours of study will become one hundred percent more effective if it is spread out over a week or at least several days, instead of doing it all in one sitting. Recognize that the human brain requires time in order to assimilate new material, so frequent breaks and a span of study time over several days will be much more beneficial.

Additionally, don't study right up until the point of the exam. Studying should stop a minimum of one hour before the exam begins. This allows the brain to rest and put things in their proper order. This will also provide the time to become as relaxed as possible when going into the examination room. The test-taker will also have time to eat well and eat sensibly. Know that the brain needs food as much as the rest of the body. With enough food and enough sleep, as well as a relaxed attitude, the body and the mind are primed for success.

Avoid any anxious classmates who are talking about the exam. These students only spread anxiety, and are not worth sharing the anxious sentimentalities.

Before the test also involves creating a positive attitude, so mental preparation should also be a point of concentration. There are many keys to creating a positive attitude. Should fears become rushing in, make a visualization of taking the exam, doing well, and seeing an A written on the paper. Write out a list of affirmations that will bring a feeling of confidence, such as "I am doing well in my English class," "I studied well and know my material," "I enjoy this class." Even if the affirmations aren't believed at first, it sends a positive message to the subconscious which will result in an alteration of the overall belief system, which is the system that creates reality.

If a sensation of panic begins, work with the fear and imagine the very worst! Work through the entire scenario of not passing the test, failing the entire course, and dropping out of school, followed by not getting a job, and pushing a shopping cart through the dark alley where you'll live. This will place things into perspective! Then, practice deep breathing and create a visualization of the opposite situation - achieving an "A" on the exam, passing the entire course, receiving the degree at a graduation ceremony.

On the day of the test, there are many things to be done to ensure the best results, as well as the most calm outlook. The following stages are suggested in order to maximize test-taking potential:

- Begin the examination day with a moderate breakfast, and avoid any coffee or beverages with caffeine if the test taker is prone to jitters. Even people who are used to managing caffeine can feel jittery or light-headed when it is taken on a test day.
- Attempt to do something that is relaxing before the examination begins. As last minute cramming clouds the mastering of overall concepts, it is better to use this time to create a calming outlook.
- Be certain to arrive at the test location well in advance, in order to provide time to select a location that is away from doors, windows and other distractions, as well as giving enough time to relax before the test begins.
- Keep away from anxiety generating classmates who will upset the sensation of stability and relaxation that is being attempted before the exam.
- Should the waiting period before the exam begins cause anxiety, create a self-distraction by reading a light magazine or something else that is relaxing and simple.

During the exam itself, read the entire exam from beginning to end, and find out how much time should be allotted to each individual problem. Once writing the exam, should more time be taken for a problem, it should be abandoned, in order to begin another problem. If there is time at the end, the unfinished problem can always be returned to and completed.

Read the instructions very carefully - twice - so that unpleasant surprises won't follow during or after the exam has ended.

When writing the exam, pretend that the situation is actually simply the completion of homework within a library, or at home. This will assist in forming a relaxed atmosphere, and will allow the brain extra focus for the complex thinking function.

Begin the exam with all of the questions with which the most confidence is felt. This will build the confidence level regarding the entire exam and will begin a quality momentum. This will also create encouragement for trying the problems where uncertainty resides.

Going with the "gut instinct" is always the way to go when solving a problem. Second guessing should be avoided at all costs. Have confidence in the ability to do well.

For essay questions, create an outline in advance that will keep the mind organized and make certain that all of the points are remembered. For multiple choice, read every answer, even if the correct one has been spotted - a better one may exist.

Continue at a pace that is reasonable and not rushed, in order to be able to work carefully. Provide enough time to go over the answers at the end, to check for small errors that can be corrected.

Should a feeling of panic begin, breathe deeply, and think of the feeling of the body releasing sand through its pores. Visualize a calm, peaceful place, and include all of the sights, sounds and sensations of this image. Continue the deep breathing, and take a few minutes to continue this with closed eyes. When all is well again, return to the test.

If a "blanking" occurs for a certain question, skip it and move on to the next question. There will be time to return to the other question later. Get everything done that can be done, first, to guarantee all the grades that can be compiled, and to build all of the confidence possible. Then return to the weaker questions to build the marks from there.

Remember, one's own reality can be created, so as long as the belief is there, success will follow. And remember: anxiety can happen later, right now, there's an exam to be written!

After the examination is complete, whether there is a feeling for a good grade or a bad grade, don't dwell on the exam, and be certain to follow through on the reward that was promised...and enjoy it! Don't dwell on any mistakes that have been made, as there is nothing that can be done at this point anyway.

Additionally, don't begin to study for the next test right away. Do something relaxing for a while, and let the mind relax and prepare itself to begin absorbing information again.

From the results of the exam - both the grade and the entire experience, be certain to learn from what has gone on. Perfect studying habits and work some more on confidence in order to make the next examination experience even better than the last one.

Learn to avoid places where openings occurred for laziness, procrastination and day dreaming.

Use the time between this exam and the next one to better learn to relax, even learning to relax on cue, so that any anxiety can be controlled during the next exam. Learn how to relax the body. Slouch in your chair if that helps. Tighten and then relax all of the different muscle groups, one group at a time, beginning with the feet and then working all the way up to the neck and face. This will ultimately relax the muscles more than they were to begin with. Learn how to breathe deeply and comfortably, and focus on this breathing going in and out as a relaxing thought. With every exhale, repeat the word "relax."

As common as test anxiety is, it is very possible to overcome it. Make yourself one of the test-takers who overcome this frustrating hindrance.

Additional Bonus Material

Due to our efforts to try to keep this book to a manageable length, we've created a link that will give you access to all of your additional bonus material.

Please visit http://www.mometrix.com/bonus948/priimsela5047 to access the information.